Truth, Reparations and Social Cohesion

This book addresses the effectiveness of transitional justice mechanisms for repairing social cohesion.

Truth commissions and reparation programs are implemented worldwide to enhance social cohesion, peace and democracy in post-conflict settings. Most claims about transitional justice measures are, however, normatively and not empirically based. This book questions whether attention from a truth and reconciliation commission can truly change the lives of the violence-affected people and whether monetary compensations or communal projects in the form of milk cows can ever truly "repair" the harm suffered. The within-country comparative case study analyzes the effects of the commission and reparation program in Peru. It studies the post-conflict situation and the development of social cohesion in communities affected by the internal armed conflict. Using detailed empirical data, this analysis reveals why the "reparation" of social cohesion in Peru was an impossible task. Contributing to a broader understanding of the impact of nationally applied transitional justice instruments in local settings, the book further offers a new framework for analyzing social cohesion as one of the aims of transitional justice processes.

Offering a detailed account of transitional justice processes and social cohesion on the micro level, as well as an important analysis of their relationship, this innovative monograph will be invaluable for transitional justice scholars and students, as well as for international political and societal actors who are involved in transitional justice measures.

Elisabeth Bunselmeyer is based at the GIGA German Institute of Global and Area Studies and University of Hamburg. She holds a PhD in Political Science from University of Marburg and was honored the Christiane-Rajewsky-Award 2018 by the German Association for Peace and Conflict Studies. Her areas of work and research are the social development in post-conflict settings and the impact of transitional justice processes in Latin America.

Transitional Justice

Kieran McEvoy, Queen's University Belfast, UK

For information about the series and details of previous and forthcoming titles, see https://www.routledge.com/Transitional-Justice/book-series/TRANJ

Truth, Reparations and Social Cohesion

Transitional Justice Lessons from Peru

Elisabeth Bunselmeyer

Routledge
Taylor & Francis Group
LONDON AND NEW YORK

First published 2020 by Routledge

2 Park Square, Milton Park, Abingdon, Oxon OX14 4RN
605 Third Avenue, New York, NY 10017

Routledge is an imprint of the Taylor & Francis Group, an informa business

First issued in paperback 2021

British Library Cataloguing-in-Publication Data
A catalogue record for this book is available from the British Library

Library of Congress Cataloging-in-Publication Data
A catalog record has been requested for this book

ISBN: 978-0-367-33847-3 (hbk)
ISBN: 978-1-03-217389-4 (pbk)
DOI: 10.4324/9780429330438

Typeset in Galliard
by codeMantra

to Eliah

Contents

Illustrations

Figure

Tables

Acknowledgments

This book is based on my dissertation and would not have been possible without the support of so many people during the last years.

First of all, I owe a special thanks to the people in the communities studied. I had the opportunity to get to know life in the Andes as they shared their opinions, ideas, and houses so generously. In Lucanamarca, I want to thank in particular Ignacio as well as Cesar, Maria, and the little Lisa for their open arms expecting me in Lucanamarca every time. I also thank COMISEDH for their support, in particular Gabriel. In Chuschi, I am especially grateful to Fredy and the local authorities for welcoming me there.

I would like to express my gratitude to Prof. Thorsten Bonacker, who has accompanied my academic life constantly for 15 years now (a real "Doktorvater") and has always provided invaluable comments and support. Prof. Susanne Buckley-Zistel was also an important advisor during my Master's thesis already and encouraged me on my way since then. I am grateful for the time working with Prof. Christoph Weller. I also want to thank my supervisor at the GIGA, Prof. Detlef Nolte that his door was always open for support and guidance.

The GIGA German Institute of Global and Area Studies funded this dissertation project within its doctoral program and offered an inspiring work atmosphere. It is here that I met the best colleague-friends I could wish for. Thank you Anne, Christoph, Janina, and Martin. I miss our wonderful time, our coffees on the balcony with talks about the PhD, the world, and the life. Thank you for being there in every moment, AM and the fat cat.

I also want to thank Sabine, Anna, and Joe for their feedback and Riccarda for taking me to the Amazonas. Furthermore, I am grateful to my research team and program as well as the Latin American Institute for their advice and financial support. The equal opportunity fund as well as the DAAD made my research trips possible.

I want to express my gratitude to the Routledge team, who assisted and advised me during the publication process, particularly to Nicola Sharpe, Colin Perrin, and Kieran McEvoy.

Thank you Rebecca for reading every word of this dissertation thoroughly and for your humorous comments.

I am also very honored and thankful to the German Association for Peace and Conflict Studies, who awarded me the Christiane-Rajewsky-Award 2018.

I also want to thank my former colleagues at the Social Science Research Center in Berlin (WZB) and especially Prof. Jutta Allmendinger, who encouraged me to undertake this dissertation. A big thank you as well to my new colleagues at the University of Hamburg, in particular Andreas, Ines, Dominik, and Karo, who supported me in the last steps of this project.

In Peru, I am also grateful to the support and encouragement of Carola and Regina, Iris and the IDEHPUCP, and many more experts in Lima. In Ayacucho, it was especially the support of COMISEDH, Apoyo para la Paz, Victor, Yuber, and Edilberto but also Jefrey and the Universidad San Cristobal de Huamanga as well as my research assistants, Gaby, Sonia, and Paulino. I would also like to express my warmest gratitude to my "family" there, Janet, Gandy, Israel, Augusto, also to Marleny, Illariq, Kari, and Cesar. A special thanks to Eva and Gaby for your support and friendship.

I am so grateful for the group of friends who not only accompanied me on this academic endeavor but also in all the other challenging times for years.

Sandra, Conny, Ben, Karen, Uwe, Cindy, Tilo, Martin, and Jorina, without you I would not be here right now. Thank you so much for sharing the most challenging time of our lives. Together we made it.

I also want to thank the volunteer crew of the sailing vessel Thor Heyerdahl, especially Moritz, Matze, Janek, and Mo. The sailing trips were always a pleasure, energizing, and helpful to get a clear mind.

Christian, Judith, and Maria, thank you for wise advice and encouragement; the Marburg connection Sarah and Susi; the Osnabrück connection Stine, Steffi, Sebastian, and particularly Iris for the final polish; my travel mates Johanna and Katrin and my oldest friends, Miri, Conny, Teena, Nina, and Lena. I am so glad and thankful to have you all around me.

I want to express my warmest gratitude to my wonderful families: Gisela and Manfred, my grandparents Hanna and Karl-Heinz, my father Achim, and little sister Linnéa, for always believing in me and in this project. And of course I want to thank my mother Astrid and Emmy for being there in every step of my life and welcoming me at home always.

My final thanks belongs to my beloved little family, Wolfgang and Karl.

Abbreviations and Spanish terms

Anexo / centro poblado	Village
Anfasep	NGO: Asociación Nacional de Familiares de Secuestrados, Detenidos y Desaparecido del Peru – National Association of the Families of Kidnapped, Arrested or Missing persons
APRODEH	NGO: Asociación pro Derechos Humanos – Association for Human Rights
Ayni	Traditional way of mutual exchanging services
Beca 18	Scholarship program for students from poor households
CAD	Comité de Autodefensa – self-defense committees
Canon Gasifero	Fund which is generated from profits of mineral exploitation projects and distributed to regional and local municipals
Chakras	Land used for agriculture
CMAN	Comisión Multisectorial de Alto Nivel – High Level Multisectorial Commission. Government entity coordinating reparation program
COMISEDH	NGO: Comisión de Derechos Humanos – Commission of Human Rights
Costa	Coastal region of Peru
Cuna Más	Social program focused on children under the age of three in regions of poverty
Juez de Paz	"Peace Judge", local authority
Juntos	Social program for families in poor living conditions
MIDIS	Ministerio de Desarrollo e Inclusión Social del Perú – Ministry of Social Inclusion and Development
Minka / faena	Traditional way of mutual exchanging services
PAR	Programa Nacional de Apoyo a la Repoblación – Program to Support the Return of Displaced People
Paz y Esperanza	Peace and Hope. NGO
PEN / Nuevo Soles	Peruvian Sol (1 PEN = 0.30 US$)

Pension 65	Pension program of the state
Peyon	Daily worker (for harvest or construction)
PIR	Plan Integral de Reparaciones – Comprehensive Reparation Plan
Puna	upper region from 3,300 to over 4,000 meters above sea level
Qali Warma	National social program providing school meals
Repared	Scholarship in the reparation program
Rondas Campesinas	Self-defense committees
RUV	Registro Único de Víctimas – National Victims' Registry
Selva	Amazon Region
Senderista	Short form for Sendero Luminoso. Guerrilla group "Shining Path"
Sierra	Highlands in the Andes
Techo Propio	"Own Roof" – Program to construct or improve houses for households with low income
TRC	Truth and Reconciliation Commission
Vaso de Leche	Government program against malnutrition
VRAEM	Valle de los Ríos Apurímac, Ene y Mantaro – Valley of the Rivers Apurímac, Ene and Mantaro, Region of Peru

Chapter 1

Introduction

Truth, reparations, and social cohesion in Peru

> [...] the Comprehensive Reparation Plan for violence-affected victims. We will continue with the effort of social inclusion and attention for our fellow citizens in situation of vulnerability, breaking the historic intergenerational transmission of poverty and social exclusion because we want to consolidate a democratic country for everyone.[1]

The former president of Peru, Ollanta Humala, claimed the comprehensive reparation program for victims of the internal armed conflict as a success of his government in his annual speech to the nation in July 2014. In Peru, a truth and reconciliation commission (TRC) investigated past atrocities and a reparation program was implemented to attend to the needs of the victims of the internal armed conflict that occurred in the country from 1980 to 2000.

Interest in the concept transitional justice (TJ) has grown as well as the number of truth commissions, reparation programs, and trials implemented in post-conflict countries worldwide since the 1980s. The United Nations and other international organizations are promoting and financing TJ. Nowadays, we can observe that there is almost always an imperative for TJ, which is based on the normative assumption that a country has to deal with its violent past, victims, and perpetrators in order to secure a peaceful and democratic future. However, these assumptions about TJ are as yet unverified. Research on the impact of TJ has only evolved over the last decade to question whether the applied measures indeed affect politics and society as intended.

This book joins in this discussion and studies the impact of TJ in Peru. In the Peruvian internal armed conflict (1980–2000), two rebel organizations were fighting violently for a new "fair" and inclusive state. The democratically elected governments of that time responded with military and police forces and a violent counterinsurgency strategy to the revolts. Legitimized by the fight against the rebel groups, Alberto Fujimori installed a quasi-dictatorship by dissolving the congress as well as the judiciary in 1992. Fujimori was in power until he left the country because his massive network of corruption was revealed in 2000. The fights among rebel groups, state forces, and self-defense committees resulted in approximately 70,000 dead and disappeared, mainly in rural areas. Within local villages, the lines between victims and perpetrators are blurred as are the lines between these two categories.[2] Villagers are living next door to their loved ones' murderers. As a consequence of the violence, social cohesion within the communities was damaged. Values such as solidarity and trust were eroded.

In Peru, as in more than 80 post-conflict societies worldwide, TJ measures were applied to address these legacies of past violence.[3] In 2001, a TRC (or commission hereafter) was installed by the interim government that followed the authoritarian presidency of Alberto Fujimori. The commission of national experts worked for two years with international support, collected testimonies, carried out exhumations and public audiences, and published an extensive report in 2003. As part of its recommendations, a comprehensive reparation program was developed. Ever since 2007, the Peruvian government has been giving collective reparations to affected communities with the aim to enhance social cohesion and democracy, as proposed by the TRC and also mentioned by Humala cited earlier. The first individual payments to affected people and families were realized in 2011. While the design of the program as such is generally regarded as a success, its critics are concerned about its late and incomplete implementation. Even now, not all of the affected communities and individuals have received their reparations. Questions arise concerning the effectiveness of the TJ measures applied in Peru. Critical voices doubt that attention from a TRC can truly change the lives of the people affected. Skeptics also question whether monetary compensations or communal projects in the form of milk cows or fish farms can ever compensate for the harm suffered.

This book addresses these questions in a comparative case study in Peru. I investigate the post-conflict situation and the development of social cohesion in communities that were hit by worst of the internal armed conflict. It is a study of a government program and its aims, limitations, and effects. But most of all, it is a study of the people in these communities, their post-conflict lives and their perception of the past, the present, and the future. The study investigates whether the truth commission and reparation program were able to have a positive influence on the development of social cohesion in post-conflict times. It is a study of the micro level of the society where the TJ measures are meant to have a positive impact.

Transitional justice and why it matters

The concept of TJ refers to a "set of practices, mechanisms and concerns that arise following a period of conflict, civil strife or repression, and that are aimed directly at confronting and dealing with past violations of human rights and humanitarian law" (Roht-Arriaza 2006, 2). It has become more important in the debates, and measures to deal with past have been applied by national and international actors all over the world. The origins of TJ can be traced back to the

Second World War and the trials of Nuremberg and Tokyo (Bickford 2005; Kritz 1995; Teitel 2000). Mechanisms of TJ include trials or other forms of criminal prosecution, truth commissions, reparation programs, institutional reforms, and memory projects as well as amnesties. One characteristic of TJ is that it combines aspects from many different disciplines such as sociology, psychology, law, political science, and philosophy. Furthermore, it is a very dynamic field, which derived from the practice and is still hard to capture. So far, there is no theory of TJ, which would show what TJ intervention would result in a specific outcome in a given situation nor is there consent on the question whether a theory is needed. There is not even a common notion of what TJ is nor a clear definition of its key factors: truth, justice, and reconciliation. The concept is, however, based on implicit theoretical assumptions. Some recent works made attempts to create a theory and to disentangle those assumptions, but the discussion is still ongoing in this heterogeneous, young, and moving field (Buckley-Zistel et al. 2014; Corradetti, Eisikovits, and Rotondi 2015; Olsen, Payne, and Reiter 2010, 25–28). The present study aims to empirically analyze the assumption that truth commissions and reparation programs enhance social cohesion. By doing so, it further contributes to theory building.

Truth commissions cover a wide field:

> Truth commissions are tasked with some or all of the following goals: to discover, clarify, and formally acknowledge past abuses; to address the needs of victims; to "counter impunity" and advance individual accountability; to outline institutional responsibility and recommend reforms; and to promote reconciliation and reduce conflict over the past.
>
> (Hayner 2010, 20)

Hayner (2010, 35–38) classified the Peruvian commission as one of the broadest in its mandate.

Reparation programs to address social, psychological, and economic consequences of violent conflicts have also been applied in many post-conflict societies worldwide. The design of the Peruvian reparation program is classified as very extensive program as well (Laplante 2014, 76–77). Reparations are expected to contribute to individual satisfaction and acknowledgment, and to restore social cohesion within communities and society as a whole. Laplante (2014, 70–79) explains the wide range of possible goals of reparations, reaching from reparative justice with the aim of compensation to socio-economic justice and an equal society in her model "plural justice aims of reparations".

It becomes apparent that the aims of these two measures and the whole concept of TJ are manifold. The "triumvirate" of truth, justice, and reconciliation is perhaps the most prevalent (Gready 2010). While some see those rather as short-term aims, peace and democracy are categorized as the long-term goals of TJ. The normative origin of TJ is based on Western hemisphere ideas of the state, society, and state-society relations. Overall, TJ measures are supposed to contribute to a peaceful, democratic future (Skaar, Garcia-Godos, and Collins 2016, 27). Whether TJ should focus on democracies can, however, reasonably be questioned.

It is important to note that some of the aims of TJ can contradict each other. Prevalent in the literature was the peace vs. justice as well as the truth vs. justice debate. A very relevant fact is also that the accomplishment of individual rights with certain benefits does not necessarily support social dynamics within a group or society in a positive way but can also have contradictory effects when causing new reasons for envy. This is crucial for the debate about individual reparations in this book.

Skaar and Malca (2015) make clear that most of the aims of TJ are based on normative or philosophical ideas and are not empirically grounded, critical research began only fairly recently. It questions whether TJ achieves what it promises and whether it really has the deterring effect it is meant to have in view of the continuing high number of human rights violations worldwide (Thoms, Ron, and Paris 2008, 19). Furthermore, requests to "localize" TJ and focus more on local conditions and needs, especially the necessities of conflict-affected people, are increasing (Baines 2010; Hinton 2010; McEvoy and McGregor 2008; Méndez 2016; Shaw, Waldorf, and Hazan 2010). Baines (2010, 413) points to the increasing awareness on the unintended effects: "Transitional justice mechanisms are increasingly scrutinized for their impact on the lives of those most affected, the 'victims'". Sriram, Martin-Ortega and Herman (2009, 34) hint at a risk: "If the population of a country perceives that the [TJ] strategies and tools are being imposed on them and are not locally appropriate, such practices lose their legitimacy and efficacy". On the other hand, Lambourne (2009, 47) highlights the possible positive effects of TJ when applied appropriately: "Democratisation of the transitional justice process, which results in local ownership and capacity building, is more likely to contribute to sustainable peacebuilding".

Within the constantly growing body of scholarship on TJ, an increasing number of studies are questioning whether the respective instrument fulfilled its theorized and mandated aims and objectives in the societies. Van der Merwe, Baxter and Chapman (2009, 4) stress the importance of such evaluations in order to advance both research and TJ practice:

> Empirically based research can make a vital contribution to understanding what it means for a society to go through a transitional justice process, and it can help analyze the process's short- and long-term impact. Such research can serve as the basis for more informed policy decisions in the future.

Skaar (2013, 98) also demands more high-quality research: "More in-depth studies of single cases employing two or more TJ mechanisms, looking at how these interact and affect the process of reconciliation".

Good overviews of existing research addressing theoretical and methodological challenges are provided by Skaar, Malca, and Eide (2015), special issues (Bonacker and Buckley-Zistel 2013; Duggan 2010; Reiter and Wiebelhaus-Brahm 2016) as well as the article by Thoms, Ron, and Paris (2010). Despite growing attention, however, a profound and sustained understanding of how best to do TJ impact research remains arguably limited.

In TJ research, qualitative single case studies analyzing mechanisms in one country are still predominant. Such studies provide detailed and local insights into the work of TJ mechanisms. Comparative studies, on the other hand, can cover more cases such as Hayner's (2010) impressive comparison of 40 truth commissions and their impact regarding reforms, prosecutions, and reparations. There are only few studies analyzing several TJ mechanisms together. Remarkable developments in this regard are large-sample comparative studies with newly developed databases (Binningsbø et al. 2012; Olsen, Payne, and Reiter 2010) including multiple TJ instruments. They still struggle, however, to find convincing causal relations between TJ and democracy or peace (Lie, Binningsbo, and Gates 2007; Binningsbø et al. 2012). The findings of these quantitative studies are still limited and face problems of endogeneity, selection bias, and limitations of the information used in the datasets (Thoms, Ron, and Paris 2010). Mixed method designs are another answer to the challenge of assessing TJ impact (Pham et al. 2016; Salehi and Williams 2016; Wiebelhaus-Brahm 2010). Moreover, surveys are another promising tool to measure attitudes toward TJ processes and the overall impact of TJ measures (Gibson, Sonis, and Hean 2010; Nussio, Rettberg, and Ugarriza 2015; Pham et al. 2007; 2011; Samii 2013; Stover and Weinstein 2004; Sulmont 2007). Longitudinal data through which changes over time can be observed are especially revealing, such as Backer's (2010) and Gibson's studies (2006; 2009; 2004) on South Africa. These are the very few works that analyze how TJ measures are actually perceived by the people who constitute the target group of the measures. The usefulness of surveys in TJ research has recently been emphasized also by Backer and Kulkarni (2016). However, for most countries, available survey data are not sufficient for these kinds of analyses and impact evaluations.

Addressing these weaknesses of the available databases and the sometimes limited explanatory power of some qualitative single case studies, I propose a structured, focused sub-national comparison of individuals and communities with and without attention from a TJ measure: in my case, the Peruvian TRC and the reparation program. I argue that in specific transitional contexts in which only parts of the population are exposed to TJ programs, as it is indeed the case for the majority of such measures, the proposed methodology constitutes a useful approach of accounting for the impact of those programs while controlling for other potentially intervening factors. The within-country comparison of regions and individuals with and without "treatment" by the TRC and the reparation program constitutes the quasi-experimental design, which has not been applied in this form in TJ impact research so far (Bunselmeyer and Schulz 2019).[4]

Repairing social cohesion

Social cohesion is concerned with the relationship between people in a community or society as well as how they relate to the state. In the words of Chan, To and Chan (2006, 290):

> Social cohesion is a state of affairs concerning both the vertical and the horizontal interactions among members of society as characterized by a set of attitudes and norms that includes trust, a sense of belonging and the willingness to participate and help, as well as their behavioural manifestations.

The indicator I developed for the community level covers the horizontal dimension of social cohesion within the community and the vertical dimension of state-citizen cohesion. Furthermore, I include subjective attitudes as well as objective behavior in the indicator. Social cohesion includes social and political trust, the basic norms of living together within the communities as well as social and political participation and the relation with the state. It is a comprehensive and adequate concept for this study because of these different dimensions and the focus on relationships and interactions.

Social cohesion is one of the aims of TJ, while it is not necessarily always called social cohesion. Some authors refer to social reconstruction or reintegration (Greiff 2009; Vinck and Pham 2010). There is, moreover, a certain overlap with the concept of reconciliation. The concept captures several aims of the TRC and the reparation program in Peru, which were meant to enhance civic trust within society, reestablish citizenship, and be part of a new social pact (CVR 2003, Vol. IX, Ch. 2.2, 138). Former president Humala quoted earlier also claimed that the reparation program would contribute to social inclusion and democracy for all Peruvians. The concept of social cohesion also draws this link to the concept of democracy, as the overall aim of TJ, with a focus on state-society relations and as such offers the possibility to analyze democracy on the basis level of society instead of using macro indicators as other studies on TJ impact have done. This macro data have often difficulties to capture the local level (Skaar, Malca, and Eide 2015, 53–55). Malca (2015) describes that in Peru macro indicators for the level of democracy are fairly high in contrast to the weaknesses the Peruvian democracy has in reality. So more research on the real situation is necessary which I deliver with this study.

While research agrees that higher social cohesion is positive for a society, there is no certainty about how to enhance it. TJ could be one way. Although social cohesion is often mentioned as one of the aims of TJ measures, there are no studies on the effects of TJ on social cohesion that I am aware of. My work delivers an important contribution with the analytical and empirical connection of both concepts.

Research focus and framework

The question in the center of this book is how the Peruvian TRC and the reparation program affected social cohesion in post-conflict communities.

The logical chain underlying the study is as follows: First, I assume that social cohesion was weakened (by the conflict and by other factors); second, TJ is applied to enhance social cohesion; third, I assess how TJ worked in the communities; fourth, I assess the level of social cohesion in the community and individuals; and finally, I draw the connection on how TJ influenced social cohesion. In methodological terms, my first independent variable is the work of the commission in the villages. The second independent variable is the attention from the reparation program for the communities and individuals. My dependent variable is the level of social cohesion, measured with the indicators elaborated for the community and for the individual level. Based on the claims of TJ, I assume a positive effect of the TRC and reparation program on individual attitudes and communal social cohesion. Within the quasi-experimental research design, I would expect higher social cohesion in the communities with "treatment" from the TRC and reparation program.

To structure the analysis, I developed an analytical framework with different stages of TJ impact based on Pham and Vinck (2007) and Skaar, Malca, and Eide (2015): (I) conception, (II) implementation, and (III) impact of TJ measures, which were extended with two more sub-stages: (IIa) awareness and (IIb) perception (see Chapter 3). Many existing studies focus on the conceptualization, planning, and design of TJ measures, followed by the implementation. The added stage awareness has hardly been researched at all. My pre-field study conducted made clear that not all people in the villages had heard about the TRC and/or reparation program. There exists a difference between objective exposure to TJ measures (there was a project implemented in the community) and subjective exposure to TJ (the person is aware about the TJ project). For analyzing the effects on the people, it was, therefore, necessary to assess the level of awareness and knowledge that the community members and authorities have regarding the TJ measures. Very important is, following, the perception and evaluation regarding the two measures by the affected people. It is obvious that only a positive evaluation of the TRC and reparation program can lead to a positive effect of the measure on social cohesion. The last step then is the assessment of social cohesion within the communities and for the individuals. On this basis, finally, the effects of the TRC and reparation program can be analyzed.

In the first part of the analysis, I compare four rural communities with different levels of attention of the TRC and the reparation program in detail. In the second part, I widen this analysis and include six more communities that received different levels of attention in the comparison. In the third part, I compare groups of individuals such as reparation receivers and non-receivers as well as victims and non-victims regarding their opinions about the past, their perception of TJ measures, and their attitudes toward social cohesion. This combined analysis allows studying the impact of the Peruvian TRC and the reparation program on social cohesion from different angles.

The analysis is based on extensive first-hand data from extended periods of fieldwork from 2014 to 2016. With my assistants, I conducted 160 semi-structured interviews in 11 communities of Peru. Half of them were conducted with communal authorities such as communal presidents, governors, mayors, and teachers and the other half with ordinary community members. Furthermore, the ethnographic field research involved participant observation, two focus groups, and a special form was the presentation and discussion of preliminary results of my study that I organized in five occasions.[5] Moreover, I conducted 43 additional expert interviews with former TRC members, representatives from the Ministry of Justice and Human Rights who were responsible for the reparation program, universities, and NGOs. In the analysis, I use this qualitative data but include some descriptive statistics next to qualitative analysis methods.

Transitional justice and social cohesion in Peru

> Internationally, Peru is well known for its impressive and sound truth commission, for the impeccable trials of Fujimori, for its collective reparations programme, and for professionalism in preparing the national victims' registry. These are all examples of advances on the road from impunity towards accountability. Yet, as we have seen, much more needs to be done to build on these achievements.
>
> (García-Godos and Reátegui 2016, 248)

Within the political circumstances of Peru, it is rather surprising that such a broad commission and reparation program were applied. Compared to other post-conflict cases, Peru experienced an internal armed conflict with some special characteristics: The TRC identified poverty as well as social, economic, and political exclusion as structural root causes of the conflict. These factors were combined with an important structural characteristic: the inequality that had marked the country for centuries. This is an important factor when investigating economic reparations. The second principal factor is that the conflict started and took place mostly in marginalized rural parts of the country. Seventy-five percent of all victims were people with indigenous roots and Quechua as their mother language, occupied in agriculture, with rather low levels of education (CVR 2003, Vol. I, Ch. 3; CVR 2010: 14–16). Not the whole country was affected in the same way. Huge parts of society have not been harmed directly. Public interest in dealing with the past was therefore rather low. The third aspect concerns the end of the conflict. The rebel groups were defeated by state forces and civilian self-defense committees, and no power-sharing or peace-agreements were concluded as in other cases. The rebel group Shining Path,[6] as the most important force in the conflict, was not visible in this TJ process apart from trials

against some of their leaders. Moreover, after the armed conflict ended, the new political elite entering office was the old elite already in charge during the violent time and also responsible for the escalating violence. This meant that the political support for dealing with the past was also rather low.

Regarding these political and societal circumstances, it was surprising that Peru installed such a broad TRC at all in 2001, which still holds as example worldwide. The commission was created only thanks to a small "window of opportunity" (Root 2009) and pressure from the human rights movement during the transitional government under interim president Valentin Panigua (2000–2001).

Following its installation, there were high expectations toward the TRC and its reparation program on the part of the affected people. The most important task of the commission was the collection of testimonies of those who had lived through the violence. This was a huge undertaking as Root (2012, 75–76) and Hayner (2010, 36–37) explain. Mainly in rural zones of the country, about 500 people collected approximately 17,000 testimonies from victims of massacres, torture, and sexual violence, family members of disappeared, former members of the rebel groups, political leaders, authorities, and members of the *rondas campesinas.*[7] The local personal had to cover a huge territory in a short time. An important source of support was the previous work done by human rights groups, which had been collecting information on victims, massacres, and other crimes for years. Also, many of those working for the commission had been involved in NGO work before. This is an important factor for the analysis of the perception of the commission later on in this study.

The commission also decided to hold public hearings in various regions of the country to make the Peruvian public aware of what their fellow citizens had lived through. Moreover, victims should be given a stage, the opportunity to feel heard in public after they already gave their testimony privately.

The exhumations carried out in three villages in the Ayacucho region – Lucanamarca, Chuschi, and Totos – were also part of the work of the commission. The TRC chose three emblematic cases in which NGOs had already collected a history of events, identified the locations of graves, and compiled lists of victims and their family members. Only with this preparatory work done, the TRC was able to complete the exhumations in such a short time frame. All three communities are situated in the marginalized rural part of the Andes and were presented as villages of victims (Exp32; Exp36; Exp37, also Rojas-Perez 2017, 41–50). The exhumations served, as declared by the commission, to find evidence for these cases but also as a sign for the villages and their inhabitants that the commission would uncover the truth and give attention to the happenings of the past.[8]

The TRC presented its 8,000-page report to the president and congress in August 2003. The commission analyzed the conflict's progression, its causes as well as the degree of responsibility of its different actors, delivered profound case studies, analyzed the consequences of the violence, and, in the last part, developed a set of recommendations.

One of the main recommendations in the final report of the TRC was the comprehensive plan for reparations: "Applied evenhandedly, reparations must also generate civic trust, reestablishing the damaged relationship between citizens and the state, so that democratic transition and governance are consolidated and new scenarios of violence are prevented" (CVR 2010, 252). Reparations were meant to contribute to social cohesion (see Chapter 2). The program included seven different forms of reparations:

1 Restoration of Citizen's Rights
2 Reparations in Education
3 Reparations in Health
4 Collective Reparations
5 Symbolic Reparations
6 Promotion and Access to Housing
7 Individual Economic Reparations

The design of the Peruvian program fulfills the categories developed by de Greiff (2006, 6–13), Laplante (2015, 162–71), and the "Basic Principles on Reparations" passed by the United Nations. In its design, it is comprehensive, complete, and integrated with the other TJ instruments and includes measures for compensation, rehabilitation, and satisfaction. In 2004, the High Level Multisector Commission (*Comisión Multisectorial de Alto Nivel – CMAN*) was established, which today falls under the Ministry of Justice and Human Rights. This commission was in charge of further coordinating the actions toward peace, reparations, and reconciliation. A second entity was installed in charge for registering affected people in 2006: the Reparations Council (*Consejo de Reparaciones*).

The first challenge was to define victims and potential beneficiaries of the reparation program. For individual reparations, all potential beneficiaries had to register with the Reparations Council. The Council tried to make use of different existing TRC registers and others, but every person had to submit again to be in the National Registry of Victims (*Registro Único de Víctimas – RUV*). Once the affected person wanted to register, it was necessary to provide evidence for the case reported in the form of witnesses, photos, or other documentation. For many people, especially from rural areas, it was very difficult to provide the evidence required, and they were stuck in this step.

The success of the registration process depended on being recognized as a victim. Those who finally registered in the RUV did receive a certificate acknowledging that they were indeed victims of the internal armed conflict. After registering, it took until 2011 for the first beneficiaries to receive individual financial reparations, 31 years after the beginning of the internal armed conflict. By 2017, around 83,600 victims with first priority had received individual economic reparations with a monetary amount of up to 3,000 US$ per person. In total, about 223,000 people were registered as victims or relatives, but not all of those are eligible for economic reparations (CMAN 2017). The number of potential beneficiaries is still a lot higher. As for reparations in health, education, housing, and citizens' rights, there is little progress, as I will further discuss in the analysis of the communities.

The objective of collective reparations was to contribute to the reconstruction and consolidation of collective institutions in the communities that lost part of their social and physical infrastructure in the violence and to compensate for their suffering. Communal projects within the reparation program are, furthermore, meant to contribute to social cohesion by uniting the community members in this work (CVR 2010, 311).

The procedure for collective projects is as follows: First, the community has to be registered as a community affected by violence. Second, the community needs to apply for a collective reparation project and be prioritized within the program. Third, the community needs to choose a project. Last, CMAN transfers the money to the local municipality, which then implements the project.

These steps already hint to the fact that collective reparations depend on the local authorities. Requests for being considered for the reparation program have to be made by the local authorities. Only if they have the knowledge and the capacity (or are assisted by an NGO) to apply for the program, can the village profit from it. The communities are prioritized according to recently developed criteria. These criteria place rigid demands on the project plans and the compliance of local authorities.

By July 2017, more than 2,400 communities out of 4,790 registered to have been severely affected have received collective reparations with projects of up to 30,000 US$ for each community (CMAN 2017).

The Peruvian case was chosen for this study because of its worldwide rating as one case with a very broad commission's mandate (Bakiner 2016, 36–37; Hayner 2010, 35–38) and reparation program. The commission followed the vision of a macro-reconciliation with the reconstruction of a social and political pact. The reparation program is an important measure in this process (Laplante 2014, 76). I expected such comprehensive measures to have a high impact as well. Moreover, Peru offered the possibility to find communities and individuals, who had received reparations already, as well as those still awaiting attention and this created perfect conditions for a within-country comparison in a quasi-experimental design.

Coming back to the different stages of TJ impact, the first phase conceptualization, design and establishment of the commission in Peru, has been investigated already (most extensively in Root 2009, 2012; Malca 2015; García-Godos and Reátegui 2016). The implementation of the recommendations of the commission has been analyzed by Macher (2014) and within an edited volume by Huber and Del Pino (2015). There are also several critical studies on memory and truth-telling as well as on truth-building by the commission, questioning whether the impact of the commission was only positive (Degregori 2004; Lambright 2015; Laplante and Theidon 2009; Mendoza 2016; Yezer 2008; Winter 2008). Two surveys conducted by the IDEHPUCP (Instituto de Democracia y Derechos Humanos de la Pontificia Universidad Católica del Perú) on attitudes of the society toward the conflict and the TJ process are also included in my analysis (Barrantes 2007; IDEHPUCP 2014; Sulmont 2007). Theidon (2006, 2007, 2013) offers profound ethnological insights into Peruvian communities and their situation during and after the conflict. Her studies on repentance and reconciliation processes in different communities are especially relevant as are her gender-focused contributions (Theidon 2007; see also Barrera 2015; Boesten 2010; Mantilla Falcón 2005).

The reparation program in Peru was topic of various reports regarding its design and implementation published on behalf of the International Center for Transitional Justice (APRODEH and ICTJ 2002, 2009; Barrantes 2012; Correa 2013; Guillerot and Magarrell 2006b; Guillerot 2008; Paredes 2010; Paredes and Correa 2011; Rubio-Marín, Paz y Paz Bailey, and Guillerot 2009) and other institutions (Barrenechea Carpio 2010; Defensoria del Pueblo 2014; Guillerot and Magarrell 2006a; Laplante 2014; Waardt 2013). There are also very valuable studies by Ulfe (Ulfe 2013, 2015; Ulfe and Málaga Sabogal 2015) on reparations in different communities, and the articles by Guillerot (2006), Laplante and Theidon (2007), and Theidon (2016) address the topic of reparations from a gender perspective. García-Godos (2008) and Laplante (2016) who have been following the process of reparations for more than a decade analyze the challenges within the Peruvian reparation program. De Waardt (2013, 2016) developed important contributions on the role of victims and their associations within the reparation process.

My study focuses on the micro level of violence-affected communities, which has not been investigated intensively and not in a comparative manner. Only very few reports exist for certain regions (Paredes and Correa 2011; Ulfe 2013). What is still missing are works on the second and third stages, the perception and the actual effects TJ has had on social cohesion on the community and the individual level. Moreover, until today, there are no systematic comparisons of the TJ processes in different areas of Peru, so I can offer a new perspective in this field. Lastly, the link between the processes of TJ and social cohesion has not yet been drawn.

Based on the assumptions of the concept of TJ, I expected higher social cohesion in communities and individuals that have received more attention from the TRC and reparation program.

Findings and contribution

My main findings suggest that the impact of the Peruvian TRC and the reparation program on social cohesion was rather limited and in some cases even negative. My analysis demonstrates that there was more awareness of the commission where the TRC worked more intensively which was to be expected. But most of the interviewed people connected the commission only to the reparation program and disregarded other measures such as testimony giving, exhumations, and public audiences. Only very few people, affected and non-affected, had heard of the final report that was published, and this alone did not lead to satisfaction. I found low awareness of collective reparations as some were perceived as development programs without symbolic component and with no reference to the violence suffered in the community. Problems with the technical implementation of the projects further hindered their positive effects. One alarming consequence that I observed was discontent because of the "unjust" and "unsatisfying" implementation of the individual reparation program causing new envy and resentment. The overall perception of reparations was in most cases negative, which contradicts the conception and aims of reparations. Finally, I discovered nearly the same if not lower levels of solidarity and trust in the communities with higher TRC and reparation work compared to those with lower engagement. The analysis on the individual level confirmed these findings. While awareness and knowledge of the two measures is highest in male authorities, this is not necessarily connected to the level of attention. And a high level of attention does not automatically lead to positive impact. The way in which people perceive the measure is the decisive factor for its impact. Only a very few people showed high levels of satisfaction with the TRC and the reparation program. Some of those also showed high attitudes toward social cohesion, but the link was not as strong as expected.

This finding challenges the assumption of TJ's positive effects on social cohesion. The commission and following reparations were unable to support the development of social cohesion in the rural areas under investigation, and the relationship between the state and communities still shows the existence of various social rifts, resulting in an ongoing challenge for enhancing social cohesion and democracy.

The analysis contributes to understanding the impact of nationally applied TJ instruments on social cohesion in local settings. My findings highlight the connection between implementation, awareness, and perception and their influence on the impact of TJ mechanisms. The contribution of this book is threefold: First, this study combines the concepts of TJ and social cohesion analytically and empirically. With the operationalization and empirical analysis of theoretical claims, I contribute to theory development. Second, I contribute to the discussion on how to conduct impact assessments of TJ measures with the new methodological approach. And finally, I deliver an in-depth comparative impact analysis of how the TRC and reparation program worked, how they were perceived, and what impact they have had on social cohesion on the micro level of society.

An important asset of this study is the high number of data collected in different settings. Together with the different levels of analysis and different methods and frameworks developed and applied, this allows to draw conclusions also regarding other regions of Peru and the processes in other countries. Finally, the findings of the book regarding problems and opportunities of the respective TJ measures are important to actors still working in the implementation of the reparation program in Peru. A summary and recommendations derived from this study were handed over to the responsible officials in the Ministry of Justice and Human Rights in Peru and used as a basis for the restructuring of the reparation program. Furthermore, conclusions drawn from the Peruvian case can be relevant for other cases as well, where TRCs or reparation programs are still in the early stages.

The plan of the book

The remainder of the book concentrates on the analysis as the basis for these conclusions. In Chapter 2, I develop the social cohesion indicator to capture this social phenomenon. Following, I theorize possible effects of truth commissions and reparation programs on social cohesion in an innovative framework, which is later applied to the Peruvian case but can be easily adopted from other researchers for other TJ contexts.

In Chapter 3, I briefly introduce the methodological framework for the analysis: the quasi-experimental research design. Beginning with sketching the stages for measuring the effects of TJ measures, I then elaborate on the operationalization for my study. The small-n comparative research design with the quasi-experimental comparison is introduced. With this method, I deliver an answer on the debates on how to assess TJ impact. Again, this method shall be applied in the analysis of other TJ contexts.

The core of the book is the empirical part in Chapters 4–6. In Chapter 4, I focus on the situation of four post-conflict villages. With the help of the indicator developed, I elaborate sociologies of the villages. Every village has its own history of violence and its distinct set of circumstances. According to the research design, some have higher levels of attention from TJ measures, while others have lower levels of attention. The in-depth comparison offers new insights on the micro level of TJ and social cohesion processes. In Chapter 5, I broaden the analysis to ten villages to demonstrate that the same patterns apply in other settings.

Chapter 6 proceeds to a comparison on the level of the individuals interviewed in the villages. Groups of individuals are compared first, with respect to the levels of attention received. Here, I want to find out whether those who participated in the TRC and received individual and collective reparations, have different opinions on TJ, social cohesion, and the situation of the village from those that did not benefit from the measures. Following on from that, I compare victims and non-victims, men and women as well as authorities and non-authorities to challenge common assumptions. Finally, I focus on the people who show the highest satisfaction with the TRC and reparation program and the interviewees with the highest attitudes toward social cohesion, in order to analyze their characteristics and exposure to TJ attention.

Finally, Chapter 7 combines the results of the analysis on the community level with patterns found on the individual level. This multilevel comparison allows a broader discussion of the findings and the connection with other studies. While

it is common sense that the form of implementation of TJ measures has implications as to their impact, I want to focus on the importance of its perception for its success. The book concludes with this discussion of the ambiguity of truth and reparations, its limits but also the possibilities of TJ.

Notes

1 Ollanta Humala, Mensaje a la Nación, 28.07.2014, translation by the author, original available in: http://rpp.pe/politica/actualidad/lea-todo-el-mensaje-a-la-nacion-del-presidente-ollanta-humala-noticia-711728.

2 This study uses the term "victim" synonymously with "affected people" with a broad understanding following the commission:

> The CVR believes that victims include all people or groups of people who, because of the internal armed conflict experienced by the country between May 1980 and November 2000, have suffered from actions or omissions that violate norms of international human rights law.
>
> (CVR 2010: 309)

I do not propose a perpetrator-victim dichotomy and do not classify victims as people without agency or as passive or innocent. I use the term as analytical category being aware of the discussion around it. For the analysis in Chapters 4–6, I classify people according to their self-definition as victims and non-victims.

3 https://transitionaljusticedata.com/.

4 To my knowledge, Philipp Schulz is the only other researcher who has applied this method in TJ scholarship in his analysis of the International Criminal Tribunal for Rwanda (ICTR). In a joint article, we discuss quasi-experimental research designs in more detail: Bunselmeyer and Schulz (2019).

5 Thanks to funding, I was able to return to two of the communities. I organized three little presentations in the villages, connecting my research with a general comparison of the life in Germany and Peru. People were very interested in this and perceived it as a good initiative.

6 Shining Path (*Partido Comunista del Perú – Sendero Luminoso (PCP-SL)*) was protagonists of the internal armed conflict in Peru. The aim of the rebel organization was to overthrow the Peruvian state in a peasant revolution, to set off an international revolution against capitalism, and to establish communism. Its ideology was based on Maoism and did not have an explicit ethnical dimension.

7 *Rondas campesinas* or civilian self-defense committees have a long tradition in some peasant communities and were especially important in the fight against Shining Path in the rural areas. They became a main actor as well and were also incorporated in the strategy of the armed forces that trained them and provided them with weapons at the end of the 1980s (CVR 2003, Vol. II, Ch. 1.5).

8 www.cverdad.org.pe/apublicas/exhumaciones/index.php.

References

APRODEH, and ICTJ. 2002. "Design Parameters for a Reparations Program in Peru." ICTJ. www.ictj.org/publication/design-parameters-reparations-program-peru.

———. 2009. "Reporte Nacional de Vigilancia Del Programa de Reparaciones Colectivas – Etapa II." ICTJ. www.ictj.org/sites/default/files/ICTJ-Aprodeh-Peru-Collective-Reparations-2009-Spanish.pdf.

Backer, David. 2010. "Watching a Bargain Unravel? A Panel Study of Victims' Attitudes about Transitional Justice in Cape Town, South Africa." *International Journal of Transitional Justice* 4 (3): 443–56.

Backer, David, and Anupma Kulkarni. 2016. "Humanizing Transitional Justice: Reflections on the Role of Survey Research in Studying Violent Conflict and Its Aftermath." *Transitional Justice Review* 1 (4): 187–232.

Baines, Erin K. 2010. "Spirits and Social Reconstruction after Mass Violence: Rethinking Transitional Justice." *African Affairs* 109 (436): 409–30.

Bakiner, Onur. 2016. *Truth Commissions Memory, Power, and Legitimacy.* Philadelphia: University of Pennsylvania Press.

Barrantes, Rafael. 2007. "Memoria y Justicia En La Opinión Pública Peruana. Reflexiones a Partir de La Encuesta Nacional Sobre Percepciones de Memoria y Reconciliación." *Memoria. Revista Sobre Cultura, Democracia y Derechos Humanos,* Lima: IDEHPUCP, no. 2: 29–38.

———. 2012. "Reparations and Displacement in Peru." Case Studies on Transitional Justice and Displacement. ICTJ / Brookings-LSE. www.ictj.org/sites/default/files/ICTJ-Brookings-Displacement-Reparations-Peru-CaseStudy-2012-English.pdf.

Barrenechea Carpio, Rodrigo. 2010. *Políticas locales de reparación en Ayacucho: ¿Reparaciones sin reparadores?* Lima: IEP.

Barrera, Anna. 2015. *Violence Against Women in Legally Plural Settings: Experiences and Lessons from the Andes.* Abingdon, Oxon; New York: Routledge.

Bickford, Louise. 2005. "Transitional Justice." In *Encyclopedia of Genocide and Crimes Against Humanity,* edited by Dinah Shelton, 3:1045–47. Detroit: Macmillan Reference.

Binningsbø, Helga Malmin, Cyanne E. Loyle, Scott Gates, and Jon Elster. 2012. "Armed Conflict and Post-Conflict Justice, 1946–2006: A Dataset." *Journal of Peace Research* 49 (5): 731–40.

Boesten, Jelke. 2010. "Analyzing Rape Regimes at the Interface of War and Peace in Peru." *International Journal of Transitional Justice* 4 (1): 110–29.

Bonacker, Thorsten, and Susanne Buckley-Zistel. 2013. "Introduction: Transitions from Violence. Analysing the Effects of Transitional Justice." *International Journal of Conflict and Violence* 7 (1): 4–9.

Buckley-Zistel, Susanne, Teresa Koloma Beck, Christian Braun, and Friederike Mieth. 2014. *Transitional Justice Theories.* Abingdon, Oxon; New York: Routledge.

Bunselmeyer, Elisabeth, and Philipp Schulz. 2019. "Quasi-Experimental Research Designs as a Tool for Assessing the Impact of Transitional Justice Instruments." *The International Journal of Human Rights,* online first, doi:10.1080/13642987.2019.1672663.

Chan, Joseph, Ho-Pong To, and Elaine Chan. 2006. "Reconsidering Social Cohesion: Developing a Definition and Analytical Framework for Empirical Research." *Social Indicators Research* 75 (2): 273–302.

CMAN. 2017. Informe de Avances en la Implementación del Plan Integral de Reparaciones. Comisión Multisectorial de Alto Nivel. CMAN. Lima.

Corradetti, Claudio, Nir Eisikovits, and Jack Volpe Rotondi. 2015. *Theorizing Transitional Justice.* Farnham: Ashgate.

Correa, Cristián. 2013. "Reparations in Peru: From Recommendations to Implementation." ICTJ. www.ictj.org/sites/default/files/ICTJ-Report-Peru-Reparations-Spanish-2013.pdf.

CVR (Comisión de la Verdad y Reconciliación). 2003. "Informe Final." Lima.

CVR (Comisión de la Verdad y Reconciliación). 2010. "Hatun Willakuy: Abbreviated Version of the Final Report of the Truth and Reconciliation Commission." Lima.

Defensoria del Pueblo. 2014. "Balance Del Nivel de Cumplimiento Del Programa de Reparaciones Económicas Individuales (PREI)." Lima. www.defensoria.gob.pe/modules/Downloads/informes/varios/2014/Informe-de-Adjuntia-008–2014-ADHPD-DP.pdf.

Degregori, Carlos Iván. 2004. "Heridas abiertas, derechos esquivos: Reflexiones sobre la Comisión de la Verdad y Reconciliación." In *Memorias en conflicto: aspectos de la violencia política contemporánea*, edited by Raynald Belay, Jorge Bracamonte, Carlos Iván Degregori, and Jean Joinville Vacher, 75–85. Lima: Embajada de Francia en el Perú, Red para el Desarrollo de las Ciencias Sociales en el Perú, IEP, IFEA.

Duggan, Colleen. 2010. "Editorial Note. Special Issue: Transitional Justice on Trial - Evaluating Its Impact." *International Journal of Transitional Justice* 4 (3): 315–28.

García-Godos, Jemima. 2008. "Victim Reparations in the Peruvian Truth Commission and the Challenge of Historical Interpretation." *International Journal of Transitional Justice* 2 (1): 63–82.

García-Godos, Jemima, and Félix Reátegui. 2016. "Peru: Beyond Paradigmatic Cases." In *Transitional Justice in Latin America: The Uneven Road from Impunity Towards Accountability*, edited by Elin Skaar, Jemima Garcia-Godos, and Cath Collins. Abingdon, Oxon; New York: Routledge.

Gibson, James L. 2004. "Overcoming Apartheid: Can Truth Reconcile a Divided Nation?" *Politikon* 31 (2): 129–55.

———. 2006. "The Contributions of Truth to Reconciliation Lessons From South Africa." *Journal of Conflict Resolution* 50 (3): 409–32.

———. 2009. "Taking Stock of Truth and Reconciliation in South Africa." In *Assessing the Impact of Transitional Justice: Challenges for Empirical Research*, edited by Hugo van der Merwe, Victoria Baxter, and Audrey R. Chapman, 173–90. Washington, D.C: United States Institute of Peace Press.

Gibson, James L., Jeffrey Sonis, and Sokhom Hean. 2010. "Cambodians' Support for the Rule of Law on the Eve of the Khmer Rouge Trials." *International Journal of Transitional Justice* 4 (3): 377–96.

Gready, Paul. 2010. *The Era of Transitional Justice: The Aftermath of the Truth and Reconciliation Commission in South Africa and Beyond*. New York: Routledge.

Greiff, Pablo de. 2006. "Introduction: Repairing the Past: Compensation for Victims of Human Rights Violations." In *The Handbook of Reparations*, edited by Pablo de Greiff, 1–18. Oxford: Oxford University Press.

———. 2009. "Articulating the Links Between Transitional Justice and Development: Justice and Social Integration." Research Brief. ICTJ.

Guillerot, Julie. 2006. "Linking Gender and Reparations in Peru: A Failed Opportunity." In *What Happened to the Women? Gender and Reparations for Human Rights Violations*, edited by Ruth Rubio-Marín, 136–91. New York: Social Science Research Council. www.ssrc.org/publications/view/D6D99C02-EA4A-DE11-AFAC-001CC477EC70/.

———. 2008. "Reparaciones En La Transición Peruana:?` Dónde Estamos y Hacía Donde Vamos?" Reparaciones Para Las Víctimas de La Violencia Política. Estudios de Caso y Análisis Comparado. Bogotá: ICTJ, 233–291.

Guillerot, Julie, and Lisa Magarrell. 2006a. "Reparación En La Transición Peruana: Memorias de Un Proceso Inacabado." ICTJ. www.ictj.org/sites/default/files/ICTJ-Peru-Memory-Process-year-2006-Spanish.pdf.

———. 2006b. *Reparaciones en la Transición Peruana. Memorias de un Proceso Inacabado.* Edited by APRODEH and ICTJ. www.ictj.org/sites/default/files/ICTJ-Peru-Memory-Process-year-2006-Spanish.pdf.

Hayner, Priscilla B. 2010. *Unspeakable Truths: Transitional Justice and the Challenge of Truth Commissions.* New York: Routledge.

Hinton, Alexander Laban, ed. 2010. *Transitional Justice: Global Mechanisms and Local Realities after Genocide and Mass Violence.* Genocide, Political Violence, Human Rights Series. New Brunswick, NJ: Rutgers University Press.

Huber, Ludwig, and Ponciano Del Pino, eds. 2015. *Políticas En Justicia Transicional. Miradas Comparativas Sobre El Legado de La CVR.* Lima: IEP, Instituto de Estudios Peruanos.

IDEHPUCP. 2014. "Encuesta: Impacto Psicosocial de La CVR En El Perú." Lima: IDEHPUCP.

Kimberly Theidon. 2006. "Justice in Transition. The Micropolitics of Reconciliation in Postwar Peru." *Journal of Conflict Resolution* 50 (3): 433–57.

Kritz, Neil J. 1995. *Transitional Justice: How Emerging Democracies Reckon With Former Regimes : Laws, Rulings, and Reports.* Washington, D.C: United States Institute of Peace Press.

Lambourne, Wendy. 2009. "Transitional Justice and Peacebuilding after Mass Violence." *International Journal of Transitional Justice* 3 (1): 28–48.

Lambright, Anne. 2015. *Andean Truths: Transitional Justice, Ethnicity, and Cultural Production in Post-Shining Path Peru.* Liverpool: Liverpool University Press.

Laplante, Lisa J. 2014. "The Plural Justice Aims of Reparations." In *Transitional Justice Theories*, edited by Susanne Buckley-Zistel, Teresa Koloma Beck, Christian Braun, and Friederike Mieth, 66–84. Abingdon, Oxon; New York: Routledge.

———. 2015. "Just Repair." *Cornell International Law Journal* 48: 101–74.

———. 2016. "From Theory to Practice: Implementing Reparations in Post-Truth Commission Peru." In *Waging War, Making Peace: Reparations and Human Rights*, edited by Barbara Rose Johnston and Susan Slyomovics, 75–94. Abingdon, Oxon; New York: Routledge.

Laplante, Lisa J., and Kimberly Theidon. 2007. "Truth with Consequences: Justice and Reparations in Post-Truth Commission Peru." *Human Rights Quarterly* 29 (1): 228–50.

———. 2009. "Commissioning Truth, Constructing Silences: The Peruvian Truth Commission and the Other Truths of 'Terrorists.'" In *Mirrors of Justice: Law and Power in the Post-Cold War Era*, edited by Kamari Maxine Clarke and Mark Goodale, 291–315. Cambridge: Cambridge University Press.

Lie, Tove Grete, Helga Malmin Binningsbo, and Scott Gates. 2007. "Post-Conflict Justice and Sustainable Peace." *World Bank Policy Research Working Paper*, no. 4191. http://papers.ssrn.com/sol3/papers.cfm?abstract_id=979663.

Macher, Sofía. 2014. *¿Hemos avanzado? a 10 años de las recomendaciones de la Comisión de la Verdad y Reconciliación.* 1a ed. Estudios sobre memoria y violencia 6. Lima: Instituto de Estudios Peruanos.

Malca, Camila Gianella. 2015. "Peru: Changing Context for Transitional Justice." In *After Violence. Transitional Justice, Peace, and Democracy*, edited by Elin Skaar, Camila Gianella Malca, and Trine Eide, 94–124. London; New York: Routledge.

Mantilla Falcón, Julissa. 2005. "The Peruvian Truth and Reconciliation Commission's Treatment of Sexual Violence against Women." *Human Rights Brief* 12 (2): 1.

McEvoy, Kieran, and Lorna McGregor, eds. 2008. *Transitional Justice from Below: Grassroots Activism and the Struggle for Change*. Oxford: Hart Publishing.

Méndez, Juan E. 2016. "Editorial Note. Special Issue: Victims as Protagonists in Transitional Justice." *International Journal of Transitional Justice* 10 (1): 1–5.

Mendoza, Rafael Ramírez. 2016. "Una Lectura Crítica de La Memoria Emblemática de La CVR Desde Los Testimonios de La Masacre de Lucanamarca." In *Dando Cuenta: Estudios Sobre El Testimonio de La Violencia Política En El Perú (1980–2000)*, edited by Francesca Denegri and Alexandra Hibbett, 211–36. Lima: Pontifica Universidad católica del Perú.

Nussio, Enzo, Angelika Rettberg, and Juan E. Ugarriza. 2015. "Victims, Nonvictims and Their Opinions on Transitional Justice: Findings from the Colombian Case." *International Journal of Transitional Justice* 9 (2): 336–54.

Olsen, Tricia D., Leigh A. Payne, and Andrew G. Reiter. 2010. *Transitional Justice in Balance: Comparing Processes, Weighing Efficacy*. Washington, D.C: United States Institute of Peace Press.

Paredes, Sonia. 2010. "Sistema de Vigilancia de Reparaciones Situación de Las Mujeres Que Han Recibido Reparación Colectiva Tercer Reporte de Vigilancia de Reparaciones Colectivas." ICTJ. www.ictj.org/sites/default/files/ICTJ-Peru-Women-Reparations-2010-Spanish.pdf.

Paredes, Sonia, and Cristián Correa. 2011. "Perú: ¿Cuánto Se Ha Reparado En Nuestras Comunidades?" ICTJ. www.ictj.org/publication/per%C3%BA-%C2%BFcu%C3%A1nto-se-ha-reparado-en-nuestras-comunidades.

Pham, Phuong, and Patrick Vinck. 2007. "Empirical Research and the Development and Assessment of Transitional Justice Mechanisms." *International Journal of Transitional Justice* 1 (2): 231–48.

Pham, Phuong, Patrick Vinck, Mychelle Balthazard, and Sokhom Hean. 2011. "After the First Trial: A Population-Based Survey on Knowledge and Perceptions of Justice and the Extraordinary Chambers in the Courts of Cambodia." SSRN Scholarly Paper ID 1860963. Rochester, NY: Social Science Research Network. http://papers.ssrn.com/abstract=1860963.

Pham, Phuong, Patrick Vinck, Bridget Marchesi, Doug Johnson, Peter Dixon, and Kathryn Sikkink. 2016. "Evaluating Transitional Justice: The Role of Multi-Level Mixed Methods Datasets and the Colombia Reparation Program for War Victims." *Transitional Justice Review* 1 (4): Article 3.

Pham, Phuong, Patrick Vinck, Eric Stover, Andrew Moss, Marieke Wierda, and Richard Bailey. 2007. "When the War Ends: A Population-Based Survey on Attitudes about Peace, Justice, and Social Reconstruction in Northern Uganda." Berkeley, CA: Human Rights Center. http://papers.ssrn.com/sol3/papers.cfm?abstract_id=1448368.

Reiter, Andrew, and Eric Wiebelhaus-Brahm. 2016. "Editorial Note." *Transitional Justice Review* 1 (4): 1–6.

Roht-Arriaza, Naomi. 2006. "The New Landscape of Transitional Justice." In *Transitional Justice in the Twenty-First Century: Beyond Truth Versus Justice*, edited by Naomi Roht-Arriaza and Javier Mariezcurrena, 1–16. Cambridge: Cambridge University Press.

Rojas-Perez, Isaias. 2017. *Mourning Remains: State Atrocity, Exhumations, and Governing the Disappeared in Peru's Postwar Andes*. Stanford, CA: Stanford University Press.

Root, Rebecca K. 2009. "Through the Window of Opportunity: The Transitional Justice Network in Peru." *Human Rights Quarterly* 31 (2): 452–73.

———. 2012. *Transitional Justice in Peru*. New York: Palgrave Macmillan.

Rubio-Marín, Ruth, Claudia Paz y Paz Bailey, and Julie Guillerot. 2009. "Indigenous Peoples and Claims for Reparation: Tentative Steps in Peru and Guatemala." Claudia Paz y Paz Bailey. ICTJ. www.ictj.org/publication/indigenous-peoples-and-claims-reparation-tentative-steps-peru-and-guatemala.

Salehi, Mariam, and Timothy Williams. 2016. "Beyond Peace vs. Justice: Assessing Transitional Justice's Impact on Enduring Peace Using Qualitative Comparative Analysis." *Transitional Justice Review* 1 (4). doi:10.5206/tjr.2016.1.4.4.

Samii, Cyrus. 2013. "Who Wants to Forgive and Forget? Transitional Justice Preferences in Postwar Burundi." *Journal of Peace Research* 50 (2): 219–33.

Shaw, Rosalind, Lars Waldorf, and Pierre Hazan, eds. 2010. *Localizing Transitional Justice: Interventions and Priorities after Mass Violence.* Stanford Studies in Human Rights. Stanford, CA: Stanford University Press.

Skaar, Elin. 2013. "Reconciliation in a Transitional Justice Perspective." *Transitional Justice Review* 1 (1): 54–103.

Skaar, Elin, Camila Gianella Malca, and Trine Eide. 2015. *After Violence. Transitional Justice, Peace, and Democracy.* London; New York: Routledge.

Skaar, Elin, Jemima Garcia-Godos, and Cath Collins. 2016. *Transitional Justice in Latin America: The Uneven Road from Impunity Towards Accountability.* Abingdon, Oxon; New York: Routledge.

Sriram, Chandra Lekha, Olga Martin-Ortega, and Johanna Herman. 2009. "Evaluating and Comparing Strategies of Peacebuilding and Transitional Justice." Jad-PbP Working Paper Series No. 1. www.researchgate.net/profile/Olga_Martin-Ortega/publication/228914875_Evaluating_and_comparing_strategies_of_peacebuilding_and_transitional_justice/links/5728930008ae0acc4f493336.pdf.

Stover, Eric, and Harvey M. Weinstein, eds. 2004. *My Neighbor, My Enemy: Justice and Community in the Aftermath of Mass Atrocity.* Cambridge: Cambridge University Press.

Sulmont, David. 2007. "Las Distancias Del Recuerdo. Memoria y Opinión Pública Sobre El Conflicto Interno En El Perú, 1980–2000." *Memoria. Revista Sobre Cultura, Democracia y Derechos Humanos*, Lima: IDEHPUCP, no. 2: 9–28.

Teitel, Ruti G. 2000. *Transitional Justice.* Oxford: Oxford University Press.

Theidon, Kimberly. 2007. "Gender in Transition: Common Sense, Women, and War." *Journal of Human Rights* 6 (4): 453–78. doi:10.1080/14754830701693011.

———. 2013. *Intimate Enemies: Violence and Reconciliation in Peru.* Pennsylvania Studies in Human Rights. Philadelphia: University of Pennsylvania Press.

———. 2016. "A Greater Measure of Justice. Gender, Violence, and Reparations." In *Mapping Feminist Anthropology in the Twenty-First Century*, edited by Ellen Lewin and Leni M. Silverstein, 191–210. New Brunswick, NJ: Rutgers University Press.

Thoms, Oskar N. T., James Ron, and Roland Paris. 2008. "The Effects of Transitional Justice Mechanisms." *Center for International Policy Studies, CIPS Working Paper* April. http://conflictrecovery.org/bin/CIPS_Transitional_Justice_April2008.pdf.

———. 2010. "State-Level Effects of Transitional Justice: What Do We Know?" *International Journal of Transitional Justice* 4 (3): 329–54. doi:10.1093/ijtj/ijq012.

Ulfe, Maria Eugenia. 2013. *¿Y después de la violencia que queda ? víctimas, cuidadanos y reparaciones en el contexto post-CVR en el Perú.* Buenos Aires: CLACSO.

———. 2015. "Neoliberal Reforms, Reparations, and Transitional Justice Measures in Torn-Apart Peru, 1980–2015." CRPD Working Paper No. 41. Leuven: Centre for Research on Peace and Development (CRPD). http://soc.kuleuven.be/crpd/files/working-papers/working-paper-ulfe.pdf.

Ulfe, Maria Eugenia, and Ximena Málaga Sabogal. 2015. "Los Nuevos Suplicantes Del Estado Peruano: Las Víctimas y El Programa Integral de Reparaciones (PIR)." In *Políticas En Justicia Transicional. Miradas Comparativas Sobre El Legado de La CVR*, edited by Ludwig Huber and Ponciano Del Pino, 169–89. Lima: IEP, Instituto de Estudios Peruanos.

Van der Merwe, Hugo, Victoria Baxter, and Audrey R. Chapman. 2009. *Assessing the Impact of Transitional Justice: Challenges for Empirical Research*. Washington, D.C: United States Institute of Peace Press.

Vinck, Patrick, and Phuong Pham. 2010. "Building Peace, Seeking Justice: A Population-Based Survey on Attitudes About Accountability and Social Reconstruction in the Central African Republic." Berkeley, CA: Human Rights Center. http://papers.ssrn.com/abstract=1652997.

Waardt, Mijke de. 2013. "Are Peruvian Victims Being Mocked? Politicization of Victimhood and Victims' Motivations for Reparations." *Human Rights Quarterly* 35 (4): 830–49.

———. 2016. "Naming and Shaming Victims: The Semantics of Victimhood." *International Journal of Transitional Justice* 10 (3): 432–50.

Wiebelhaus-Brahm, E. 2010. *Truth Commissions and Transitional Societies: The Impact on Human Rights and Democracy*. New York: Routledge.

Winter, Franka. 2008. *Die Wahrheit Sagen. Perus Wahrheits- Und Versöhnungskommission 2001–2003. Eine Kritische Würdigung*. Tectum Verlag. www.tectum-verlag.de/die-wahrheit-sagen.html.

Yezer, Caroline. 2008. "Who Wants to Know? Rumors, Suspicions, and Opposition to Truth-Telling in Ayacucho." *Latin American and Caribbean Ethnic Studies* 3 (3): 271–89.

Chapter 2

Transitional justice and social cohesion

A new framework

The relationships within a society and toward the state are crucial for daily life. Armed conflict affects these relationships mostly negatively. Enhancing or re-constructing social cohesion is often mentioned as one of the aims of transitional justice in post-conflict settings. Moreover, social cohesion is strongly connected with the overall goals of transitional justice: peace and democracy. This chapter aims to entangle this link between transitional justice and social cohesion and concretize the possible effects. First, I develop the social cohesion indicator to then elaborate on the relation between social cohesion and conflict. Finally, I draw the connection between the two concepts, theorizing possible effects of transitional justice on social cohesion and developing the analytical framework for the analysis. This framework shall be adopted by other researchers as there are no works up to date that assess this relationship conceptually or empirically.

Social cohesion indicator

The social cohesion indicator is developed to grasp this social phenomenon. It is based on Chan, To, and Chan (2006) and complemented with some factors relevant for assessing the impact of transitional justice. The indicator is divided into a horizontal and vertical dimension[1] as well as a subjective and objective component, which is very useful to capture the processes on different levels. The horizontal subjective dimension refers to cohesion within the society, or in this study within the community. It describes the process of trust and identity building as well as the presence or absence of solidarity or envy. I added the development of narratives and perceptions of the past. The vertical subjective dimension refers to the state-society cohesion and captures political trust and confidence in institutions. I added the role of the state and expectations toward the state as important indicators for the state-citizen relationship. Furthermore, I included identity on this level as well because the self-identification of the people as citizens or its opposite is a further key factor.

The objective component of the indicator complements the observation of behavior. It includes social participation, voluntarism, and the presence or absence of inter-group cleavages. Active membership in social or community

Table 2.1 Social cohesion indicator

	Subjective component (People's state of mind)	*Objective component (Behavioral manifestations)*
Horizontal dimension (Cohesion within society/ community)	General trust with fellow citizens Willingness to cooperate and help → *solidarity* Sense of belonging or identity *Common narrative and perception of the past*	Social participation Voluntarism *Relation toward communal authorities* Presence or absence of major inter-group alliances or cleavages *Crime*
Vertical dimension (State-citizen cohesion)	Confidence in political institutions *Role of the state* *Expectations toward the state* *Sense of belonging or identity*	Political participation *State presence* *Corruption* *Provision of basic services/ public goods*

Note: Indicator based on Chan, To, and Chan (2006, 294), additions of the author are in *Italic*.

organizations, for instance, would be a sign of high social cohesion on the horizontal dimension, violent disputes, or other crimes a negative indicator. I added the relationship toward communal authorities as another expression of within-community relations.

On the vertical objective dimension, the indicator refers to political participation on the citizens' side (see Bollen and Hoyle 1990; Chan, To, and Chan 2006). I added state presence, corruption, and basic service provision on the vertical dimension as well because these are meaningful for the state's side of state-citizen cohesion and complement the expectations or role seen on the subjective citizens' part (Table 2.1).

This indicator should not describe a static situation but a dynamic process. The central characteristic that scholars find for reconciliation (Bloomfield 2003, 12–13; Lederach 2001, 847) is true for social cohesion as well, it is a dynamic and changing process, which is influenced by many different factors.

Social cohesion and armed conflict

Conflicts and disputes are normal within a society or community and can generate positive change. Armed conflict, however, is a very different situation. I assume that armed conflict has negative effects on social cohesion because of its social, political, economic, and psychological consequences. Whitt and Wilson (2007, 656) state:

> A second barrier to healing is posed by high levels of fear and uncertainty in postconflict environments. Research indicates that fear and uncertainty are likely to increase distrust, competition, and threat perceptions among ethnic groups, which can lead to recurrent conflict.

Other research also found that violent conflicts affect social cohesion negatively as they cause divisions between different conflict groups, destroy social cooperation and institutions, cause marginalization, and erode trust. At the same time, state capacity is undermined, the rule of law and state monopoly on violence are weakened (Cox, Orsborn, and Sisk 2015; Fearon, Humphreys, and Weinstein 2009). De Juan and Pierskala (2016) find also that exposure to violence results in diminishing trust in the national government. Most scholars follow this idea, but some recent studies find positive effects on inner cohesion caused by an external threat (Gilligan, Pasquale, and Samii 2014) or higher political participation after conflicts (Blattman 2009). Whitt and Wilson (2007, 666) also find in their experimental study "strong evidence for a norm of fairness across ethnicity in the aftermath of Bosnia's civil war". In some cases, "the shared experience of violence unifies groups" (Cox, Orsborn, and Sisk 2015, 26).

There is no general rule about how armed conflict and social cohesion are connected; it depends on the circumstances and form of armed conflict. There can certainly be these unifying effects on social cohesion depending on the context, but I did not observe those in Peru. In many rural areas, parts of the villages first supported the fight of Shining Path and only later turned against them. None of the selected villages opposed them directly, but over time the disapproval of the violent and authoritative methods used by the rebel group grew. The joint venture of the so-called *rondas campesinas* – civilian self-defense committees –were also operating against fellow community members, and at the end of the internal armed conflict, in all of the ten studied villages there have been supporters and victims of Shining Path, the state forces and also self-defense committees. I assume therefore that social cohesion in these villages was weakened through the armed conflict, leading to distrust and causing divisions between community members as the analysis of the truth commission (CVR 2003, Vol. VIII, Part 3) and other studies (Isbell 1994; Theidon 2013) observed. These findings were confirmed in many interviews as well as the following quote of a community leader indicates: "The topic of the violence has marked some components of the social live, has fragmented, weakened the social cohesion – this is very clear" (L9: 47).[2]

My assumption is that armed conflict in these cases had negative effects on social cohesion within the communities. Further, I argue that armed conflict had negative effects on the relationship toward the state because the state itself did not prevent the violence by the rebel groups and many community members also suffered violence from the state. The interpretation of the past and the role of the state as an actor are important in this regard, and therefore, form part of my social cohesion indicator.

Social cohesion and peace are positively correlated. Researcher agree that in case of high social cohesion the probability of peace is also higher (Cox and Sisk 2017). Moreover, lack of social cohesion can be a cause of severe conflict. People satisfied within community and society are unlikely to start conflicts. Active citizens use political and social institutions to express their interests and when the state is fulfilling expectations its citizens are unlikely to rebel against it. There are also studies highlighting the positive effects of social cohesion on economic outcomes (Osberg 2003).

Only very few studies have been conducted to investigate how social cohesion can be enhanced in post-conflict societies. Examples are the studies of Cox, Orsborn, and Sisk (2015) and Fearon, Humphreys, and Weinstein (2009) looking at the effects of peace building, development and other programs, finding slightly positive effects on social cohesion. Factors influencing social cohesion are manifold: economic well-being (Catterberg and Moreno 2006) as well as globalization and crime (Blanco and Ruiz 2013) are some of the factors identified in previous studies, which are included in my analysis.

The central question of this book is whether and how transitional justice can contribute to social cohesion. As far as I am aware, there are only two works which draw this link. Bradshaw (2008, 184–85, 192) makes the strong point that distributive justice is indispensable for social cohesion. And Cox (2014) analyzes the TRC as one program within many others, but only for the state-society relation and without finding direct results. My study is an important contribution with the connection of both concepts.

The impact of transitional justice on social cohesion

There are still only few studies looking at the positive and negative effects transitional justice can have, in particular on individuals. I will briefly elaborate on existing studies on the effects of truth commissions and reparation programs in particular to then develop the conceptual framework.

The first extensive analysis of all existing truth commissions was published in 2001 (the second edition Hayner 2010). Hayner analyzes the design, mandate and work of the commissions, and also how the recommendations were implemented and whether reparation programs or trials followed the truth commissions. The results are mixed. Some commissions were followed by large reforms or reparations programs, others nearly disappeared after the publication of the final report (Hayner 2010, 91–110, 163–81). Wiebelhaus-Brahm (2010) goes a step further and does not only investigate the implementation of recommendations but asks for the effects of truth commissions on human rights and democracy in a mixed methods study analyzing four commissions qualitatively and 29 commissions quantitatively. Concerning the effects on human rights, he finds a diverse picture in between reparations as fulfillment of a right and amnesties granted, which hindered prosecutions. The influence of truth commissions on democracy was not as high as supposed or expected according to Wiebelhaus-Brahm. Chile was the only negative case where a commission led to new conflicts. He, therefore, concludes: "the destabilizing potential of truth commissions appears to be overstated" (Wiebelhaus-Brahm 2010, 146).

Bakiner (2014) compares other cases and finds that nearly all commissions had direct political impact as well as indirect political impact, especially when supported by civil society organizations. According to his results, they had a limited positive judicial impact and negative judicial impact only in South Africa and Liberia. Olsen et al. (2010, 457) draw on a new database and present "a 'justice balance' explanation, whereby commissions, incapable of promoting stability and accountability on their own, contribute to human rights improvements when they complement and enhance amnesties and prosecutions". Truth commissions that achieved a balance between amnesties and trials, stability and accountability worked best (Olsen et al. 2010). Kim and Sikkink (2010, 962), on the other hand, find a positive effect of truth commissions on human rights. Mendeloff (2004) questions these positive effects of truth commissions and concludes that they are overstated. Vinjamuri and Snyder (2003, 20) put forward a similar argument and even find negative effects of truth commission if the pre-conditions are not fulfilled: "Truth commissions contribute to democratic consolidation only when a prodemocracy coalition holds power in a fairly well institutionalized state".

The different findings on truth commissions can be explained in the different cases chosen, databases used, and concepts defined. There is no certainty about which method is adequate for measuring impact. Another major problem in research on transitional justice impact is to connect a certain outcome such as an improvement in democracy to one single measure such as a truth commission. So, there is an ongoing debate on whether and if so, to what extent, truth commissions are indeed providing what they are supposed to. Most existing studies focus on the society as a whole. Wiebelhaus-Brahm (2010, 161), therefore, stresses that with all the studies on truth commissions, what is still missing is a sound analysis of the effects on individuals. This study is a contribution to this discussion because it offers exactly this perspective on the effects of the Peruvian truth and reconciliation commission and its reparation program on the individual and on the community level.

Regarding reparation programs, there are even fewer notable impact studies. I already discussed the fundamental works on reparations, which discuss the idea of reparations on the one hand and the implementation in different settings on the other hand including their possible effects (Elster 2006; Ferstman, Goetz, and Stephens 2009; Feyter, Parmentier, and Bossuyt 2006; Greiff 2006b; Rubio-Marín 2009; Wemmers 2014). All those edited volumes are very valuable collections. However, they do not provide a systematical analysis of the effects of reparations on the target group – the affected population of the respective country. Well-implemented impact studies on the local level are still rare.

An exemption are the studies of Firchow (2014, 2017) for the Columbian case. She analyzes the implementation of the program and the impact using a survey conducted in two communities and finds only little variance between the community with and the one without a reparation program. Moreover, she discovered discontent because of the form of implementation of the program (Firchow 2017). Moreover, Firchow and Mac Ginty (2013) coordinated a special section of *Human Rights Review* exploring the relationship between reparations and peacebuilding, as one of the aims of transitional justice. The same applies to the connection between reparations and development projects. At the end of his study on the connection of reparation programs and development assistance, Dixon (2016, 107) states: "Perhaps the most fundamental question, which I have not attempted to answer, is how victims' consciousness of the reparations process affects their healing and broader experience of reparative justice".

With my study, I contribute to the discussion on transitional justice impact, focusing exactly on the perception of the measures by the affected people.

There are general claims on the effects of transitional justice, namely truth, justice, peace, and democracy. Many of these claims aim at the macrolevel of politics or society. On this basis, I developed assumptions about the possible effects of truth commissions and reparations on social cohesion on the community level in Table 2.2. These are based on the more general claims made by Skaar and Malca (2015, 7–12), Greiff (2006a, 460–66), Roht-Arriaza (2004), Laplante (2015), and Mendeloff (2004, 2009).

The Peruvian truth commission, however, did not do much of its work on the communal level, due to time constraints and a lack of resources. The commission worked mainly directly with the affected people by carrying out exhumations and collecting testimonies. Exhumations, the identification of disappeared people and the dignified re-burial can be very important. Knowing what had happened to the victim and to be sure that the person is buried in an adequate place can contribute to inner healing and peace for the relatives. Truth-telling can, as Mendeloff (2009) analyzes, at best contribute to healing and a heightened sense of justice. However, truth-telling can also lead to re-traumatization and, for those not participating, to a heightened sense of injustice and a continued victimization.

I assume that the horizontal level of cohesion within the community is affected by individual and collective reparations as well as by truth-telling and exhumations. The pre-field study showed already that reparations had a more direct effect than the truth commission, which was hardly known or confused with reparations. In theory, working together in a communal reparation project could enhance interpersonal trust and solidarity between community members and generate higher interest in communal work in general. Satisfaction and recognition via individual reparations or truth-telling could turn individuals into more content and active community members. To contribute to satisfying basic needs on the economic level could open new avenues for community cooperation. The vertical cohesion is also influenced by collective and individual reparations, as well as by truth-telling and exhumations. These measures can enhance political trust in the state for fulfilling its promise to attend to victims. Receiving reparations or seeing their own history taken seriously can contribute to the feeling of being a full citizen with full civil rights.

Table 2.2 Conceptual framework: the possible effects of the TRC and reparations on social cohesion

	Horizontal cohesion (Within society)			
	Trust within comm.	*Solidarity within comm.*	*Narrative/identity within comm.*	*Social participation*
Positive effects of TRC and reparations	Increasing trust through common work in communal collective project Individual: satisfaction/ acknowledgement	Increasing solidarity through common work in collective project Individual: satisfaction/ acknowledgement	Strengthening a unifying identity/inclusive narrative Individual: satisfaction/ acknowledgement	Increasing interest in communal work through communal projects Individual: satisfaction/ acknowledgement
Negative effects of TRC and reparations	Decreasing if perceived as unjust or excluding	Decreasing if perceived as unjust or excluding	Excluding narrative/ victims category	Decreasing interest if project is not working
	Vertical cohesion (State-society)			
	Political trust	*Role/Importance of the state*	*Narrative/identity*	*Political participation*
Positive effects of TRC and reparations	Legitimization through responsibility taken over by state/ recognition and acknowledgement	Increasing through attendance of the state/feeling part of state/citizen's rights	Strengthening a unifying identity/ inclusive narrative acknowledgement	Increasing for gaining interest in the state/ civil rights
Negative effects of TRC and reparations	Decreasing if unfulfilled expectations	Decreasing if low level of attendance	Excluding narrative/ victims category	Decreasing if disappointment

Source: Author's own elaboration, based on Skaar and Malca (2015, 7–12), Greiff (2006a, 460–66), Roht-Arriaza (2004), Laplante (2015), and Mendeloff (2004; 2009).

On the other hand, if perceived as unjust or if expectations are not fulfilled reparations and truth commissions can lead to a further distancing of such groups from the state, less trust toward the state and also within the community. Narratives can be unifying and inclusive such as "we Peruvians (or community members) have survived the time of the conflict". But they can be excluding if some victims are not recognized as victims and lead to further rifts. Truth-telling can also inflame existing divisions.

In summary, these are the main effects but I should also note that other TJ measures such as trials could have effects on community cohesion as well. However, participation in trials was not mentioned by anyone. Therefore, the effects of the truth commission and especially those of the reparations constitute the focus of this study.

I concentrate on the effects on the community level also including the individual level. As explained I assume that when individuals are satisfied and feel acknowledged within the community and by the state, they are more likely to participate in communal events and show trust and solidarity. The focus of this study is on the social relationships within the villages and the relationship toward the state. The strong psychological component of reparations and truth-telling will not be assessed in detail within this book. This would be a topic for further investigation. Hamber (2006, 564) hints to the problem that needs or expectations of affected people sometimes contrast to what is politically possible and prioritized. This study investigates whether the Peruvian commission and reparation program were able to meet the needs and expectations of affected people.

Notes

1 The term "vertical" dimension for the description of the state-citizen cohesion should be understood as an analytical category only and not as an expression about a certain (autocratic) state model.

2 Interviews conducted for this study are cited anonymously with a code, where the first one or two letters are referring to the community or an expert interview; see the list of all interviews in Annexes 1 and 2. Translation from Spanish to English was made by the author.

References

Bakiner, Onur. 2014. "Truth Commission Impact: An Assessment of How Commissions Influence Politics and Society." *International Journal of Transitional Justice* 8 (1): 6–30.

Blanco, Luisa, and Isabel Ruiz. 2013. "The Impact of Crime and Insecurity on Trust in Democracy and Institutions." *American Economic Review* 103 (3): 284–88.

Blattman, Christopher. 2009. "From Violence to Voting: War and Political Participation in Uganda." *American Political Science Review* 103 (02): 231–47.

Bloomfield, David. 2003. "Reconciliation: An Introduction." In *Reconciliation after Violent Conflict: A Handbook*, edited by David Bloomfield, Terri Barnes, Lucien Huyse, and International Institute for Democracy and Electoral Assistance, 10–18. Handbook Series. Stockholm: International IDEA.

Bollen, Kenneth A., and Rick H. Hoyle. 1990. "Perceived Cohesion: A Conceptual and Empirical Examination." *Social Forces* 69 (2): 479–504.

Bradshaw, Gavin. 2008. "Social Cohesion in a Post-Conflict Context: Case Study of South Africa 12 Years On." *International Social Science Journal* 59 (192): 183–95.

Catterberg, Gabriela, and Alejandro Moreno. 2006. "The Individual Bases of Political Trust: Trends in New and Established Democracies." *International Journal of Public Opinion Research* 18 (1): 31–48.

Chan, Joseph, Ho-Pong To, and Elaine Chan. 2006. "Reconsidering Social Cohesion: Developing a Definition and Analytical Framework for Empirical Research." *Social Indicators Research* 75 (2): 273–302.

Cox, Fletcher D. 2014. "Fostering Social Cohesion in Deeply Divided, Conflict-Affected Countries." Conference Paper, Toronto: ISA International Studies Association.

Cox, Fletcher D., Catherine R. Orsborn, and Timothy D. Sisk. 2015. "Religion, Peacebuilding, and Social Cohesion in Conflict-Affected Countries." Research Report. Sié Chéou-Kang Center for International Security and Diplomacy at the Josef Korbel School of International Studies. www.du.edu/korbel/sie/media/documents/faculty_pubs/sisk/religion-and-social-cohesion-reports/rsc-researchreport.pdf.

Cox, Fletcher D., and Timothy D. Sisk. 2017. *Peacebuilding in Deeply Divided Societies.* New York: Palgrave Macmillan.

CVR (Comisión de la Verdad y Reconciliación). 2003. "Informe Final." Lima.

De Juan, Alexander, and Jan Henryk Pierskalla. 2016. "Civil War Violence and Political Trust: Microlevel Evidence from Nepal." *Conflict Management and Peace Science* 33 (1): 67–88.

Dixon, Peter J. 2016. "Reparations, Assistance and the Experience of Justice: Lessons from Colombia and the Democratic Republic of the Congo." *International Journal of Transitional Justice* 10 (1): 88–107.

Elster, Jon, ed. 2006. *Retribution and Reparation in the Transition to Democracy.* New York: Cambridge University Press.

Fearon, James D, Macartan Humphreys, and Jeremy M Weinstein. 2009. "Can Development Aid Contribute to Social Cohesion after Civil War? Evidence from a Field Experiment in Post-Conflict Liberia." *American Economic Review* 99 (2): 287–91.

Ferstman, Carla, Mariana Goetz, and Alan Stephens, eds. 2009. *Reparations for Victims of Genocide, War Crimes and Crimes against Humanity: Systems in Place and Systems in the Making.* Leiden; Boston: Martinjus Nijhoff.

Feyter, Koen De, Stephan Parmentier, and Marc Bossuyt. 2006. *Out of the Ashes: Reparation for Victims of Gross and Systematic Human Rights Violations.* Antwerp: Intersentia.

Firchow, Pamina. 2014. "The Implementation of the Institutional Programme of Collective Reparations in Colombia." *Journal of Human Rights Practice* 6 (2): 356–75.

———. 2017. "Do Reparations Repair Relationships? Setting the Stage for Reconciliation in Colombia." *International Journal of Transitional Justice* 11 (2): 315–338.

Firchow, Pamina, and Roger Mac Ginty. 2013. "Reparations and Peacebuilding: Issues and Controversies." *Human Rights Review* 14 (3): 231–39.

Gilligan, Michael J., Benjamin J. Pasquale, and Cyrus Samii. 2014. "Civil War and Social Cohesion: Lab-in-the-Field Evidence from Nepal." *American Journal of Political Science* 58 (3): 604–619.

Greiff, Pablo de. 2006a. "Justice and Reparations." In *The Handbook of Reparations,* edited by Pablo de Greiff, 451–77. Oxford: Oxford University Press.

———. 2006b. *The Handbook of Reparations*. Oxford: Oxford University Press.

Hamber, Brandon. 2006. "Narrowing the Micro and Macro: A Psychological Perspective on Reparations in Societies in Transition." In *The Handbook of Reparations*, edited by Pablo de Greiff, 560–88. Oxford: Oxford University Press.

Hayner, Priscilla B. 2010. *Unspeakable Truths: Transitional Justice and the Challenge of Truth Commissions*. New York: Routledge.

Isbell, Billie Jean. 1994. "Shining Path and Peasant Responses in Rural Ayacucho." In *The Shining Path of Peru*, edited by David Scott Palmer, 77–99. New York: Palgrave Macmillan.

Kim, Hunjoon, and Kathryn Sikkink. 2010. "Explaining the Deterrence Effect of Human Rights Prosecutions for Transitional Countries." *International Studies Quarterly* 54 (4): 939–963.

Laplante, Lisa J. 2015. "Just Repair." *Cornell International Law Journal* 48: 101–74.

Lederach, John Paul. 2001. "Civil Society and Reconciliation." In *Turbulent Peace: The Challenges of Managing International Conflict*, edited by Chester A. Crocker, Fen Osler Hampson, and Pamela Aall, 841–54. Washington, D.C: United States Institute of Peace Press.

Mendeloff, David. 2004. "Truth-Seeking, Truth-Telling, and Postconflict Peacebuilding: Curb the Enthusiasm?" *International Studies Review* 6 (3): 355–80.

———. 2009. "Trauma and Vengeance: Assessing the Psychological and Emotional Effects of Post-Conflict Justice." *Human Rights Quarterly* 31 (3): 592–623.

Olsen, Tricia D., Leigh A. Payne, Andrew G. Reiter, and E. Wiebelhaus-Brahm. 2010. "When Truth Commissions Improve Human Rights." *International Journal of Transitional Justice* 4 (3): 457–76.

Osberg, Lars, ed. 2003. *The Economic Implications of Social Cohesion*. Toronto: University of Toronto Press.

Roht-Arriaza, Naomi. 2004. "Reparations in the Aftermath of Repression an Mass Violence." In *My Neighbor, My Enemy: Justice and Community in the Aftermath of Mass Atrocity*, edited by Eric Stover and Harvey M. Weinstein, 121–40. Cambridge: Cambridge University Press.

Rubio-Marín, Ruth, ed. 2009. *The Gender of Reparations: Unsettling Sexual Hierarchies While Redressing Human Rights Violations*. Cambridge: Cambridge University Press.

Skaar, Elin, and Camila Gianella Malca. 2015. "Transitional Justice Alternatives: Claims and Counterclaims." In *After Violence. Transitional Justice, Peace, and Democracy*, edited by Elin Skaar, Camila Gianella Malca, and Trine Eide, 1–28. London; New York: Routledge.

Theidon, Kimberly. 2013. *Intimate Enemies: Violence and Reconciliation in Peru*. Pennsylvania Studies in Human Rights. Philadelphia: University of Pennsylvania Press.

Vinjamuri, Leslie, and Jack L. Snyder. 2003. "Trials and Errors: Principle and Pragmatism in Strategies of International Justice." *International Security* 28 (3): 5–44.

Wemmers, Jo-Anne M., ed. 2014. *Reparation for Victims of Crimes against Humanity: The Healing Role of Reparation*. London: Routledge.

Whitt, Sam, and Rick K. Wilson. 2007. "The Dictator Game, Fairness and Ethnicity in Postwar Bosnia." *American Journal of Political Science* 51 (3): 655–668.

Wiebelhaus-Brahm, Eric 2010. *Truth Commissions and Transitional Societies: The Impact on Human Rights and Democracy*. New York: Routledge.

Chapter 3

The challenge of measuring social impact

The quasi-experimental research design

Quasi-experimental research designs are an innovative answer on the highly discussed question of how to assess transitional justice impact. In this book, I analyze whether the assumption underlying transitional justice that TRCs and reparation programs contribute to social cohesion holds true. Hereby, this study contributes to the ongoing methodological debate on how to assess the impact as there is still a lack of methodologically sound studies. Based on the conceptual framework elaborated earlier in which I connected the concepts of transitional justice and social cohesion, this chapter develops the methodological approach for this study. Again, the analytical framework with the stages of measuring transitional justice impact and its operationalization as well as the quasi-experimental research design are presented in a manner that allows other researchers to apply them to other transitional justice contexts.

The analytical framework: stages of measuring transitional justice impact

I argue, based on Pham and Vinck (2007) and Skaar et al. (2015), that the impact process can be captured in three stages with two sub-stages: First, the TJ instrument is designed, then second, it is implemented. It is important to note that gaps can already occur between these two phases. In this study I focus on the local level of implementation. The deciding factors are then the awareness of the respective measures, which influences its perception before reaching its final impact in the last stage. Informing people forms part of the implementation as they need to be aware of any commission or reparation programs. So as to be able to participate in or benefit from the TRC or reparation program, all affected people need to know of the scope, target groups, procedures, etc. For reparations, it is crucial that they are understood as reparations and not as development programs. If this distinction is not communicated clearly, the compensatory effect will be rather low. Awareness and perception of TJ measures are, therefore, integrated as in-between-stages

Figure 3.1 Analytical framework – stages of transitional justice impact.

IIa and IIb as they are crucial to the program's impact, which is the level of social cohesion. I already noticed the importance of these two factors in the pre-field study. It is important to distinguish here between objective exposure and subjective exposure to TJ measures. In objective terms, a community might have been granted a collective reparation project but if some people are not aware of the project as reparation this would result in absence of subjective exposure. The study further distinguishes between awareness and knowledge. The expectations of the affected people toward the TRC and reparation program are also included in the awareness stage IIa. Those expectations are usually very high and influence the perception and impact of the respective measure. In order to have a positive impact, TJ measures must meet the expectations of affected people, they need to be aware of them and have certain knowledge to perceive measures as good, fair, and adequate. If this is achieved, then TJ measures can have a positive impact. When people do not know or understand the ideas behind truth commissions or reparation programs, however, and when they are perceived as unjust or hard to get, measures have a rather negative impact on social cohesion (Figure 3.1).

In this study, I will mainly focus on the second and third stages because the first one has been investigated already. On the local level, the implementation (II) and, most importantly, the awareness (IIa), the perception (IIb), and impact (III) of transitional justice measures have scarcely been researched so far.

The analytical framework allows for an investigation of this connection of transitional justice and social cohesion in the single cases in the first step of the analysis. In the second step, it provides a framework for the comparison and identification of differences and similarities across cases, thereby facilitating the understanding, explanation, and interpretation of various processes.

In order to apply this framework to a case, it is necessary to operationalize it. For every stage and the corresponding research questions, I developed sub-indicators, to be able to summarize and compare the stages between cases. The table in Annex 5 demonstrates the operationalization of the analytical framework. Every stage is analyzed for the TRC and the reparation program divided in collective in individual reparations. I developed measures for each category which are divided into three common categories: high, medium, and low. The table in Annex 6 displays the results within the framework for the ten communities.

The table with the categories is an abstract way to summarize and structure findings for the different cases. However, these summarized values should not be understood as absolute numbers, instead they are rather an abstract summary of extensive case analysis displayed in Chapters 4 and 5. The transitional justice and social cohesion literature reviewed previously suggest that it seems unlikely that a comprehensive explanation of the phenomenon of interest (effect of TJ on social cohesion) can rely on a linear relationship between the independent and the dependent variable. Nor will the same patterns hold true in all contexts, or the outcomes of interest be present in a straightforward manner. Instead, it is probable to find a complex interaction of several independent and intervening variables over longer periods of time. The concrete paths leading to an outcome will vary according to the setting. Still, the framework lays a strong foundation for the analysis of various cases and for tracing the effects of transitional justice on social cohesion in different contexts.

These stages guide the analysis of the specific cases with the method of structured, focused comparison with a quasi-experimental design, to be introduced next.

Quasi-experimental research design[1]

Quasi-experimental research designs are an innovative answer on the highly discussed question of how to assess transitional justice impact (Bunselmeyer and Schulz 2019). They offer the unique possibility to assess the impact of TJ mechanisms by comparing theorized effects of respective measures between selected target and control groups grounded in empirical data. This methodological approach thus enables researchers to evaluate whether or not the respective transitional justice instrument under investigation worked as suggested by theoretical assumptions and policy mandates, while holding constant and controlling for a variety of potentially intervening factors. It allows to investigate causal relationships between TJ measures and their respectively theorized outcomes – something which existing approaches largely fall short off.

Once a specific theoretical assumption of the transitional justice instrument and its intended outcome have been identified, a dependent variable (y = the conceptualized outcome) as well as an independent variable (x = the respective transitional justice mechanism) can be recognized. These then permit for comparative and systematic measurements. The comparative elements of such methodologies are introduced through the application of deductive assessments among target groups and control groups. Whereas target or treatment groups will have been involved in, or affected by, the transitional justice mechanism, the control groups in comparison will not (or only to a lesser extent) have previously been confronted with activities by the transitional justice instrument, but are otherwise as similar as possible to the initial group. This is critical to ensure accurate matching and omit selection bias. In theory, for the transitional justice mechanism to be deemed successful, the results between the target and the control group must be expected to vary; the intended outcome – i.e. higher social cohesion – should ideally be fulfilled among the target groups of the instrument.

The set-up and construction of a control group is what gives the research design its quasi-experimental character (Cook and Campbell 1979; Harmon et al. 2000; Reichardt 2009). This design thereby differs from natural experiments (Dunning 2012) because treatment and control groups are not randomly chosen. Quasi-experimental research designs are generally applied in situations where "controlled" experiments with random assignments of a treatment are not feasible due to ethical, political, or practical reasons. In quasi-experimental settings, the decisions of who receives a treatment are most often made through policy-makers, politicians, and practitioners responsible for the respective programs. This lack of random assignment is "always the case for ex-post impact evaluation designs" (White and Sabarwal 2014, 2). Quasi-experimental designs can generally be planned or unplanned. Unplanned quasi-experiments are settings, which evolve out of the fact that transitional justice measures implemented in one country do not attend the whole population in the same way. This gives the situation of treatment groups with high exposure to transitional justice instruments, e.g., benefit from a reparation program, and control groups not benefitting from such measures. These settings are especially useful when pre- and post-test scenarios or data are not available (Reichardt 2009, 50). The systematic use of quasi-experimental situations that are already given by the nature of the program within a quasi-experimental structured, focused comparison is a fruitful possibility to measure the impact of transitional justice processes. It shall help to understand the connection between transitional justice and social cohesion.

Within the quasi-experimental research design, the control group has to be as close to identical as possible to the target groups in all other denominators, with the only exception being the exposure to the activities of the transitional justice mechanisms. In the next part, I will illustrate how this materializes in practice. While the design is meant to exclude the influence of other factors than the transitional justice mechanism, this is still a challenge. Aiming for equal characteristics of compared cases is worth striving for, but in most real-life situations, it is not possible to achieve exactly identical conditions.

Based on the assumptions of the concept of transitional justice, the study sets out to investigate whether (a) communities involved in TRC's work and reparation program show higher levels of social cohesion, in comparison to non-involved communities; and (b) people involved in the TRC's work and reparation receiver show higher levels of attitudes toward social cohesion, in comparison to non-receivers.

With the focus on the sub-national level of affected communities I follow the recommendation of Sonis (2009) to focus on the target group of transitional justice instruments for measuring their impact as do the claims to "localize" TJ. The affected local communities were certainly the focus of the truth and reconciliation commission and, even more, of the reparation program. A within-country analysis offered the best possibility to find places with similar characteristics for the comparison.

Within Peru, ten rural communities were selected in the Ayacucho region, the rural region most affected by the conflict, according to the level of attention from the TRC and reparation program. I chose two districts as emblematic cases that have experienced the highest levels of attention from the TRC and the reparation program. In practical terms, for the treatment groups I chose communities that were visited by the TRC, where an exhumation was carried out and/or testimonies collected from 2001 to 2003, that had received a collective reparation project from 2007 to 2014 and/or had a high number of community members that received individual reparations between 2012 and 2016. For the comparison, I chose cases without TJ attention according to my information, that, however, turned out to be cases with low or medium attention later (see Chapters 4 and 5). All the communities have experienced strong repercussions from different sides of the conflict. They have similar social characteristics but different economic dynamics due to the existence of coca and drug trafficking in three communities. The idea behind this selection was to investigate TJ impact under different conditions.

It is important to bear in mind that even within the most advanced research design it is not possible to omit all influencing factors. In the real world, there are no perfect conditions for comparison but researchers make use of the best possible option. Being aware of those factors and including them in the analysis allows me to extract the effects of transitional justice on social cohesion.

Furthermore, I address this difficulty by combining the comparison of the communities on a more summarized, abstract level with the in-depth study of the processes within the communities. That means that in the first instance, I deliver very detailed case studies. Second, I compare these cases carefully to define common factors in the transitional justice processes and the development of social cohesion. Third, I analyze the individuals interviewed regardless of which villages they come from to discover more about their characteristics and opinion toward transitional justice and social cohesion.

Data

The main source for the analysis is the extensive first-hand data from extended periods of fieldwork from 2014 to 2016. With my assistants, I conducted 160 semi-structured interviews in 11 communities of Peru with 43 additional expert interviews with former TRC members, representatives from the Ministry of Justice and Human Rights who were responsible for the reparation program, universities, and NGOs. Half of the 160 semi-structured interviews were conducted with communal authorities such as communal presidents, governors, mayors, and teachers and the other half with ordinary community members. Furthermore, the ethnographic field research involved participant observation, two focus groups, and a special form was the presentation and discussion of preliminary results of my study that I organized in five occasions. Moreover, I analyzed 42 testimonies collected by the TRC in the communities in 2001/2002 which are electronically available at the *Defensoría del Pueblo* (Peruvian Ombudsman) in Lima. The interview guide was created on the basis of the social cohesion indicator that I developed.

In order to analyze the level of social cohesion, I considered applying an experiment from behavioral economics such as Whitt and Wilson (2007) with the dictator-game design in post-war Bosnia.[2] However, the interference caused by experiments in the form of money or a program is highly dubious ethically. I decided not to implement a real experimental design but include an experimental hypothetical question in my interviews instead. I asked the interviewed people:

> If you had ten sacks of corn (the most widely grown agricultural product) which you cannot consume alone, with whom would you share it? Please indicate how much you would give to your family, your neighbors, local authorities, NGOs, and the state.

The idea behind this question was to discover different priorities and attitudes, especially toward other community members. With this design, I gained important insights without interfering by offering money or other incentives. The question worked fairly well and revealed attitudes toward the different actors.

The individuals in the communities were chosen to represent a variety of characteristics such as authority and non-authority, age, gender, victim and non-victim, receiver and non-receiver of reparations. This permits an analysis of the factors causing different attitudes toward social cohesion.[3] The interviews were conducted in Spanish or in Quechua – the primary language of many interview partners. The dataset includes the 160 interviews, and in total I had about 12 different topics and 45 questions. These formal interviews are supplemented by more than 50 informal talks I had with community members or authorities on the street or at communal events and other occasions. These informal talks are of high importance for the study. I discovered a significant amount of information and opinions not only on the transitional justice process but also the situation of the village in a larger sense.

Table 3.1 Types of reparation receivers

	Victim	*Non-victim*
Reparations	Receiver	Receiver
No reparations	Non-receiver	Observer

All the interviews were transcribed in Spanish and the transcriptions were inserted in the program MAXQDA[4] and coded along a coding scheme. The answers to open questions were coded according to the structured, qualitative, content analysis (Kuckartz 2016, 97–121). For other questions, I used the deductive category building with scale structuring ("skalierende Strukturierung") (Mayring 2010, 92–109). Within this method, material is coded according to the developed categories following the operationalization (see Annex 5). In my case, for example, the category "knowledge of the truth commission" with the categories "high", "medium", and "low". The use of the codings for the social cohesion indicator was made as displayed in Annex 4.

For the analysis of individuals, the method for the typification ("Typenbildung") was used (Kuckartz 2016, 143–61). The types of receivers, non-receivers, and observers were developed as well as the classification "contended" and the "socially minded". All types were developed on the basis of the coded data and developed categories. I developed three types of people affected by the reparation program for the comparative analysis: (1) the receivers of individual or collective reparations; (2) the non-receivers, who were also affected by the violence but did not receive anything; and (3) the observers, those who were not affected by violence and not within the focus of the program. These categories follow the idea of the quasi-experimental research design as well. The receivers are the treatment groups and non-receivers the control group. The third group of observers is another control group because they have not been affected by the conflict (Table 3.1).

This study uses a specific research design, which can either be exclusively based upon qualitative or quantitative data, or which implies the potential to combine both types of data and thereby constitutes a mixed-method approach. I decided to use qualitative data but included some descriptive statistics next to qualitative analysis methods. The indicator for social cohesion is compared on the community and the individual level using descriptive statistics. The combination of different data analysis methods permits the identification of patterns for the connection of transitional justice and social cohesion based on in-depth case analysis.

Notes

1 Part of this subchapter is based on a joint article, which focuses on the quasi-experimental research design: Bunselmeyer and Schulz (2019).

2 Participants had to allocate money to other people from different ethnic backgrounds. With this experiment, the researchers gained knowledge on trust and identity toward the in-group and the out-group in this post-conflict setting.
3 I pursued a kind of purposive sampling to find people who will provide useful perspectives on the phenomenon of interest. Another strategy pursued was that of the snowball sampling in the sense that some interview partners, especially in the local municipalities or NGOs working in the villages, recommended people or introduced me to people, whose opinion would be of interest for the study. The sample was then completed with randomly selected people. In each village, I aimed to interview a balanced number of authorities/non-authorities, men/women, victims/non-victims, etc. However, I was not able to anticipate whether people would classify themselves as victims for example. And in many communities, I could not find individual receivers or only fewer receivers than anticipated, also not with the help of local authorities. Although interviewed people were selected very carefully, I cannot claim that the interviewed people are a representative sample, but I am convinced that the picture that emerged is very close to reality.
4 MAXQDA is a professional Software for Qualitative & Mixed Methods Research, www.maxqda.com/.

References

Bunselmeyer, Elisabeth, and Philipp Schulz. 2019. "Quasi-Experimental Research Designs as a Tool for Assessing the Impact of Transitional Justice Instruments." *The International Journal of Human Rights*, online first, doi:10.1080/13642987.2019.1672663.

Cook, Thomas D., and Donald Thomas Campbell. 1979. *Quasi-Experimentation: Design & Analysis Issues for Field Settings*. Boston: Houghton Mifflin.

Dunning, Thad. 2012. *Natural Experiments in the Social Sciences: A Design-Based Approach*. Cambridge: Cambridge University Press.

Harmon, Robert J., George A. Morgan, Jeffrey A. Gliner, and Robert J. Harmon. 2000. "Quasi-Experimental Designs." *Journal of the American Academy of Child & Adolescent Psychiatry* 39 (6): 794–96.

Kuckartz, Udo. 2016. *Qualitative Inhaltsanalyse. Methoden, Praxis, Computerunterstützung*. 3rd ed. Weinheim: Beltz Juventa.

Mayring, Philipp. 2010. *Qualitative Inhaltsanalyse: Grundlagen und Techniken*. 11, aktualisierte und überarb. Aufl. Beltz Pädagogik. Weinheim: Beltz.

Pham, Phuong, and Patrick Vinck. 2007. "Empirical Research and the Development and Assessment of Transitional Justice Mechanisms." *International Journal of Transitional Justice* 1 (2): 231–48.

Reichardt, Charles. 2009. "Quasi-Experimental Design." In *The SAGE Handbook of Quantitative Methods in Psychology*, edited by Roger E. Millsap and Alberto Maydeu-Olivares, 46–71. London: SAGE.

Skaar, Elin, Camila Gianella Malca, and Trine Eide. 2015. *After Violence. Transitional Justice, Peace, and Democracy*. London; New York: Routledge.

Sonis, Jeffrey. 2009. "Survivor Studies. The Importance of Evaluating the Effects of Truth Commissions on Survivors of Human Rights Violations." In *Assessing the Impact of Transitional Justice: Challenges for Empirical Research*, edited by Hugo van der Merwe, Victoria Baxter, and Audrey R. Chapman, 191–225. Washington, DC: United States Institute of Peace Press.

White, Howard, and Shagun Sabarwal. 2014. "Quasi-Experimental Design and Methods." *UNICEF Office of Research Methodological Briefs: Impact Evaluation* 8. http://devinfolive.info/impact_evaluation/img/downloads/Quasi-Experimental_Design_and_Methods_ENG.pdf.

Whitt, Sam, and Rick K. Wilson. 2007. "The Dictator Game, Fairness and Ethnicity in Postwar Bosnia." *American Journal of Political Science* 51 (3): 655–668.

Chapter 4

Four villages, truth, reparations, and social cohesion

How did the Peruvian truth and reconciliation commission and reparation program affect social cohesion in post-conflict communities? This chapter analyzes this question in an in-depth comparison of four rural communities and offers new insights on the micro level. With the help of the developed social cohesion indicator, I elaborate on sociologies of the villages. Every village has its own history of violence and its distinct set of circumstances. According to the research design, some have higher levels of attention from transitional justice measures, while others have lower levels of attention. The empirical findings of the different settings challenge the widely shared assumptions behind the search for truth and reparations. The comparison allows to understand how the TRC and reparation program worked there, how they were perceived in different settings, and how to analyze the effects the two measures had. The analysis will be conducted case by case according to the stages of the analytical framework developed earlier: implementation, awareness, knowledge, and perception of the transitional justice measures and, finally, the impact on social cohesion.

All four communities are situated in the Ayacucho region, were strongly affected by the internal armed conflict and suffered violence from different sides: Shining Path, the state forces, and self-defense committees. Two communities, Lucanamarca and Chuschi, received high levels of attention from the truth commission and the reparation program. The other two, Santa Rosa and Kimbiri, received only medium or low levels of attention, and this is why they lend themselves to a comparison according to the quasi-experimental research design (see Chapter 3).

Chuschi and Lucanamarca are emblematic cases that were in the focus of the TRC and the reparation program, accompanied by human rights organizations. In Lucanamarca, Huanca Sancos province, Shining Path committed its first massacre. About 70 people were killed in April 1983, as revenge because the village had revolted against Shining Path. In Chuschi, Cangallo province, Shining Path began its violent fight burning ballot boxes in 1980. In the years that followed, it was one of the places where confrontations between Shining Path and the armed forces took place (CVR 2003, Vol. VII, Ch. 2.46, 2.6). The two villages in this remote Andean area have similar socio-economic conditions, are reliant on agriculture with high levels of malnutrition and poverty as well as high dependency on social programs. The TRC's decision to work extensively in the two communities and carry out exhumations there was made according to both political and practical considerations. The fact that Lucanamarca was an example for Shining Path's violence and Chuschi had been the starting point of this violence was the political reason for these communities being chosen. The practical reason was the preparatory work that had been done by human rights organizations already such as the collection of testimonies, reconstruction of events, and location of burial sites that enabled the commission to complete these cases in the short time available. The testimonies were, however, collected once again this time by the TRC. Following the high number of testimonies the TRC collected, the awareness created and the support of the NGOs, a higher number of people also registered for the victims' register RUV and some individuals have received reparations already. With the support of the NGOs, local authorities implemented collective reparation projects as well.

The other two communities, Kimbiri and Santa Rosa, are located in the remote jungle region of Ayacucho. They are part of the VRAEM region and also rely on agriculture as main income opportunity, but here it is mainly coca. The VRAEM is one of the main coca-producing regions in Latin America. Nevertheless, the two villages still face similar socio-economic problems, have still high poverty and malnutrition rates and they also benefit from social programs although to a lesser extent than Lucanamarca and Chuschi. In the region of the VRAEM, furthermore, there are still remnants of Shining Path. No human rights organization has been working there, and the TRC barely reached that area. This was due among other factors to Shining Path's ongoing presence who were, not surprisingly, opposing the work of the commission. Santa Rosa and Kimbiri also suffered many losses in violence from the military, rebel groups, and self-defense committees. The two villages may only be separated by a river, but Santa Rosa belongs to Ayacucho and Kimbiri to Cusco. The most important difference is that the department of Cusco has a higher budget from the *Canon*[1] and is supposedly able to create better infrastructures and services. However, it also faces high levels of corruption. This was a problem during the collective reparation project as well, that was approved for Santa Rosa in 2008 but never implemented. There were also some recipients of individual reparations in Kimbiri and Santa Rosa, and here the level of attention through the reparation program was similar to Lucanamarca and Chuschi, which I had not expected.

Lucanamarca: transitional justice overload in the Andes

Santiago de Lucanamarca is the district capital of Lucanamarca, which is made up of a total of nine villages (two *comunidades campesinas* and seven *anexos*), situated in the Huanca Sancos province in Ayacucho. It was designated as a district in 1965 after the agrarian reform and already acknowledged as *comunidad campesina* in 1941, but its origins date back to the sixteenth century. Geographically, it is part of the Andean region at 3.400 m above sea level and still marginalized in the rural part of Ayacucho, a five hours' drive from the regional capital of Ayacucho (before the completion of the new road in 2014 it had been a nine hours' drive). These days transport is available four days a week. Infrastructure also improved in the last years with roads, electricity, water, and drain systems being built. Projects were carried out by national, regional, and local government. The capital overlooks a steep valley, and the landscape is characterized by wide rugged areas of largely uninhabited land. This upper region *puna* (up to 5,000m) is used for the breeding of vicuñas (a lama species) and other animals such as sheep and cattle; only the lower and middle altitudes are at least partly suitable for agricultural purposes. Andean terraces were already constructed by the Incas, but a high percentage of the terraces were abandoned and the cultivation is not considered as important as in the past. The main crops are potatoes, corn, beans, and, to a lesser extent, quinoa; in the lower altitudes, peaches and apples can also be grown. Most of the harvest is used for personal consumption; only a small percentage is sold on local or regional markets. In the past community, members used to visit markets in neighboring districts, also Chuschi, to exchange products (Falconí, Jímenez, and Alfaro 2007, 13–16). According to the community members, the land is not as fertile as it used to be in and climate change and water shortages have further reduced harvests. Moreover, the population is growing and as land is divided between family members, it becomes smaller and smaller (L17: 29; L7: 38; L5: 69; L10: 61; L12: 37; L5: 19). "If you have agriculture and livestock farming the village should consume and export those products. Here it is only for subsistence farming and they are not producing more" (L14: 21). Traditionally, the region was known for high-quality sheep breeding, but this breeding has declined. The breeding of guinea pigs, a delicacy in Peru, is another business opportunity that some people are investing in. Half of the population has an income of less than 100 PEN (30 US$) per month. Apart from agriculture and animal husbandry, there are barely any other opportunities. Only very few people work as professionals in schools, the municipality, NGOs, or social programs; for women, there are even fewer opportunities: "Here in Lucanamarca there is no work for women. Before, there was an NGO who brought work; we were decorating tablecloths, with this there was work. But now there is nothing" (L13: 17). There is no restaurant in Lucanamarca and only few little shops. These are mainly run by women.

Many of the women I interviewed complained about the male-dominated society and ongoing machismo in the community but stated at the same time that there had been some changes. Women now appear in positions of authority, albeit still in small numbers. Men care more about their children than they did before (L12: 21; L4: 19). The Catholic faith is still dominant with about 80% of the population and the Evangelical church at about 20%. However, there are hardly any regular services and the importance of the church has decreased.

The economic situation of Lucanamarca is very weak. The census 2007 counted 2675 inhabitants of the whole district, some later reports list similar numbers, and the capital has about 1200 inhabitants.[2] Poverty rate is 63%, rate of extreme poverty is 32%, and the rate of malnutrition is 40%. Nearly 90% of the population is in the focus of social programs of the MIDIS.[3]

A high percentage of the population is bilingual (Spanish and Quechua) while some of the elderly people are monolingual only. But all inhabitants still speak Quechua and are aware of their indigenous roots. They continue to practice some cultural traditions and to wear traditional clothing. The anniversary of the community, the carnival, and water festivals are some of the traditional festivities when those who left often return to Lucanamarca.

Lucanamarca is acknowledged as *comunidad campesino* with its own statute passed in 2011. This statute regulates the communal life, communal work, assemblies, rights, and obligations of the community members and their authorities. Local authorities are the municipality with its mayor and council consisting of five members, the governor, the local president with the communal board (*junta directiva*), and the *juez de paz* (justices of the peace). The traditional authority of the *varayoc* used to organize communal works and activities but is not present anymore. There are still presidents of the different sections of the community and the *cobradores*, young people who take care of the communal land and cattle in cooperation with the communal board. With its district status, the authorities changed when the mayor and the council's members received salaries and managed the budget of the *FONCOMUN* since 1995 (Falconí, Jímenez, and Alfaro 2007, 16–18; Ulfe 2013, 25–30).

Education has become more important. There is a pre-, primary, and secondary school in Lucanamarca. It was thanks to the engagement of local authorities and community members that the national and regional government agreed to construct a secondary school in 1983 so that children did not have to travel to other places. The conditions for education are very difficult; however, the infrastructure is missing, teachers are sometimes not motivated or drink a lot, students cannot dedicate themselves to their studies but have to help at home in agriculture or care for younger siblings (L14: 20). The number of families sending their children to study in the cities has grown. Only some of those studied "professionals" return to Lucanamarca later.

There is a permanent health post in the community with a doctor, a dentist, and nurses, inaugurated by then president Alberto Fujimori. People use these services but many are still skeptical toward anything medical, including vaccinations. Another problem is that some treatments remain unaffordable to community members, especially treatment in hospital. The free insurance for poor people, introduced by the government in 2001, does not cover specialist treatment and neither does the insurance available via the reparation program.

The huge problem of malnutrition and anemia could not be solved. As one doctor explained, it is due to poverty (L10: 61). An NGO worker in the area stated, however, that the low quality of alimentation was the main problem.

Families buy rice, noodles, and sweets in the shops instead of cultivating quinoa, vegetables, and other nutritious products (Exp9).

Regarding the institutions present in the communities, the most pressing issue for the community members is that there is no ATM or other bank services. There is only the office for national registration (*Registro Nacional de Identificación y Estado Civil – RENIEC*). The national government started a new program to service remote areas in 2014. These *Tambos* are supposed to deliver services to rural populations, especially in the housing, construction, and sanitation sectors. The *Tambo* in Lucanamarca was installed in 2014 in the presence of senior ministers. But for as long as I was able to observe it, it did not serve for more than internet access, for those willing to walk 45 minutes uphill from the village. The people had hoped that the Tambo would bring access to facilities such as ATMs and institutional support for the agrarian sector. Interviewees state that a bank presence would attract more people on the "pay days" of the social programs, a market could be established and that this could create micro business opportunities, especially for women preparing food or products to sell (L12: 67).[4] Up to then, it appeared to be an *elefante blanco* (white elephant)[5] (L11: 59).

There is no police station because the community forced the police to leave in 1994 after they had abused the community in the 1980s. Community members reported that:

> There have been violations of children, married women, they knocked the community down. Therefore, the previous leaders of the community of Lucanamarca have reached to remove the bases of the national police. Thanks to that the violence here could come to an end.
>
> (L5: 43; see also L11: 41)

In Lucanamarca, today the levels of attention received by the social programs are high: *Juntos, Qali Warma, Vaso de Leche, Cuna Más, Pension 65*. Lucanamarca was one of the first villages in the implementation of the program *Juntos* in 2005. The MIDIS lists for August 2017 the following numbers of beneficiaries of the different programs: 278 families in *Juntos*, 220 people in *Pension 65*, 86 families in *Cuna Más*, and 175 children in *Qali Warma* in six educational institutions.[6]

These state programs are, however, met with skepticism. On the one hand, it is a support for families with small children and obliges the families, especially the mothers, to take their children for health checks and to make sure that they attend school (L1: 87; L3: 75; L4: 62; L5: 67). On the other hand, people state in the interviews that families got used to receiving this money every month and had fewer incentives to work. There need to be projects to reeducate locals in the production and cultivation of nutritious foods and for this money only be used for additional products, explained one young community leader (L6: 78; L12: 30). Some criticize the program *Juntos* as an indirect incentive to have more children and say that it enforces assistentialism and dependency. Moreover, interviewees criticize that the program was not able to combat malnutrition (L1: 87).

Lucanamarca has a long history of NGOs and other programs working in the community, notably COMISEDH since 2002. They were mainly involved in the work of the TRC. At first COMISEDH focused on human and civil rights, published a memory book, opened a local library, organized the commemoration days, and so on. After that their focus shifted to a project supporting traditional agriculture and to distributing seeds and materials for the construction of greenhouses or stables for guinea-pigs. The most successful project was the establishment of a "school of leaders" in which selected community members took part and were educated in civil rights, agriculture, and animal husbandry and which was based on an exchange of experience. COMISEDH has turned into an authority within Lucanamarca over the years and has a strong influence on the local politics. Ulfe (2013, 31–32) characterizes the NGO as an intermediary communicating and lobbying between the community and local, regional, and national institutions and state entities and is very critical of their work. This is important to have in mind when analyzing the transitional justice process. Due to the end of funding from the German development cooperation, COMISEDH withdrew from the community in 2016 and only maintains a minimal presence today.

Before the conflict began, people describe life in Lucanamarca as peaceful and happy. This positive memory is described extensively in the book *Lucanamarca: memorias de nuestro pueblo* (Lucanamarca: memories of our village) elaborated and published by the NGO COMISEDH in 2007 (Falconí, Jímenez, and Alfaro 2007). For the book, various workshops were organized, paintings commissioned, and interviews conducted. The communal life in Lucanamarca is described as having been very active. Building the road to connect to the next provinces was organized via the communal authorities and with the help of all community members because there were no state programs. Neighboring villages also participated in these collective activities called *minka* or *faena*. Of course, there were small conflicts present usually regarding cattle or land, within the villages and with neighboring villages, but in general, there was strong social cohesion. The local authorities were elected in local assemblies, worked on a voluntarily basis and were highly respected. Conflicts were solved in accordance with the local *juez de paz* (Falconí, Jímenez, and Alfaro 2007, 25–68). It seems that this perception is influenced by certain narratives and perhaps also influenced by COMISEDH. Some of my interviews suggested that the time before the conflict was not an entirely "happy time" and there is reason to question how it is presented. However, there are no other sources available.

What is certain is that in the 1950s migration began toward the cities. This was mainly temporary migration as farmers moved to work in the harvest in the coastal areas. Permanent migration is associated with the hope for better living conditions: "All my brothers went to the cities to work there. [...] If there would be work here they would stay" (L18: 22). All of the community members have relatives in the city and are in permanent contact. There are associations of Lucanamarquinos in Ayacucho, Lima, and Ica. The influence of those associations is significant as they engage in lobbying and fundraising.[7] This migration increased during the conflict.

Some return to the village after studying in the cities, but they are in the minority. Those, who return as "professionals" can be very important for a change in Lucanamarca when they continue to work in positions of authority or create associations or small businesses. One interview partner stated that people returning from the city "know how to survive, how to make progress, how to develop" (L6: 19).

The main factors that make people leave the village are the lower production rate of the *chakras* (land used for agriculture) and the lack of paid work opportunities. Before, it was not that important to earn a lot of money as the main products for consume were home-grown or exchanged with neighbors or other communities. Now people do need money for alimentation, housing (people don't help with construction for free anymore), for school books, and so on. This relatively new emphasis on money is crucial for understanding the significance of individual economic reparations as well.

It is important to mention, however, that not all of these developments began with the conflict and that many rural communities face similar changes as I will discuss later. The conflict has, however, reinforced some of those developments.

The internal armed conflict was very present in Lucanamarca. Shining Path's ideas circulated in the village very early on – partly via the college "Los Andes" in Huancasancos, the provincial capital, where Lucanamarca's elite studied. In 1982, the whole zone was declared as "red zone" by Shining Path – a region that was governed by their group. But the population's discontent with the authoritarian leadership of Shining Path, their ways of distributing goods, and their violent methods grew. The neighboring village of Sacsamarca was one of the first to stand up against Shining Path in February 1983. They killed some of the rebels and then called in the military for help (Ulfe 2013, 32–35).

In Lucanamarca, community authorities also decided to kill one of Shining Path's regional leaders, a fellow Lucanamarquino. As a reaction to this "revolution", Shining Path committed the 1983 massacre to make an example of Lucanamarca. This explanation was given later by Shining Path' leader Abimael Guzmán. On April 3rd, about 60–80 Shining Path fighters entered the village and killed everyone in their path. Many peasants were killed while working in the communal *minka* constructing the road above Lucanamarca. Twenty people were killed in the village center, in front of the church on the main square. A total of 69 people lost their lives. The youngest victim was only two months old. The rebels stopped only because a little boy shouted "the army is coming" – or at least this is the story told by members of the community. A day after this massacre, the surviving villagers decided to kill the Shining Path leader's parents in vengeance. The TRC describes this dynamic that turned villagers into murderers of their neighbors or even family members (CVR 2003, Vol. V, Ch. 2.2; Vol. VII, Ch. 2.6). In total, Lucanamarca lost more than 120 people in the internal armed conflict. After the massacre, a police base was installed in Lucanamarca but the troops were abusive and very authoritarian and left in 1994 (see earlier). There were further events during the conflict in Lucanamarca such as the disappearances of three authorities in 1994 (Ulfe 2013, 53–56). However, the village decided to focus only on the massacre and remain silent about other acts and the involvement of fellow community members. This is when the narrative of the "innocent victims' village" started to unfold.

In the late 1990s, the situation calmed down as was the case across the whole country. The villagers reorganized their lives. Consequences of the conflict, however, were manifold. All families had been affected, lost relatives, houses were damaged or destroyed, and animals were stolen or killed. For several years, the land had not been cultivated and people missed the harvest. Many local leaders had lost their lives and thus communal order had been destroyed (L5: 41, 52). Education was suspended for some years. Communal participation declined, while distrust and egotism spread: "The topic of the violence has marked some components of the social life, has fragmented and weakened social cohesion – this is very clear" (L4: 47). Another local leader has the same impression: "Maybe, this [the violence] has separated us, before we had been united. Without that maybe we would not have been separated" (L7: 62). And, importantly, the violence affected the whole village, not only individuals or families:

> It's not two or three that have been suffering but it is the whole village. Because, when they say it's only two or three victims, the others are marginalized. Therefore, every support of an NGO should be for the whole village, for the common good.
>
> (L14: 60)

Interview partners state that they could not finish school because of the violence, this is particularly true for those who lost one or even both of their parents and take their place as main providers for the family. So there are consequences in all areas – social, political, psychological, physical, in education, housing as well as the loss of animals and agricultural products (Exp9).

The number of deaths documented by the TRC stands at 106 (CVR 2003, Annex 5).

Many of the interviewees state that the violence still holds a lot of importance until today [10 high, 2 med, 1 low].[8] The majority of the interview partners classify themselves as victims or as having been affected by the violence [14 yes, 6 no]. Nevertheless, there are significant differences in their approach to the past. Some say that it is important to remember but the majority says that it would be better to forget what happened [3 remember, 8 forget]. In almost all annual celebrations, speeches, and communal assemblies, some reference is made to the conflict and the suffering.[9]

Among the developments after the conflict ended, the infrastructure improvements are the most important and they continue to this day. The interviewees cite malnutrition, the economic situation, lack of work, and lack of good education as the most significant problems in the community today: "The most important problem is education, most of all the alimentation and malnutrition of the children. Malnutrition is above 61% in children, it is very tough" (L3: 20).

The implementation of transitional justice in the community

Lucanamarca has seen various transitional justice measures. The first one was the *PAR* repopulation program of the Fujimori administration. Ulfe (2013, 63) states that about 30 houses were built in Lucanamarca for those affected by the conflict by 2000. The precise number and criteria for receiving a new house remain unclear. The questions I put to various people did not yield any clear answers for this program. Community members also did not refer to this program when asked about reparations, only one woman mentioned the houses.

In 2002, COMISEDH started working in Lucanamarca in cooperation with the TRC. As member of the Peruvian human rights movement since the 1980s, they had been involved in the preparation of the national truth and reconciliation commission. The commission had to choose some exemplary cases, and locations where they would conduct a deeper analysis and implement exhumations. They chose Lucanamarca as an example of the extreme violence committed by Shining Path. This was also due to the preparatory work that was conducted by COMISEDH. They had already collated lists of victims and identified the locations of burial sites that served as a basis for the exhumations (Exp36; Exp37). Exhumations were carried out by the TRC in November 2002. However, only the victims of the massacre of the April 3rd were exhumed, not all victims of the internal armed conflict. The exhumed bodies were transferred to Lima for DNA analysis. They were returned for a re-burial ceremony in the newly constructed cemetery, funded by the German development cooperation. The then president Toledo visited the village to participate in this ceremony in January 2003 (Rojas-Perez 2017, 46–50). The process is recorded in the documentary "Lucanamarca" including its impressive final ceremony.[10] The TRC also collected many testimonies, and community members were participating in the trial against former Shining Path leaders that took place in Lima from 2004 to 2006. While the villagers were scared of revenge acts by Shining Path at that time, today the trial seems to hold no significance. At least, none of my interview partners mentioned it. No one from Lucanamarca participated in public audiences.

About 20 cases were recorded and 70 testimonies collected in Lucanamarca itself and about 30 cases in the whole district. The massacre is the main case with 45 testimonies. In the 24 testimonies studied, people demanded reparations, justice, and development. There was a high expectation to receive reparations. This misinterpretation of the aims of the TRC might be connected to the work of NGOs and the idea of telling the story in return for something.[11] Regardless of the presumed influence of NGOs, an important factor for the expectation of material reparations is the precarious economic status of the victims in Lucanamarca. Root (2012, 86–87) also states: "In Lucanamarca, as in communities throughout Peru, the CVR's work was answering questions but also creating the expectations of justice and reparations".

With the support of COMISEDH, a victims' association was formed in Lucanamarca in 2004.[12] Its aim was to unite families of the victims of the massacre. Again, other victims were excluded (Ramirez Castillo 2007). With assistance from COMISEDH, the victims' association received an oven to produce bread, funded by a German NGO. The idea behind the project was to improve access to food as well as provide an income for the families. But the bakery was only run for two weeks and the new oven has been stored in a shed since. According to a former representative of the association, families did not want to work together and some refused to participate (Exp10; L7). A former member states that she did not receive the money promised and, therefore, withdrew from the association (L16: 50). So, this project did not work, and the association did not fulfill its aims either. Their members blame the leaders now for not receiving reparations as they expected.

In terms of official reparations, there were both collective and individual reparations in Lucanamarca. Lucanamarca was one of the first communities nationwide to receive a collective reparation project in 2007. The project was a fish farm for trout implemented in the upper part of the district. Fishing was only common in the lower part before. The necessity of such a project can already be called into question. According to my interviews, the population was not consulted about the choice of project. The main problem was then that the municipality did not manage it well, there were some technical problems and people claim that the project was not suited to the area. The farm produced only very limited numbers of fish, and it was closed shortly after (L4: 55). Furthermore, half of the villagers perceived it as project initiated by the mayor and not as reparations as I will explain in the next part. There were accusations that the mayor was selling the fish to other villages. He explained that a plague killed the fish instead. "The projects are not working. The fish farm did not work out. The invested capital was lost" (L1: 75). In summary, this project was not seen as a success.

A CMAN representative in Lima explained that Lucanamarca was thought to be an ideal case for a holistic reparation program. But when it came to starting it, it was already too late: too much work had already been done, and people were sick of yet more memory projects (Exp26). Former president Humala visited the community in 2013 to announce more collective reparation projects for the *anexos* and inaugurated a plaque in the central place of the village in commemoration of the victims of the internal armed conflict. Out of the symbolic checks, given to the neighboring communities in this event, resulted the projects giving cattle to the communities of Carmen de Alanya and San Antonio de Julo, analyzed in Chapter 5. There are nine communities in the district of Lucanamarca registered as affected communities, and all of them have received a collective reparation project by now (CMAN 2017).[13]

Regarding individual reparations about 290 people were registered in the RUV by July 2017, among them 184 victims and 106 family members. This is a very high number because registering was supported by the NGO COMISEDH. Still, some remain who are not registered but have been affected by the violence:

> They do not want to register me although I have been affected, abused, and they even took my land. This is why I did not complete secondary school that time, later I did it with my own effort, with my own work I started to study.
>
> (L5: 52)

Out of the 20 people interviewed, 14 declared themselves to be victims of the internal armed conflict. Only four are registered in the RUV, following their own testimonies or that of their parents to the TRC. Only three of them received individual economic reparations. In the first round in 2011, seven people from Lucanamarca were chosen to receive reparations. CMAN lists 119 people as beneficiaries of individual economic reparations until June 2017. However, not all of them have received their reparation yet.

Regarding the other areas of the reparation program, I found the situation to be fairly mixed. The restoration of citizens' rights did not have priority in Lucanamarca because no documentation was destroyed during the conflict.

In health, many people are eligible for the health insurance (180 potential beneficiaries according to CMAN). However, staff in the local health center did not know about the different types of insurance for victims and the free insurance for poor people, and neither did the staff in the hospital in Huancasancos. Moreover, there was no psychological support available in Lucanamarca, apart from single visits by a psychologist, organized by COMISEDH.

In the housing sector, the PAR was implemented in 2000. Apart from that, there was hardly any progress in this area. Moreover, this is often confused with the *Techo propio* program, implemented since 2014 as a support in housing for poor people. The idea was that registered victims would get an extra financial support within this program. *Techo propio* was also met with many problems during its implementation. The requirements were not easy to fulfill because a piece of free land with land title was required as was a co-payment that many cannot effort. Still, there were about 20 families who were interested in the program. They did, however, not get a special offer or discount with their victims' certificate although CMAN lists six beneficiaries. Moreover, the person in charge of the process and of collecting the co-payments disappeared with the money in the winter of 2016 and was not heard again to date (Exp8).

In education, there have been some improvements recently as I explained in the previous chapter. The first regulation granted scholarships only to direct victims, who were mostly adults by that time with no interest in further studies. This regulation was changed only in 2015, and scholarships can now be transferred to the children and grandchildren of victims. CMAN lists 180 possible beneficiaries in Lucanamarca, but to my knowledge no one has benefited from the scholarship program so far. There was a lot of confusion with the program *Beca 18* even at the level of the authorities and even less information was available to the public; even the president of the victims' association was not aware of the different programs. The lack of information, even among the authorities and leaders of the victims' association is shocking.

As far as symbolic measures are concerned, two memorials were constructed on the main square and in the upper part at Muylla Cruz where the massacre started. This was thanks to the initiative by COMISEDH, financed by the German Cooperation. During the construction, a heated debate broke out about whose names should appear on it, and whether it should only include massacre victims or of all victims of the conflict – including members of Shining Path and the leader's parents killed in the revenge attack. Today, the names on the memorial can barely be deciphered and it seems as no one cares much about it. The former project leader stated: "they don't feel it's theirs – so they don't care" (Expl3). He continues to explain that it was not the community who requested the memorial but rather the idea of the NGO. Weissert (2016) mentions this difficulty as well. The cemetery – another symbolic measure – lies abandoned, and the area is covered in animal excrement and trash. Only a few people usually attend the annual commemoration ceremony for the victims on the April 3rd, mainly older women and a handful of members of the authorities. In 2015, when I participated, it was also organized by COMISEDH. It was the NGO that brought flowers from the city. It does not seem to be that important to the people. In the commemoration in April 2016, a regional congressman participated but community members complained later that it was just another political visit for taking the photo and without complying with the reparation program or any other promises.[14] COMISEDH organized also the work for a memory book in which community members tell the story of what happened to the village with paintings created by them. A local library was installed, and the paintings exhibited there. When the project came to an end, no one took care of the library. A university group arrived in 2015 to restore the library but again with little success. Again, people do not feel it is "theirs". Today, this memory book does not seem to be very important either; at least no one mentioned it in my interviews.

The awareness and perception of transitional justice

In Lucanamarca, I certainly found high levels of awareness of the TRC and the reparation program. The TRC is known by nearly all community members [16]. Nevertheless, some confused the work of the commission with the reparation program [5]. Not all interviewees remember the testimonies and exhumations. In Lucanamarca, as in all the other villages, there exists the perception that the TRC came to pay reparations. Out of 20 people asked, only four people refer to the exhumations and collection of testimonies: "Sure, in the beginning they did surveys to find out who the victims were" (L13: 58).

> When we were in college we went to interview all the old people, we made a little documentary with the students. We wanted to understand. So we went to look for information. The commission came as well to investigate some cases.
>
> (L14: 65)

"When we were young they came to investigate, by doing the exhumation and acknowledging the victims" (L6: 66). Even within some of the authorities, the perception persists that the "TRC came to bring support to the victims" (L3: 63). In-depth knowledge of the aims of the TRC is very low. Only three people were well informed about the work of the commission, two of them members of the authorities and the third had studied in Ayacucho.

There were high levels of awareness of the reparation program as well. Nearly all people affirmed that reparations had been paid in the community [19]. However, as with the TRC, they had limited knowledge of the program. Half of the people talk about rumors or something they have heard of. "Yes, they say that some community members have received roofs for their houses" (L18: 58). She was referring to the PAR program and did not know about other reparation programs. But in comparison, people in Lucanamarca are better informed than in the other three villages [4 high, 5 medium, 10 low knowledge]. This could be due to the work of COMISEDH.

When asked directly, only three people said that they received reparations and refer only to individual reparations. Collective reparations are not perceived as reparations. Of the 20 interviewed people, only eight knew that there was a collective reparation project when asked directly about it, and those were nearly all authorities. As already mentioned, the majority of the community members perceived it as project organized by the municipality or it had been forgotten because it didn't work. When asked about reparations, they refer mainly to individual reparations. Reparations in health, education, and housing are not well known and were only mentioned by one authority (L7: 49–53). There might be a change now because regulations in education changed, and there are many new potential beneficiaries.

So, in fact, the whole village received a collective reparation project and participated in the exhumations so that the objective exposure to the transitional justice measures is high. But only eight collective receivers were aware of the reparations given and subjective exposure to TJ is lower than expected.

Awareness of the TRC is fairly high in Lucanamarca. However, most of the people interviewed do not know the different aspects of the work of the commission. They remember that the TRC spoke to the victims but some link it with the aim of providing some form of reparations. In-depth knowledge is rare in the community. The commission is perceived as an entity formed to give support to the victims. Most of the information the TRC tried to disseminate did not reach the people, even in a community like Lucanamarca that received such high levels of attention. The commission as an entity was not perceived as a state entity but rather as an NGO by many people. In Lucanamarca, COMISEDH played the role of an intermediary and further reinforced this perception. Therefore, some now blame COMISEDH for the commission's shortcomings and for the lack of reparations (Exp1; Exp10).

Some of my interview partners mentioned the problem of mistrust toward the TRC (L10: 50). Moreover, community members demand that its work should continue and further investigations be conducted because a lot of cases have not yet been investigated: "They did not see the problems and all the people that have been violated" (L5: 47). And another interviewee confirms:

> Last year we found a body buried in the countryside, in the 'puna' of Tiopampa. They demand to know, whose family member this was and the truth commission hasn't investigated this. Until today they do not know who it was.
>
> (L3: 68)[15]

People complain about the unequal weighting of some stories compared to others. In Lucanamarca, mainly the massacre of the April 3rd has been investigated and community members complain that further investigation would be necessary for other incidents. Another problem occurs because it seems like "the truth" has different forms and villagers complain about neighbors telling a different story to also be included in the "victim-group" which led to an over-victimization. These results are confirmed by the study of Mendoza (2016) who questions as well whether the TRC captured the whole story of incidents in Lucanamarca.

There were only very few people who were positive about the commission and voiced that the attention the village and the affected people received from the commission was important: "The people were more or less happy that their rights had been noticed and their story had been listened to" (L1: 70). This fact of listening to their stories, this feeling of being heard was also one of the aims that are mentioned in transitional justice literature: the benefits of truth telling (see 2.1.1). However, those who gave their testimony most certainly had other expectations tied to telling the truth (see above). In the later rating of the work of the commission, this led to rather negative evaluations.

The TRC's overall role was assessed as being important but as not having achieved its task. Others criticize that the village did not profit from it:

> I think that it is good what it has done, the bad thing is that with this investigation, they collected information, books, videos of the interviews. But the benefit for the village, what was it? I don't know of a single thing they have given.
>
> (L14: 67)

In summary, the perception of the TRC according to my interviews is rather negative [5 low, 2 med, 0 high].

The presence of so many external professionals who were connected to the work of the TRC must have had an impact on the population that never experienced this sort of attention before. However, it was also the starting point for high expectations of support or development of the village. This perception is reinforced by the studies of Weissert (2016) and Ramirez (2007).

The perception of the collective reparation project, which was supposed to be a form of direct economic support for the community, was negative as well. First, there was discontent because it did not work, and the money was wasted. Villagers also referred to projects in neighboring villages and of those some worked better (communal house) or were seen to be worse (milk cows in two communities analyzed in the next chapter):

> The fish farm was a poor choice. They did not conduct a feasibility study. There were problems right from the start because of the high start up costs: the fish food, the staff salaries of the person who cares about the fish. Furthermore, the people did not get involved and this is why the municipality decided to abandon the project. This is how we lost it, the reparation of 130,000 Soles: 100,000 Soles from the state and 30,000 Soles from the municipality. That means we have lost it on this project.
>
> (L7: 49)

Second, the project was perceived by some people as a mayoral project and not as reparation for the following reasons. The municipality was responsible for carrying out the project. Then, there was no symbolic part associated with the project that would refer to the violence suffered. Neither did the fish farm have any communal character, which would bring families to work together.[16] President Humala's visit in 2011 where he announced more reparation programs for the *anexos* and revealed a memorial plaque was not mentioned by any of my interview partners. This symbolic event did not seem to matter much. It could be that the perception of projects in other villages as being more successful reinforced disappointment about the money that had been wasted on the fish farm.[17]

Regarding the symbolic measures implemented by COMISEDH, it is difficult to say what impact this work had. Definitely, Lucanamarca is a village that reflected on its history but this did not lead to a more united village. According to the interviewees, the most important measures were the exhumations and the re-burial of family members. But as not all victims have yet been exhumed, some are still awaiting the exhumations of their loved ones. In all the memorialization efforts with initiative of COMISEDH, local ownership of the projects is missing. Weissert (2016, 260) detects in his study of the memorialization efforts in the community as well that measures were imposed externally and only few people were satisfied with it. He also points out that the case of Lucanamarca was used for political gains not only by the TRC but also by state entities such as the Ministry of Defense during a visit in April 2009 to emphasize the heroism of the armed forces during the war. In my interviews, only one person of the local authorities mentioned symbolic reparations and stated:

> when we look at the topic of the monument, I think that it permitted the population in some form to reflect the topic of symbolic reparations and that it restructures the topic of social cohesion, that beginning from all the difficulties and pain they have reflected, they said 'we were wrong' and that it should not be like that now, in some way contributed the topic of civil symbolic reparations.
>
> (L4: 55)

In conversations with COMISEDH staff, they were also skeptical of the memory projects implemented. None of the community members mentioned these measures in my interviews. In all the time I spent in the community, no one referred to the memorial.

The perception of reparations being received is focused on individual economic reparations. For analyzing this perception, I divide interviewees into three groups – those not affected by the violence and not expecting to receive anything: observers; those, affected who have not received reparations: non-receivers; and those who received individual or collective reparations: receivers (see Chapter 3). In Lucanamarca, there were 10 receivers who were aware of this status, here three had received individual and the rest collective reparations; six non-receivers, of those only one was registered in the national registry RUV and four observers, among whom only one person did not know of the reparation program at all. The observers and non-receivers are receivers of the collective project as well, in terms of objective exposure. But, as mentioned before, they did not know of the fish farm at all or did not perceive it as a project linked to reparations, and thus there was no subjective exposure. So, in this classification, they are non-receivers because they are not aware of it.

The observers find reparations as such a good idea but note that they are not distributed equally within the village: "Yes, there was something, in some form they were compensating the families but it does not reach to all of them" (L14: 71). And another woman states her discontent:

> I heard that they made houses for some, not for others, some got 10,000, others 5,000. I don't know how much but not all of them got it. And that is inequality [...] therefore the people feel bad, they say why did they get it and I didn't? Therefore, I say that everything that comes should come for everyone, if not, then it is better that nothing comes. So they are not jealous or feeling bad.
>
> (L11: 50)

She demands that reparations be for everyone instead of for some individuals, which only creates new conflict.

The non-receivers do not understand why they didn't receive any reparations and perceive this as unjust.

> Some received money with the registration paper. Why? With this paper 'papelito' we received, I went to Huancasancos to receive something. But nothing, they don't want to give anything, I did not receive anything, this paper is not valid, they say, there is nothing for me. Why is that? Others received something for no reason ('por gusto'). We all suffered the same violence.
>
> (L16: 44)

The victims of the massacre received higher attention in the form of exhumations, new graves provided, and reparations. So, there is a perceived hierarchy of victims: "There are some people that have been affected but are not registered and there are others that were not affected but are in the register. Some have received reparations already" (L11: 58). Then, there is the special case of the brother of said Shining Path leader whose brothers and parents were killed. He knows exactly who the murderers of his parents were and sees himself as a victim. He asked for reparations in his testimony to the commission. But as relative of members of the subversive groups he falls into the category of people who will not receive anything. His case is also mentioned in the documentary.

The receivers were not satisfied either, either because of the amount or the late payment or the regulations in the education program:

> Individual reparations, yes we have them, some have been repaired but the amount that we received is not solid. If we are many brothers and sisters, in practical terms it is not equal that was has happened to us. It does not bring back our dearest ones. They had the idea to increase the money but until today nothing. In the topic of reparations in education, equally for the question of the age it is a problem for us. Therefore we are demanding to be able to transfer it on to our children.
>
> (L7: 52–53)

At least this demand was met now with the new regulations.

In one case, someone's father died and the child is eligible for reparations. According to the regulations, 5,000 PEN will be paid to the mother, the widow, and 5,000 PEN to all the children. He is his father's only son but his mother remarried after his father died, and he has a half-sister who registered for reparations as well. Therefore, he had to share the 5,000 PEN with this half-sister even though it was not her father who died. His wife told me that it was really upsetting for him, and he was not sure if he should start a family fight over this but remained unsatisfied and perceives it as unjust (L21). Instead of providing relief for the family, it created new resentments.

In another case, a part of the family reparation was meant to be for a woman who had passed away already, my interview partner's mother-in-law. She tried to get this part for her husband but failed because of the regulations (L13). Others as well could not receive the reparation when their parents passed away before receiving the reparation as the reparations were not transferable.[18] Finally, there are also few people who question the whole idea of reparations, of compensating the harm suffered, the loss of a family member with money, a cow or a tractor (L6: 70).

The level of satisfaction with reparations is very low in the majority of the interview partners, in receivers, non-receivers, and observers alike [0 high, 4 med, 14 low]. They expected reparations to come for all of them, not for some individuals only, because the whole population suffered during the violence: "For example in the case of the family members of my mothers who have been affected and the support does not come [...] for others they have been constructing houses, they have given 10,000 Soles, I heard all of that [...] why do they not give in a general way because the whole village has been affected" (L14: 60; also L11: 52). Due to this negative evaluation, hardly any positive impact on social cohesion to be expected.

The impact on social cohesion

The social cohesion indicator for the community of Lucanamarca shows that the overall level is relatively low. The situation in the community was perceived as having improved in terms of development and infrastructure [11 positive], but in terms of social cohesion, it was worse than before according to the interviewees [13 less solidarity].

On the horizontal level, I observed that the community lacks trust and solidarity which exists only in extreme cases such as accidents or deaths; in those cases, half of the interviewees would help. The *ayni* – a traditional way of mutual exchanging services – is hardly practiced anymore. Traditionally, when someone built his house or brought in a harvest, neighbors would help. Next time, it would be the other neighbor's turn and so on. Community members explain this with the increase in paid work and say that people got used to working for money only: "Before there was [solidarity] but now everything they do for money only" (L13: 27). "The people here are not trusting at all. Because some say something to you and behind you they are talking badly. How is the saying: 'there is no trust in your own shadow'" (L6: 25). The authorities noticed the low solidarity levels and trust as well: "I see it [solidarity] only very little, maybe the whole situation that happened in the year 83 seems that there is fear. No, they do not trust us either" (L10: 23). Envy is really high, some see envy even as a cause for the outbreak of terrorism (L11: 31). "When you are improving in something, the people think it is bad. When you are not doing anything, they speak ill of you as well. If you want something done, you have to do it yourself" (L15: 36).

Only two of my interview partners, both authorities and one of them receiver, see a positive process of reconstruction of social cohesion within society (L4: 22; L7: 27).

The identity or sense of belonging is still strong in Lucanamarca: "definitely, we emphasize that, for example in other cities such as Ica, Lima, Ayacucho, we have our reunions, we assemble together, we are Lucanamarquinos, this pride remains forever" (L5: 60). There is no common narrative or perception of the past. Some interview partners state that the violence of the 1980s is still important today but the majority wants to forget about it instead. When asked who caused violence, they mention Shining Path or both, the rebel group, and state forces. As already mentioned, there is this notion of Lucanamarca as a "victims village". This is, in some form, used politically but not in the way to build agency but rather as a reason to demand support. Many community members speak of a "trauma" or that they have been "traumatized", this occurs more often than in the other communities: "Many stayed traumatized, orphaned. [...] Because of this, the COMISEHD came" (L17: 44; also L5: 42; L6: 70; L7: 20; L11: 38; L22: 47). I suppose this is also due to the fact that some realized that this helped gain support from the TRC or NGOs (Ramirez Castillo 2007; Theidon 2013). This narrative, however, is not a unifying one because a hierarchy of victims was created with the unequal treatment or levels of attention for different victims.

There is a high level of membership in social organizations but only to receive benefits such as the programs Juntos and vaso de leche. People participate in fiestas when there are presents or food and drink.[19] Community members explain this once again with the increase in paid work, and I observed a decrease in participation in communal work as well. Participation in assemblies and communal minkas or faenas is only high if there is a penalty for non-attendance.[20] This equals a payment for the day.

> Previously, there was this solidarity how do you call it 'one for all and all for one' they were working, there were minkas, aynis. But all these minkas, aynis have been lost, the custom has been lost because many times, here from the community of Lucanamarca we are migrating to the city of Lima. Therefore, there is not such a solidarity, no help between neighbors, between districts, there is not such organization. Fairly, we are disorganized politically, culturally, economically we are disorganized.
>
> (L5: 26)

One authority explains the low participation with the lack of perception of civil rights: "There are limitations, it is not 100% the topic of participation in assemblies. There are a few reasons, but this involves the issue of empowering citizens. If they do not know how to exercise a true citizenship, they will not feel part of these spaces of participation. One thing is if you do not know how you could participate, then there are fears behind that. [...] If they do not take it as their spaces, it will be very difficult. One, to participate and exercise the issue of citizenship, has to feel that the space belongs to him and that he has to participate, even that is still missing. There are well-developed structures but they are often discriminatory" (L4: 32).

The lack of interest in communal activities and participation is also linked to the perception of the authorities. Confidence in local authorities stands only at medium level [3.8], lower than the trust in the own family [5.2]. People expect the local authorities or the state to do the work that they completed together before such as constructing and maintaining roads and canals. Local authorities have to fight the problem of disinterest of the people. To find people for voluntary communal authority posts or as patrons for activities and fiestas is sometimes difficult. I also observed a polarization into the municipality on one hand and the village on the other. The authorities noted this problem and mention that they should reunite with the population to work together (L4: 25). As authorities caring most about the village are the major and municipality mentioned. The former communal president was found drunk on the street once a month. This role model is beyond questionable. Some community members state that the municipality was not doing enough and that they would always contract people from outside and not from Lucanamarca (L22: 24). So, they are not satisfied. In response to the corn question, people would give most to their family and neighbors and less to authorities, NGOs, and the state.

Conflicts are still present in Lucanamarca, mainly about territory. These are solved with local authorities or higher legal instances. Violence is also widespread in the community, mainly as domestic violence but also between community members and mostly alcohol-related. Interviewees are divided in their opinion on whether the violence of the 80s could occur again.

The state-society relationship is interesting in Lucanamarca. Trust in the state is very low. Also the importance of the state for the village is evaluated as very low because people do not see its presence. Expectations toward the state on the other side are very high but the only form in which the state's presence is perceived is in social programs and some infrastructure work.

It is interesting to see the narrative of the state not being present before the conflict started. However, the secondary school was constructed with state support in the 1980s already. It was only thanks to the initiative of local authorities who traveled to Lima to ask for support, but it was granted, so there was awareness of state support. The narrative of "Fujimori as the pacificator" is not as dominant in Lucanamarca as in other villages. However, in the perception of the community members, the military had defeated the rebel group, not they themselves. There, the image of the "passive victims" is created. The memory of Fujimori exists as the one who came and constructed schools and the health post.

Interestingly, the identification with Peru as a country is very strong, but this identity relates to the country, its culture, and not to the state. Lucanamarquinos still do not see themselves as part of the Peruvian state.

Political participation in Lucanamarca is very low and limited to elections – where voting is obligatory. The participation in the second round of the

presidential elections in June 2016 was 57%, which is very low bearing in mind that there is a fine for not voting.[21] There is hardly any understanding of political rights in the community. State presence is perceived as low and only seen in construction or infrastructure work and social programs – not as a social and political construct that means and provides more than that. It was the clientelism of the Fujimori era that fostered this perception. The citizens see themselves as customers and not as citizens with civil and political rights. In Lucanamarca, COMISEDH implemented a project on civil rights and participation from 2008 onwards. In my observation, this project resulted in some minor changes on the community level toward more interest or participation of some community members, especially women. However, the political participation in the nation state was not touched or changed by it.[22]

The provision of security – a substantial task according to state theory – is not attributed to the state. This is caused in the experiences that were made with police and military during the conflict and their abusive behavior. Therefore, Lucanamarca rejected the construction of a police station in the village. Conflicts in the community are solved by local authorities – or through bribery. There is a story of a former mayor who injured someone in a drunken fight and then paid the family the next day for not making a formal accusation.

Several presidents and senior ministers visited the community, travelling to the remote Andean community by helicopter. The then President, Alejandro Toledo, visited Lucanamarca in January 2003 to participate in the ceremony for the re-burial of the victims exhumed and identified in Lima within the work of the TRC. In this occasion, he asked for forgiveness on behalf of the Peruvian state, which seems to be an important act according to transitional justice literature. In his speech, he asked for forgiveness for something "we did not do" –because the government failed to protect its citizens. He praised the courage of the community members who stood as heroes against Shining Path. But the image of the village as a "village of heroes" was not adopted by the population. Toledo focused on the justice aspect of bringing the Shining Path leader to trial – a fact, according to my interviews, not that important for the community members. Toledo promised help and support for education, health, food, security, justice, and infrastructure for the village and, importantly, he does not make a difference between the attention for poverty or for victimhood.

Hardly any community members remembered the visit when asked about visits of presidents or senior ministers, and only two mentioned Toledo's visit: "Toledo came but nothing happened" (L20: 48–49). Another authority explains that Lucanamarca would have some importance nationwide because of the violence suffered. Therefore, many politicians came but nothing happens: "Sometimes that state that comes here is tedious, sometimes they promised and do not keep the promises" (L14: 79).

The former president Humala visited the community as well in 2012 to announce more reparation projects in the neighboring communities and "revealed" a memorial plaque in the central square of Lucanamarca. It was a symbolic visit – but no community member remembered it in my interviews and the writing on the plaque has already faded. The same happened with the inauguration of the Tambo – a visit by senior ministers – and nothing happened in the perception of the interviewees: "For example, the ministers, they come to go for a walk, they do not bring anything, at least a project for the village. They came to visit no more, there is no commitment" (L10: 59).

The state is present in the community in objective terms apart from those visits it is present as it grants the budget to the local government, infrastructure such as *Trabaja Peru* (Peru is working), social programs, the health post, education, and the governor – many of those are, however, not perceived as state entities. The reparation program was also not perceived as state program by all of the people but as an NGO project by some.

The community members evaluate the situation today as better than the situation some years ago [11]. When asked which entity caused the positive changes in the community, they mention state programs [5], the municipality [5], and other local authorities [4], and the NGO COMISEDH [5], but no reference is made to the TRC or reparation program as having improved anything. Community members see some efforts on behalf of the state but are not satisfied with them. While some see reparations as just another social program, others perceive it as a present given by the NGO to some handpicked villagers. The theorized aim of reparations of feeling attended to and satisfied and therefore enhancing trust in the state and the community members could not be observed in Lucanamarca.

Summary

The level of social cohesion in Lucanamarca is relatively low today as I have demonstrated. The idea of the "happy time" before the conflict that some community members have has to be seen with caution. There were previous factors that influenced the social situation in the village: modernization and the connection with the cities with new roads and more cars, migration caused by lack of work and education opportunities – for instance, there are some pieces of land that belong to people living in the cities who do not cultivate it and do not participate in communal activities; climate change affected the harvests; and most importantly the increase in paid work and the use of money. This, in the opinion of the community members caused the separation and loss of solidarity and communal work. The conflict recognizably reinforced some of these developments; it led to higher migration, loss of social and political order, and loss of experienced leaders. Structures in education, housing, infrastructure, agriculture, and income opportunities were destroyed. The psychological consequences of the violence further weakened social cohesion.

Lucanamarca had received high levels of attention due to political and practical considerations of the TRC and the work of the NGO COMISEDH – which has also been criticized. The TRC collected testimonies, carried out exhumations and re-burial ceremonies, community members participated in a trial, and different memory initiatives were implemented. The TRC's presence generated high expectations mainly of receiving reparations or some other form of development.

In theory, on the collective level, the installation of a project like the communal fish farm in Lucanamarca could be one way to enhance the productivity of a village and encourage the community members to work together. But it did not succeed and neither did the victims' association's project. The collective reparation project is, therefore, perceived as negative and, furthermore, did not have a symbolic or communal component. Symbolic measures do not seem to be important to the people apart from the re-burial of exhumed bodies. In many of the implemented projects, local ownership was lacking.

On the individual level, the pure act of testimony giving to the TRC was not described as positive by any interview partner. The receipt of a victim's certificate seemed useless if it did not constitute an entitlement to reparations. In theory, individual economic reparations as well as individual scholarships and health insurance were meant to improve the situation of affected people. But, as shown, only few people benefited from these programs to date, and they are not satisfied with it.

I conclude that the reparation program suffered from shortcomings in the implementation, awareness, and perception within the village. Furthermore, I saw disappointment for the work of the TRC, NGO, and the state. The not transparent way of distributing reparations caused more envy and conflict in the community than helping. The high expectations were not fulfilled, and the state is rather perceived as attending in the form of social programs and infrastructure.

Receivers are discontent, but non-receivers even more as they feel an unequal attention. Even observers who were not affected by the violence in Lucanamarca criticize the implementation of the program. More than half of the interviewed people display only low levels of satisfaction with the reparation program (12). The few who assessed it with medium satisfaction are those observers with high knowledge, mainly members of the authorities.[23]

Lucanamarca is one of the emblematic cases within Peru that received a lot of attention by NGOs, the truth and reconciliation commission, and the reparation program. Within my cases, it is the one that received the highest attention of all. However, the programs were not able to enhance social cohesion as they were meant to by their design. The affected people are rather disappointed: "we were fighting for all that [reparations] for such a long time and now – nothing…" (Exp10).

Chuschi: hardly any notice of transitional justice

Chuschi is the place where Shining Path started its armed fight in 1980. The village of Chuschi is the capital of the district Chuschi, which comprises in total five *comunidades campesinas* (Chuschi, Quispillaqta, San Juan de Uchuyri, Canchacancha y Chacolla) and 58 villages, situated in the Cangallo province in

Ayacucho. Chuschi was recognized as district as early as 1857 and as a *comunidad campesina* in 1940 (Flórez Salcedo 2012, 230–33). It is also located in the Andean region at 3.500 m above sea level and still marginalized in the rural part of Ayacucho, about three hours' drive from the regional capital Ayacucho, small buses run up to four times daily. Before the road was constructed, it was a nine hours' drive from Ayacucho. In the district, there are various villages that still have no car access. Infrastructure improved in the last years in roads, electricity as well as water and drain systems. The national, regional, and local government set up several projects some in cooperation with NGOs. The landscape is dominated by the Andes; the village covers three different zones or ecological floors: the upper region, *puna*, which sits from 3,300 to over 4,000 m above sea level, is suitable for traditional livestock farming way with little technical support. Cows, sheep, alpacas, and llamas can be seen here. The second floor starts below 3,300 m and is the corn-producing area. In the lower part, apple fruits, peaches, oranges, and tunas (prickly pears) are produced. The Andean terraces had originally been constructed by the Incas, but a high percentage of these terraces are abandoned today. Most of the harvest is used for personal consumption, only a small percentage is sold in local or regional markets. According to the community members, the land is not as fruitful as it was: "[there is] a descent in production, they do not produce that much, for laziness of the people and low rendition. Before, they cultivated more and the chakra yielded more crops. Now the soil is not good anymore" (CH4: 21). Climate change and water shortages are other problems that reduce the agricultural yield. The population is also growing and land divided between family members has become smaller: "The father of the grandfathers had a piece of land, maybe one hectare, until today we are many, they divided the land for us" (CH1: 32). They do not make use of the territory as before and as much as they could (CH15: 19; CH12: 22). Some single mothers do not have their own land and depend on their parents and on the program Juntos (CH16: 19). Children got accustomed to having nice clothes and shoes and parents needed more money, and paid work: "[...] the majority of the children got used to the shop. Before they put on 'ojotas' but now our children want nice shoes, therefore we want [paid] work" (CH16: 67). There is, however, not a lot of paid work available, only in infrastructure construction, in the municipality and in some social programs. As my interview partners state, there is hardly any work available for women (CH17: 20). These are very similar problems to those in Lucanamarca. Some women started small businesses selling food or handmade products. "I want to say as well: before, the women were not seen here, in the afternoons they sell their 'mazamorita' (traditional meal), [...] which was never seen before" (CH15: 59). The women have opened themselves a new space, outside of their homes, not only for generating income but also for meeting people (Exp29). There are some projects producing handicrafts, but the majority of the products is also only for their own use. Few women did make a personal change in opening restaurants, hostels, or small shops, using the income opportunity because there are now more external people coming to

Chuschi such as teachers, professionals working for the social programs, and the municipality staff or engineers at the various infrastructure projects (CH18: 23).

Chuschi is recognized as a comunidad campesina with its own statute that regulates the communal life, communal works, assemblies, rights, and obligations of the community members and their authorities. Local authorities are the municipality with its mayor and council of five members, the governor and the local president, the communal board and the *juez de paz*. In Chuschi, there is the *juez letrado* mandated by the government and the *juez non letrado* elected by the community (CH6: 29). Moreover, there are authorities in the single barrios of the community that are organizing the barrios. And in Chuschi, the traditional authority of the *varayoc* is still present. The *varayoc* are composed of 8–20 men and their wives who organize festivities and communal activities. They also care, together with the board, about communal land and cattle (Isbell 1985). Nowadays, there are problems to recruit new volunteers for this position: “Nearly everyone has participated once, there is no one anymore that could enter. It’s voluntary. We are caring the order, bringing service to the community, in the fiestas, activities, assemblies, faenas, supporting the community” (CH10: 21).

With its status as district, the authorities changed as the mayor and members of the council got salaries and manage the budget as in Lucanamarca. The declared vision of the municipality is focused still on the basic development of the community. The authorities want to: “overcome extreme poverty and promote the integral human development of the district […] for the sustainable integral socio-economic development of the district, generating opportunities to live with dignity and a better quality of life”.[24]

Some community members complain about the ongoing male domination in the community, in authority positions and in reunions women are still underrepresented: “There are no women in high positions here in Chuschi. The problem is that we [as women] have opinions, we can speak, but we are scared. […] They hate us, we all hate ourselves here” (CH21: 45–46). Other interviewees observe at least minor changes. Men would help more in the kitchen and with the children, which was not seen before (CH13: 37).

The last census in 2007 counted 8,281 inhabitants in the whole district, the MIDIS 2012 8,108 inhabitants, the capital has about 1,400 inhabitants.[25] Poverty rate is 74%, 40% in extreme poverty and malnutrition index 42%. More than 90% of the inhabitants are in the focus of MIDIS programs.[26]

A high percentage of the population is bilingual (Spanish and Quechua) while some of the elderly people are monolingual only. Still, all the inhabitants speak Quechua and are aware of their indigenous roots. They keep practicing cultural traditions and wear traditional clothing. The hat and skirt of Chuschi are well known in the whole area and can be seen every day on the streets, especially in women’s outfits. The traditional music *Chimaycha* is well known as well, and community members are very proud of it. As in Lucanamarca, there are many special local festivities such as the anniversary of the community, a carnival,

Easter, and the water and breeding celebrations. Many of those who emigrated return to Chuschi for those festivities and are proud of these traditions.

There is temporal and permanent migration. People leave the village to study and/or work in the cities, some send their children to the cities. All families have a network of relatives in Lima, Ayacucho, Arequipa, or Ica. Some professionals who worked or studied in the cities come back to Chuschi and start businesses, submit local authority positions or as patrons for local festivities. In the cities, there are associations of Chuschinos that organize festivities and funding events. Some are also politically active.[27]

The Catholic religion is still prevalent with about 80% of the population being of the faith and about 20% belonging to the Evangelical church. In contrast to Lucanamarca, there are regular services in both churches. The *hermanas* (sisters) of the Catholic Church are an established social institution in Chuschi. There are at least three *hermanas* present in the community; they provide meals for the elderly or sick people, open a library daily where children can do their homework, and participate actively in local events. There are also Jehovah's Witnesses present in Chuschi, but they have only a few members.

Education has become more important. There is an initial, primary, and secondary school in Chuschi since the 1990s, a technical superior school opened in 2016. People are still hoping for a technical institute for higher education. Access to education has improved and now more than 90% of all children attend primary school, but secondary school is less well attended and only few go on to university every year. Scholarship programs such as the *BECA 18* opened possibilities:

> The access to education is a bit more normal, we are on about 90%. But, nevertheless, there are still sectors which do not have access to education, because of the lack of resources, economy. [...] So, with these modalities [scholarships] quite a lot of students of this zone have been able to enter university. [...] The country does show some progress [...] nevertheless, it has to be worked in the social topics, in the emotional topic, formation as citizen, as person, in the formation of values which have been lost heavily in a way.
> (CH5: 22–23)

However, like other community members the same interviewee complains, about the bad behavior and lack of strong values in students and teachers. Some teachers are very active and responsible; others drink a lot during the working week. And in the small village, the students notice this behavior. Interviewees state that it was not like that before. The teachers' behavior set a bad role model for the students (CH23: 21).

The director of the secondary school mentioned these problems as well:

> The students see that in the same way, they notice when the teacher drinks, they are missing out on learning important things, their friends too and

> there is no one to guide them. The students put pressure on their parents, if they do not get what they want, they leave. There are parents who complain that their children escaped from home, there are girls that get pregnant.
> (CH9: 21)

Teenage pregnancy is still a problem in Chuschi. Contraception is not a topic that people talk about, and young people don't go to the health post to get it. Access to health care has been improving in the last few years, and Chuschi now has a little hospital that was inaugurated in 2015. The number of health workers has increased, and the institutions grown but some community members still do not trust them. The number of hospital births has been rising and there is now also a room for overnight stays for women arriving from further away. However, the pressing problems of malnutrition and anemia are ongoing in the whole district (CH13: 19, 37).

The police station was set up during the internal armed conflict and contributed to the diminishment of Shining Path in the district. However, the police and other state forces were also responsible for disappearances and abuse during the internal armed conflict in Chuschi. A police official states that the people have a lot of distrust toward the police because of the violence of the 1980s but that they are slowly accepting the institution. Some are also asking the police for support and report some delinquencies. The police organize talks in the schools to make young people aware of different issues, especially of domestic violence. A police official explains that the way they work had changed. Abuse or violations of the law were no longer allowed, and there were controls via the national ombudsman as well (CH11: 24–27). There is also a security service that operates in the village of Chuschi, which is paid for by the municipality and, in March 2016, a new neighborhood junta was installed. They have been trained by the police and are meant to keep order in the smaller communities and prevent robberies (Exp38).

There is an ATM, which is important as social programs are paid out there for the whole district of Chuschi and for some neighboring villages such as Sarhua as well. The "pay day" is accompanied by a small market where locals and external vendors sell food or other products. It is an important income opportunity for people in Chuschi although most of vendors are external. Still, when people withdraw their payments they often go directly to the shops or restaurants. Various NGOs have worked in the district of Chuschi since 2000: *Aprodeh* and *Paz y Esperanza* as human rights organizations supporting the TRC and the *Welthungerhilfe* together with *ABA* and *Cedap* had funding from Japan and other countries to implement projects in infrastructure and agriculture (CH12: 18). However, in the interviews, only one project *Chakra Emprendedora* is mentioned positively by a community member (CH17).

The state programs implemented by the national government to combat poverty and malnutrition since the 1970s have a strong presence in Chuschi: *Juntos, Qali Warma, Vaso de Leche, Cuna Más, Pension 65*. The MIDIS lists for

August 2017, the following numbers of beneficiaries of the different programs: 978 families in *Juntos*, 630 people in *Pension 65*, 115 families in *Cuna Más* with 69 children in four daycare centers, and 443 children in *Qali Warma* in 14 educational institutions.[28]

Opinions about the social programs are diverse, however. *Pension 65* is seen as providing good support to the elderly from most interview partners. Only few state that *Pension 65* are receiving some people who have money and do not need it (CH14: 50). Others report that there are problems when children of the elderly steal their money:

> I heard of Pension 65 as well that there are some children, well their parents receive and they are giving it to them. They shout to them, abuse them. This is not right, it hurts [...] Moreover, there is a lot of corruption.
>
> (CH8: 61)

Programs like *Qali Warma* are judged to be positive and an important nutritional support while at school but did not solve the problem of the poor nutrition within the families at night or on the weekends (CH8: 22).

The most discussed program is *Juntos* – the same as in Lucanamarca. One the one hand, it is seen as a positive support for families with small children as it compels mothers to comply with health checks and make sure their children attend school. One interviewee said that it was thanks to *Juntos* that the mothers now met in reunions that they did not have before and this is seen as a positive development (CH12: 23). The beneficiaries of the program claimed that it was not enough money (CH16: 68). On the other hand, people said in the interviews that families had got used to receiving this money every month and now had fewer incentives to work as a result. Moreover, the program *Juntos* was an incentive to have more children, even for young girls: "Young girls are having children because of the program Juntos. The population is growing therefore" (CH20: 52). Another woman said: "here they are used to receive and not to give, the social programs do not show them how to give [...] I think there are students that are thinking to get pregnant to enter in these programs" (CH9: 30). They claim that the program reinforces assistentialism and getting used to receiving presents: "I think it is because of the social support [programs] that the people don't care about communal work, before there were united, now they are separated" (CH13: 19). Others even commented that *Juntos* created new problems of envy (CH4: 34). As in Lucanamarca, people demanded that the program *Juntos* should educate people how to generate their own income instead (CH1: 60). In spite of all this criticism, Chuschi has been shown as an exemplary achievement of the program *Juntos*, and this is where the program's tenth anniversary celebrations took place in 2015, accompanied by a visit of several senior ministers.[29] One member of the local authorities explained to me that the wider problem was that every national and local government changed programs frequently and introduced their own programs, so that there was little continuity and many parallel programs, which in turn impeded their efficiency (CH5: 79).

A *Tambo* of the national government program was set up in the upper part of the district, similar to the one in Lucanamarca. The program promises to reach and better service remote areas. The Tambo in the district of Chuschi, as in Lucanamarca, has only been used for internet access and accommodation for professionals so far (Exp30).

The mayor and council who are in position since 2015 are very active and participated in different new programs; in 2016, Chuschi won the *sello municipal*. This is awarded to municipalities when they complete their annual project aims and thereby improve the living conditions of their populations. In September 2017, the second *Model Intercultural of Itinerant Justice* was organized in Chuschi and offered legal assistance and guidance. In the Peruvian imagination, Chuschi is the Andean village in need and the women and children with their traditional skirts appear always in the official photographs with ministers or other functionaries of the national and regional government.[30]

Life in Chuschi before the conflict is described by Isbell (1985) who lived in the community for several years in the 1960s and 1970s. Her book is a very detailed ethnographic analysis of that time. She describes the importance of traditions and rituals in the population as well as the well-organized community structure. However, as in Lucanamarca modernization had already reached Chuschi back then. Education was improved; old structures and elites changed; people migrated to the cities and returned with new ideas. Small businesses emerged and money became more important.[31]

Chuschi is where Shining Path started the violent conflict and burnt the ballot boxes in May 1980, one day before the national elections. Shining Path also established "popular schools" to spread its ideology in various villages, formed militant groups, and took over the communal house of the municipality, local government, and *juez de paz* in 1982. They replaced the local board and confiscated all official documents. In 1983, the communal building in Chuschi was burned down and with it all its documents, which has been causing problems with missing DNIs and communal acts to date. In separate incidents, villages of the district revolted against Shining Path, which resulted in several deaths. The dispute between Chuschi and the neighboring community of Quispillacta that had been ongoing for centuries, escalated during this time. Villagers accused each other of supporting one or the other group, knowing that this would lead to the death of the accused person.

As part of its counterinsurgency strategy, the military created support bases all over the country. One of those was in the neighboring district of Totos. Many people from Chuschi were detained, tortured and disappeared there, after being accused of supporting Shining Path. At the same time, a police station was set up in Chuschi. Like elsewhere military presence saw rapidly decreasing number of Shining Path victims but the number of deaths caused by the state forces increased instead. The military base became the main site for various confrontations and deaths in the fight between Shining Path and the state forces. Together with the military, the police in Chuschi are responsible for a case of three disappeared members of the local authorities and an adolescent in 1991. As they had refused to form a self-defense group, they were suspected of supporting Shining Path. This case was brought to trial (APRODEH 2008; also CVR 2003, Vol. VII, Ch. 2.46).

In the interviews conducted people reported that the community members of Chuschi suffered from intimidation and abuse from both sides: "So it has left a total disaster, of both. We were in the middle" (CH14: 44). Another man described the difficult situation as follows:

> They [the military] blamed me, I was there involved, they arrested me. Not only me, others. [...] I wanted to stay in Chuschi but had to go to San Miguel. The situation was very bad. It was not safe to live here.
>
> (CH15: 47)

And another woman reported: "They killed my uncle, he was killed by the police and they threw him down there behind the secondary school. After one week they found him and my dad says he carried him and they buried him there" (CH16: 51). Consequences were widespread:

> The whole department was left as a disaster; a lot of progress has been destroyed. What were they thinking these people [Shining Path], with what intention have they started. They should have thought it good, they should have made it slowly, they killed innocent poor people, ignorant.
>
> (CH23: 57)

Interestingly, this woman is not in general against the ideas of Shining Path but not conform with the way they fought for it. In Chuschi, the narrative that Fujimori has ended the conflict and won the conflict, is still present (CH8: 38).

The reparation plan by the municipality lists 135 fatalities, 137 disappeared, 38 cases of sexual violence, and 552 torture victims in the whole district.[32] The TRC listed fewer victims (CVR 2003, Annex 5). It is important to emphasize that there were victims on both sides: that of Shining Path and that of the state forces.

As in Lucanamarca, the consequences of the conflict were multifold, including social, psychological, economic, political, and in education. One community member explains the impact on education.

> Yes, my uncle was disappeared and they still don't know where he is. My cousins for this reason stayed without education, they are looking for work now. If this situation had not have happened, their father maybe would have educated them and it would be different.
>
> (CH1: 45)

Also the loss of values is connected with the consequences of violence:

> Before Shining Path came the people were well educated. Now there is no respect. So I see some consequences [of the violence], maybe for the fathers of the family, like a bit violent, not all in general. Equally I see abandonment of small children, they leave them with the grandparents, they don't care. And this is maybe because they have been affected by the time of the violence.
>
> (CH8: 18)

In economic terms, "those who had recently started small businesses lost everything. They came and burnt down houses and everything. It was a disaster" (CH1: 40). Another consequence of the violence was that people could not attend to their chakras to cultivate the land. Furthermore, the violence destroyed a lot of water and electricity infrastructure (CH23: 48, 56). From a psychological perspective, people talk about the fear meant that they could not sleep in their houses because of the danger. They feel traumatized. Those, who did not lose a family member still feel affected:

> I was born in the year 1980, in this year the social internal conflict was ongoing, until 1990. So as a child I lived through that and I remember it still. That time one could not sleep in our houses but had to find another place far away, hiding to wake up alive. If not, you would wake up dead. This affected us a lot, psychologically. This cannot be deleted, it is always in the mind. We have suffered this violence.
>
> (CH2: 48)

In consequence of the violence, the social order within the communities was damaged and values such as solidarity and trust lost: "The violence that occurred in this area in the 80s and 90s has caused a setback in social terms" (CH5: 21). Many interview partners describe that the violence caused distrust in the people and that they are not that open as before, that they don't trust anymore (CH13: 19).

Community members also describe the image of Chuschi that was generated during the internal armed conflict in Peru: "They say Chuschi is the red moon of Peru, the whole world knows Chuschi because the political violence happened here" (CH16: 60). There is still a lot of discrimination in the cities toward Chuschi and other communities of Ayacucho, which further limits the locals' opportunities (CH5: 21). One of the teachers experienced this discrimination when she arrived in Lima and was called: "la terrorista de Ayacucho" (CH8: 46). The judge, who came some years ago to Chuschi, observes:

> I see that the Chuschino is calm, they do not protest, when there are problems they keep quiet about it. It seems to me that this is a consequence of the political violence. The Chuschino is humble, quiet, not a fighter; it is not a rebellious village.
>
> (CH6: 19)

The consequences of the violence are varied. Some of the interviewed people state that the violence is still important today while others have a different perception [6 high, 7 med, 4 low, 2 very low]. Less than half of the interview partners define themselves as victims [8 yes, 12 no].

After the conflict, a strong earthquake hit Chuschi in 1999 and about 500 houses and communal buildings were destroyed. At that time, then president Fujimori visited the district twice as a show of solidarity. In 2001, the interim president Paniagua also visited Chuschi declaring it an example of humanitarian politics in Peru.

Another important issue was when in the year 2000 a Mining company wanted to start explorations in an area that belonged to the community of Chuschi. The population and even families were divided into those in favor and those against the mining proposal. Those in favor were hoping that it would bring income and work and those in opposition feared the environmental consequences, especially because the population depended on agriculture and animal husbandry. Interview partners state that this situation worsened the rifts within the community and led to further distrust both within and toward authorities. There were rumors that villagers and authorities received payments from the mining company for their support: "There was a time when Chuschi was divided into two, for and against, from then on they did not trust in local authorities" (CH7: 24). Another man confirms:

> There was the division, including divisions between families, parents, children, brothers. It was chaos, [...] until today they are not united, including the authorities. Then came the corruption. Corruption is what the mine brought. The authorities received some presents, they were bribed.
>
> (CH15: 21)

The mine offered paid work and payments of an order that no one ever imagined. This reinforced the importance of paid work and made it harder persuade people to work for free or even for the "normal" daily wages in the *chakras* (Exp38).

The ongoing dispute with the neighboring village of Quispillacta is still a topic in Chuschi. Both villages are only divided by a little river. The conflict has been ongoing for centuries and was now reinforced because Quispillacta wants to be recognized as a district as well, which would grant them their own budget and control over their territories. They need a minimum number of villages and population to be able to apply for district status. I heard accusations from community members of both Chuschi and Quispillacta stating that the group of people fighting for the district was convincing other village authorities to support them by means of forged signatures and bribery. This led to distrust toward the authorities (see 6.1.3). In 2016, activists from Quispillacta started impeachment proceedings against the mayor of Chuschi, which failed. The historical roots and the process of the conflict between both communities is analyzed by Flórez Salcedo (2012) and Huaycha Cayllahua (2013).

Apart from this, the other main problems identified by the interviewees are: social problems, malnutrition, the economic situation combined with less extract of agriculture, lack of work, and lack of good education as well as domestic violence.

The implementation of transitional justice in the community

Chuschi did not experience the same level of exposure to transitional justice processes as Lucanamarca but still received a substantial amount of attention. Within the PAR program houses were constructed in the upper part of the district of Chuschi but not in the village itself (Exp38). However, this was not mentioned by any of the interview partners.

The TRC decided to conduct the first exhumation in Chuschi because as in Lucanamarca an NGO, *Paz y Esperanza*, had completed some groundwork in the area. Furthermore, this emblematic case seemed politically advantageous for the TRC. A communal grave was exhumed on a territory between the villages of Chuschi and Uchuyri in 2002. The bodies of eight victims were identified and re-buried in a ceremony with participation of TRC members and relatives of the victims from Quispillacta and Chuschi. They were victims of the state forces (Rojas-Perez 2017, 42–44).[33] As in Lucanamarca, there are many more graves that have not been exhumed. In 2016, another re-burial of bodies took place. The TRC collected further testimonies in Chuschi and investigated the case of four disappeared people in 1991 (CVR 2003, Vol. VII, Ch. 2.46). In the following trial, family members from Chuschi participated (APRODEH 2008). But few in the community are aware of this trial; none of my interview partners mentioned it, probably because those family members live in Lima today. The case is also a topic in the documentary *Caminantes de la Memoria* (Wanderer of the Memory). It describes a scene of reconciliation after a member of the military was convicted in the trial and a family member of one of the victims stated she forgave him although he could not tell them where the bones of their loved ones were.[34]

There were about 20 cases recorded and testimonies collected in Chuschi itself and about 40 cases in the whole district. In the two testimonies reviewed, people asked to know where their family members were buried because they were still disappeared. They demanded also some form of economic assistance for their families (200493; 200801). One testimony giver explained that because of his father's death, he and his siblings could not continue their education and that they would like some support now to compensate for that:

> If my father had been alive, we would at least have finished secondary school, with that we would at least be working in something, like others, and live our lives. But as we don't have our education, we are affected. Today in this time is everything for the one that has education. Therefore, we cannot find money, we just do some little works in chakras and this is how we find food. (200801: 28)

With the work of the TRC and the testimony giving was already connected the expectation of reparations.

In 2007, the municipality of Chuschi developed a local reparation plan (*Plan Integral de Reparaciones del Distrito de Chuschi 2008–2015*) with support from an NGO, and there was also a treaty signed between the *Consejo de Reparaciones* and the municipality to facilitate the cooperation. The reparation plan contains an analysis of the conflict in Chuschi and elaborates the vision for reparations in Chuschi. The plan recognizes the opportunities to acknowledge victims by awarding reparations, reinstituting the civil rights that were curtailed and contributing to the re-establishment of civic confidence and social solidarity. In the plan, reparations are connected to the development of families, work, identity, culture, social and communal participation, and the execution of civic rights. Reparations are seen as a part of the national reconciliation. The local reparation plan explains that collective reparations are a sign of acknowledgement and reaffirmation of the dignity and status of the community. Collective reparations should create civic trust and a sense of belonging and national identity, reconstruct social, institutional, economic, and material capital of the families and communities affected by the violence.

I was surprised to find such a detailed plan in the archives of the municipality. I found it by chance while looking for another document; no one remembered it or mentioned it to me. Everything in this report points to the influence of the NGO not least because of the way it was worded and how it referenced reparation theory. Unfortunately, I could not find anyone who has been part of the creation of the report. The plan has not been fully implemented to date. In Chuschi, there are similar problems as in Lucanamarca.

Regarding individual reparations, there are still people who are not registered: "My mum is registered, I did not register because when it came [the registration] I was away from the community, I was not here" (CH2: 51). The people in Chuschi faced the same problems as in other communities. They did not understand in the beginning that the registration was connected to receiving reparations, some did not know about the registration at all or could not provide the required documents:

> Many times the state puts special parameter to be able to register to the affected people. For example, I was affected, but they want evidence, maybe a wound of a bullet, something visible. Therefore, it is difficult. Imagine a woman who was violated, how can she prove now to be considered as affected and maybe receive this support? This form of parameter has nothing to do with our reality.
>
> (CH7: 49)

Community members also blame the government for not implementing the program earlier and criticize that victims had to tell their stories again:

> when they opened the register not all of the people wanted to register because in that moment they were not thinking that later they could receive

> individual reparations. And simply repeating these scenes make them remember and it affects the soul and causes pain and suffering. For those maybe it is worth more to forget and never again remember and they are, like they say, living their normal daily lives.
>
> (CH5: 70)

Out of the 20 people interviewed, 8 declared themselves to be victims of the internal armed conflict. Only two are registered in the RUV. None of them received individual economic reparations. According to the information from CMAN, 264 people are beneficiaries of individual economic reparations by July 2017 in the district of Chuschi. I tried to find one of those people to interview but even with the support of authorities and NGOs, it was not possible. In total, 759 people were registered in the RUV in June 2017, 505 direct victims and 254 family members. The municipality twice sent functionaries to training offered by CMAN to handle the RUV in the village and open an office to register the affected. Both failed the final exam though, and there is still no adequate attention or knowledge about the reparation program.

Reinstatement of civil rights such as determining the status and providing documentation for the disappeared, and the reconstruction of DNIs has been implemented only in part. There are still people whose birth certificates are missing or who have wrong DNIs, and they face problems in formal procedures with ministries.

The local reparation plan lists seven different types of reparations for Chuschi. Reparations in housing had not been implemented at the time of the interviews. According to CMAN, 33 people were entitled to these reparations in the program *Techo Propio*. But, as explained for the case of Lucanamarca, there are problems in the requirements and technical implementation of this program.

Reparation in health, such as the diffusion of the health insurance and attention in mental health for affected people, had also barely been implemented. In the mini hospital in Chuschi, there was no awareness of this insurance and when asked about the insurance for the affected it was confused with the insurance provided for poor people. Psychological support offered in the health center is only available in Spanish, and the person responsible did not seem trained in helping people who were traumatized during the violent conflict.

Reparations in education such as scholarships and extra courses for affected people have also barely been implemented. Few people knew about the new national scholarship program *Repared* and again it was confused with the scholarship for poor people. More than 600 people could potentially benefit from the *Repared* program, according to CMAN.

Symbolic reparations such as the construction of memory parks and memorials and the re-naming of streets were not implemented. In fact, nothing was realized apart from the re-burials with the TRC in 2002 and again in 2016. There is no memorial or day of commemoration. In some years, the national press came and reported from Chuschi on May 17th, the day Shining Path burnt the ballot boxes. In 2016, a short documentary was made for a TV channel. However, there is little interest in the past from outside or inside the village:

> For example, seven, eight years ago, the May 17th, the day of the first attack of the subversivos here, this day all the press came to make their reports. But in the last years we did not have visits from no one.
>
> (CH7: 40)

For collective reparations, the plan lists a huge number of projects to rebuild and improve basic services in infrastructure, education institutions, health posts, communal buildings, water and drain systems, reforestation, energy, telecommunication, churches, and nutrition. Second, it lists possible projects for the generation of income such as the breeding of small and big animals such as milk cows, alpacas, and vicunas and fish farms. There are 28 villages of Chuschi listed in the registry of affected communities by the CMAN, of those 17 have already received collective reparations (CMAN 2017).[35] A communal house was built in Chuschi in 2009, which housed the health center until the small hospital was built in 2016. However, community members were not aware that this house was built as part of the reparation program. Only one community member mentioned it in my interviews. As with the other cases, the project was executed by the municipality.

The awareness and perception of transitional justice

In Chuschi, I found relatively high awareness of the TRC [15] but some confuse it and refer directly to reparations [7], only few mention the exhumations and search of disappeared or the publication of the report. Knowledge within local authorities is a little higher, only two ordinary community members knew about the exhumation: "they came when I was 16, they were reburying bones" (CH16: 51). And another woman explains:

> [the TRC] made an investigation, talking to the people, they made re-burials because their family members did not know where their loved ones were. We wanted to know where their loved ones are, where they buried them. Yes, I heard of this truth commission.
>
> (CH21: 64)

Interestingly, all the community members refer only to the truth commission, the word reconciliation is not used. One authority explains: "Thanks to the government, the politics of a government, there came a truth commission which is in some form giving support in form of collective reparations, but still did not come the individual reparation" (CH2: 48).

The awareness of reparations is even higher [18], but knowledge about the program is low. Half of the people know only very little or only rumors.

Information about transitional justice measures is very low in Chuschi – as in the other communities. Community members and authorities are not well informed about what programs are available, how to apply, and what the regulations were or who received anything. "They say for their sons, if there is a widow, if it is a single they gave it to his mother. [Q: collective reparations as well?] Mmh, I don't know" (CH16: 53–54). There is widespread confusion with other programs as well (CH18: 50–50).

The collective reparation project in Chuschi itself is not known. They know the building, but the community members do not know that this house was built with money from the reparations fund. It does not have any memorial sign. Only one of the interviewees referred to that project (CH15: 51). Interestingly, ten interview partners refer to collective reparations as part of the reparation program, but not to the one implemented in Chuschi itself but in neighboring villages.

Regarding individual reparations, some state that reparations have already been paid to people in Chuschi: "[...] individual [reparations] it seems that some received them as well" (CH15: 50). Others state that there was nothing until today: "Collective yes but individual they say is in process but there has nothing arrived yet" (CH1: 51–52). In total, 17 people state that there have been reparations paid in the community.

None of the interviewed people said he or she received reparations because they only refer to individual ones and not to the collective project. There is no subjective exposure to the reparations although objectively they received a project. There is barely any knowledge of the different forms of reparations in health, education, and housing.

The perception of the TRC has different dimensions. First, its work is not well understood by the community members. In total, 15 people have heard of the commission but only one person knows more about its work and five have medium levels of knowledge. The concrete work of TRC is barely present in the memory of the people, but slightly more in authorities. The connection of the TRC with the reparation program by seven people has an impact on their satisfaction levels with the work. That means, if one is dissatisfied with the reparation program, they would be dissatisfied with the commission as well because it is perceived as the entity with the purpose of delivering reparations.

As in Lucanamarca, there was distrust toward the TRC in Chuschi:

> It seems to me that when the TRC came it made a superficial study, these days the people had fear, they informed only about some things. [...] they don't feel united. They thought these days that the terrorism would come back, therefore they did not give all the information and many have been silent. In Chuschi only few cases have been reported because of the fear. Right now one could receive more information.
>
> (CH6: 43)

As a conclusion, this man claims that those who did not dare to talk to the commission have also not received reparations although they would be eligible.

Others state that the commission did not conclude its work: “the outcome is missing” (CH11: 74) and further investigation would be necessary:

> The TRC in some way did work on the national level, recuperating information, with the exhumation of bodies, investigations. I consider that it has not covered 100% of the cases, maybe the most highlighted ones, the representative ones. I consider that it has covered 80%, 70% of all the cases. There are cases where maybe there were two victims, three victims, and those maybe have not been considered. Some parts where they are not that detailed in the report how the happenings were. Some things that I have seen, I have family members that have lived that period and they tell me in detail the places, names of the authorities, places where the things happened, all of that. When I compare that with the report of the TRC, it does not speak about this at length, it says two three lines and terminates there. It is a summary and in the end does not transfer the complete message. The same might be true for the whole report, other communities in other districts.
>
> (CH5: 61)

Interviewees demand further searches for the disappeared:

> There are still people looking for their loved ones [...] the government does not know what to do. A friend of mine, for example, is looking for her father, she cannot find him. She is suffering: ‘I would like to bury him, the money is not important anymore, it won’t bring back my father but I want to find my father.’ The government made it good but is delaying with everything.
>
> (CH8: 49)

And, as mentioned already, the evaluation of the commission is connected to the reparations: “After the violence of the 80s, the TRC was formed. Yes, they did work but in summary we observe now that it is maybe not in the form that we wanted, because the affected population was expecting support” (CH7: 47).

Because of these perceived shortcomings, in summary, the overall evaluation of the TRC is rather negative [0 high, 2 medium, 7 low].

The perception of the collective reparation project in Chuschi was too low to examine as only one interview partner know about the project and the others did not. They do know the building as a communal building but not that it was built within the collective reparation program. Even the person interviewed who works in the health center which used to operate from this building did not know about it. The one person aware of it is medium satisfied: “In Chuschi it seems like they gave 100,000 Soles in collective reparations and they made a little work, they built a communal house here. It is something. This is what they made. There is the health post” (CH15: 51). Some interviewees mention that they feel that reparations should be paid directly to the person affected and not collective: "so they can be satisfied and at least there is calm and peace in their hearts because now the people are resentful" (CH13: 50). Individual psychological support would also be necessary. Some of the authorities and one community member, interestingly, know about reparation projects in other communities and evaluate them critically. They reported that the local government tried to get reparation projects for the communities, but they missed the opportunity to explain why those projects were chosen and that they were indeed reparation projects. Furthermore,

> these projects do not last, maybe after they are executed they should be handed over to the local government or a commission which is formed within the community with a contract with the aim to put them in charge of the operation. There are, for example, communities that have received water systems that are still not working. And why? Because very often the people do not know how these systems work. [...] Sometimes the continuation is missing and all of that [the projects] come to nothing.
>
> (CH7: 51)

This person, who was in charge of the reparations in the district before, does not know that according to CMAN regulations, this is already part of the procedure. A commission has to be formed and people responsible for the project identified from within the community. He is referring to one project, which is not working in the neighboring community of Uchuyri (see Chapter 5). Another important point mentioned by him is that the projects are not connected to the violence of the 1980s and not perceived as reparations – as it is the case with the communal house in Chuschi. Another former responsible person for the reparation program complains a misuse of reparation money: "some people have enriched themselves with this RUV" (CH12: 52). The same person also confuses the reparation program with other development or state projects. Another woman, asked for the reparation program, explained that the program *Chacra Emprendedora* executed by the state was a huge support (CH17: 52). She too confuses the reparation program with another.

People also told me about collective reparation projects in other parts of the district that did not work out because people did not want to collaborate: "But normally associations do not work because the people do not want to work together, they do not reunite. Other projects have failed for that reason" (CH4: 51).

Another point criticized is that the same amount is given to every community:

> So, it is a minimum incentive that the government gave. It is not the same if you compare communities where there are only 25 or 20 people and they benefit from 100,000 and another community which has 800 inhabitants where 100,000 is not significant.
>
> (CH5: 63)

In view of the different sizes of the communities in the district of Chuschi but also elsewhere this seems unjust. He further mentions that the projects sometimes do not suit the village and that technical assistance is not sufficient:

> Many times populations for the lack of a definitive study of their necessities demand projects that do not have sustainability over time. [...] the reason why the majority of the projects of collective reparations are not productive is because they come with an execution of three month of technical assistance, three month of presence of the responsible person and in the fourth month all technical support disappears. [...] This is the huge problem, aggravating deficiency to make all the productive projects, over all the collective reparations, are not working. I don't know of one community that received this type of collective reparation and got good advantage out of it. The majority is negative.
>
> (CH5: 66)

Once more, these answers demonstrate the difficulties of the collective reparation projects, first in the technical operation of the project and second in the perception of the project. In Chuschi, the collective reparation project works technically for community purposes but has no connection to the reparation program or the violence suffered. Again, there is objective exposure to this TJ measure but no subjective exposure. Its impact is therefore expected to be very limited.

The perception of reparations is focused on individual economic reparations. For assessing the perception of individual reparations, I divide the interviewed people again in three groups: observers, non-receivers, and receivers (see Chapter 3). I could, however, not find beneficiaries of the reparation program in Chuschi apart from the one person who was aware of the collective project, which was surprising. There are seven non-receivers of those only two are registered in the RUV and 12 observers; of those two do not know the reparation program.

The observers judged the reparations to be a good idea but criticized the incomplete implementation as well. One person, however, questioned whether reparations can work for recuperating victims at all: "Money is not like your family. Reparations are no compensation. [Q: could it help?] No, not anymore" (CH22: 58–59). Individual reparations are perceived as unjust:

> The topic of individual reparation is controversial, on a national level, there are people with economic power. I am referring to the military, the police, many of them have lost their lives. But how much are they getting in reparations? Those are high amounts. And how much is the government giving to a peasant who gave his life or was a victim of this situation? This 10,000 and there is the huge question: 'Qué vida vale más?' (Which life is worth more?) Why is there such indifference? [...] there are judicial processes including those presented to the international courts, victims – or people that have

> been immersed, intellectuals, authors tied directly to Shining Path – are demanding their reparation of 200,000 or 700,000! Those are exaggerated cases.
>
> (CH5: 67)

The same person described how difficult the reparation process was for victims of sexual abuse: "Who will declare to have been sexually violated and demands reparations? There are children, many without parents, the children of this abuse. I believe that this would leave people very vulnerable to discrimination" (CH5: 70). He goes on to criticize the delays:

> Many of those people who suffered this in person are 60, 70, 80 years old today and the government is in a delay totally. Since the presentation of the report of the TRC they did not attend in an immediate form.
>
> (CH5: 70)

The non-receivers do not understand why others received reparations when they did not:

> No, we did not receive anything. My husband was arrested various times as well, they are not recovering anything, they did not give us anything. [...] They said they would give us something, but nothing. Not one Sol. Promises, nothing more. Some received something by lying. There are some survivors, nothing happened to them and yet received something anyway.
>
> (CH23: 66)

This woman is also not satisfied with the reparations her family members, the children, and wife of her disappeared brother, received:

> They received their money. But they did not give a lot, 800 Soles as reparations but nothing more, in the case of a wife 5,000, they said. They gave them a piece of land in Lima. They are living there. But it is a total disaster, when their mother and father were still alive, the children would live as well as professionals but now everything is wrong. Without the father, no. [Q: Do the reparations help?] I don't think that it helps a lot, 800 Soles.
>
> (CH23: 62; also CH21: 69)

Others had similar opinions: "Individual [reparations] are still missing. We are waiting for them. [...] Yes, some have received something but only very little. This is also not sufficient to recuperate psychologically, a professional psychologist could help us get stronger mentally" (CH2: 48, 59).

Another man was very frustrated because some people seemed to be receiving a lot of support from different programs, and he did not get anything although he was registered in the RUV as well: "I saw, for example, his son, a soldier, died. The spouse receives something monthly and also received Pension 65, but they cut it off because you cannot get both" (CH14: 50). In another interview, I heard about the problems with rumors and lack of transparency and also how different victim groups were created:

> Individual [reparations] it seems some have received as well. But I have a certificate, because I have been strongly affected, but for abuse and torture they say there is nothing, only for the dead ones. I fell a bit bad because psychologically I am affected. In other words, maybe they would give some help for psychological abuse. [Q: nothing?] No, there came nothing.
>
> (CH15: 50)

This man is very upset because he seems to be a second-class victim and not eligible for reparations. Although he received his certificate which acknowledges him as victim but the certificate does not guarantee him any benefits.

Moreover, both victims as non-victims criticize the requirements and technicalities:

> But sadly we see that some families still have not received individual reparations. [...] Now there is a scholarship, similar to Beca 18, Beca Repared. But often the fathers of the nation ("padres de la patria") set norms that are not based in reality. In this case of Repared – I had the opportunity to coordinate with the responsible person – they told me that those are for directly affected people. So, the directly affected are already 40, 50, 60 years old, so, at that age, why would they aspire to attend university? To enter in a higher education program is nearly impossible. Therefore, this program should be aimed at the children of the affected people.
>
> (CH7: 47)

For those who knew that others had received something when they had not, the situation seemed to be worse. They perceived the program as highly unjust. And the expectations created were very high, as was the disappointment.

It is almost impossible to judge the perception of the collective reparation program in Chuschi because only one person knew the project. Others referred to projects in neighboring villages that did not work and were therefore not judged positively either. Individual reparations were perceived as negative because they were still not fully implemented. Furthermore, the requirements, conditions, and amounts of reparations were criticized. The majority of the interviewed people had very low levels of satisfaction with the reparations [12 low, 2 med, 0 high]. There was no positive impact on social cohesion to be expected under these circumstances.

The impact on social cohesion

The social cohesion indicator for the community of Chuschi shows that the overall level is relatively low. I find very similar problems and patterns in Chuschi as in Lucanamarca. The situation in the community is perceived as having improved in terms of development and infrastructure [14 positive] but in terms of social cohesion it is worse than before [14 less solidarity].

On the horizontal level, I found that the community lacks trust and solidarity, which exists only in extreme cases such as accidents or deaths or if someone has severe problems, then all the interviewees would help. Since the epoch of the Inca until the 1990s *ayni* and *minka* had been practiced but nowadays these traditions are hardly present anymore:

> I consider that the whole topic of globalization has something positive and negative. You can say positive because it compensates the effort of work, economically vitalized the work of a community or society. [...] the negative aspect is that there is no longer this love, affection and emotion towards people, no solidarity or support for the community.
>
> (CH5: 31)

Community members explain the loss of solidarity and cohesion with the arrival of paid work – people got used to working for money only (CH2: 31–32). "Before there were all together, no we are separated. There is still solidarity when there are problems. Ayni still exists in 50% of places, now there is more work" (CH3: 28).

Others see the social programs as one reason for shrinking solidarity: "I think it is because of the social programs that the people do not care about communal work anymore, because before they were united, now there is disunity" (CH13: 19). Another authority observes the same: "the people got used to the 'facilismo', they receive money and we are losing a bit of what is ayni, you have to hire someone if you need help on the chakra, a 'peyon' (temporary worker)" (CH7: 60; also CH13: 27). Only very few people still practice ayni, within families it can still be observed:

> Only in the families, for example in the construction of houses. [Before] it was solidarity nothing else, they asked and for that they prepared food and drink and they helped. Now only close families help each other for free, the others request money. When I sow, I have to hire a 'peyon'.
>
> (CH14: 27; also CH7: 28)

The community members see the conflict surrounding the mining company as one reason for the reduction in solidarity as well: "Before, there was this union, all were united but now this tradition, the mining company that came here is the reason for the change. There, one part was in favor and the other part against it" (CH15: 21). The mining company also paid to local workers fairly high wages and so it became even more difficult to find cheap peyones (Exp38; also CH18: 21).

The people interviewed complained about the loss of values and interest in the common good. Before, people were more polite and looked out for each other. Today, this is less and parents do not teach their children these values. Some claim that the laws against violence against children restricted their education (CH12: 41). "Today you don't touch your children. Therefore, the boy does not know how to differentiate between what is bad and what is good, or learn what respect is. This is a cultural topic that is important in our societies" (CH5: 23). The lack of values is mentioned by the teachers as well who try to make a contribution. However, some teachers drink during the week and do not serve as good role models and neither do the parents (CH9: 21). And again, there is the connection to the conflict: "Before Shining Path came the people were well educated. Now there is no respect anymore" (CH8: 42).

Envy is really high and limits the development of the village in opinion of the villagers. "Yes, there is a lot. The social programs they cause envy" (CH4: 34).

> I think the majority are envious. They want for themselves no more, not for the community, they want things for themselves, for their neighbors no. They are like this. Therefore, this village cannot move forward. If we were all united with one single idea, we could advance our village. But when we are split in two, with some people against it there is no advance. There is failure. It's like that.
>
> (CH23: 43)

It is alarming that social programs are seen as causing envy and the loss of solidarity and mutual work. The intention of the programs is to strengthen families within the community.

Trust and solidarity have diminished. However, the villagers still have a strong sense of identity. They are proud because of their traditions, clothes, and music:

> We have a very special cultural life we have our song the Chimaycha, our dance, the clothing, the decorated hat, with flowers. These things are a very special tradition, which they don't have at the national level or in other communities. Therefore, there are a lot of tourists who visit and they have a beautiful experience here in the 'tourism vivencia'. This makes us proud to be Chuschino.
>
> (CH2: 62)

Only one of my interview partners observes that some professionals (those who studied in the cities) try not to be recognized as Chuschino because they fear being stigmatized but they still come to visit the community (CH13: 53). This discrimination that some Chuschinos experience in the cities is connected with the interpretation of the past. The entire country sees Chuschi as the place where terrorism began. This is still obvious in the articles and TV spots of the last years that appear at the date of the outbreak of violence, May 17th.[36]

The community members themselves also interpret things differently. Some stated that the violence was caused by a lack of state presence: "But before there was no presence of the government. I think it is for this reason that the political violence occurred" (CH1: 58). Another interviewee said that the violence was caused by a lack of attention to the basic needs of the population, in education and communication and access to state services (CH5: 53). "Before, the president was only there for the rich people no one else. The upper part of the province and the selva were forgotten, they were on their own, there was no education. This is why terrorism came" (CH14: 58).

Interviewees have different opinions on the importance the violence has until today [6 high, 7 medium, 4 low, 2 very low]. Most community members claimed that different actors committed violence. Interestingly, the police officer also expressed that violence came from different sides: "Mainly the military, police, and Shining Path. Where they came they killed. When the military and police came to support the community where those abuses took place, then, there was confusion and all that and there were victims" (CH11: 65–66). The state forces on the national level have not yet assumed responsibility for the crimes they committed against the population.

Community members said that it was be better to forget about the past to not repeat it [67%] and go forward but claim at the same time that it would be difficult for those who lived through it (CH1: 40). People should be able to get on with their lives:

> It would be better to forget, [...] when they have money and are healthy I think they will reach happiness and be at peace. If not they will be worried and do other things and from that could arise an internal conflict.
>
> (CH2: 46)

Others state that history should not be forgotten but be told to their children to learn from the past: "Well, it is always good to compare, see, pass on videos, pass them on to the young ones, touch their hearts to make them see what is changing" (CH8: 40). And another man as well: "It should be evaluated very carefully, the details, the causes [of the conflict], it is very important for all of the communities so that it won't be repeated" (CH5: 53). As mentioned already, the perception prevails that it is quiet today, thanks to Fujimori who brought the peace (CH21: 58).

Overall, I found low solidarity that is limited to extreme situations. People focus on their own well-being. Some of the community members still feel the consequences of the violence, and there are different interpretations of the past as well as a tendency to forget the past to move on. The community members mention that solidarity and traditions have been influenced by various factors: the armed conflict, the introduction of paid work and the mining company, the stronger ties to the cities, migration, and social programs.

People said that participation in communal activities was about 90% before but that today only half of the people participated (CH1: 28). "Before they say it was more, in minka, they worked, today nothing, they want money nothing else" (CH22: 31). For the same reasons as for solidarity, I observed a decreasing participation in communal works as well. Participation in communal *minka* and communal assemblies is only high if there is a penalty for non-participation, which equals a payment for the day (CH2: 35).[37] People expect the local authorities or the state to do what they completed in joint action before such as constructing and maintaining roads and canals. Local authorities have to fight the problem of disinterest. To find people for voluntary communal authority posts or as patrons for activities and fiestas is sometimes difficult: "They want the municipality to do it all with money, Foncomun, etc. but it is not enough, [...], they want to gain no more, they want the mayor to do everything" (CH15: 30). "In the past, they participated, there was more commitment. All the streets they made in faenas. [...] Today they demand everything from the municipality" (CH4: 31). Once more, it becomes very clear that providing local governments with budgets brings the opportunity to carry out projects on the one hand but seems to lower the commitment of the population to communal work on the other. In the communal work, assemblies and fiestas that I observed participation was low, only some active members attended all of the reunions and meetings and contributed. The majority did not care. Community members claimed that the community had been more organized before and that the people used to be more interested in the community (CH10: 32). Trust in local authorities has reduced as well, the local authorities themselves note this problem: "there is no trust from the people" (CH4: 25). High levels of corruption are one of the main problems (CH5: 27).

> For example, before we were more united, with the authority nearly all united, but there came other authorities, there was some loss of checks and balances and many things have happened in the municipality. The people – even if a humble or trustworthy member of the authorities arrives – the people distrust, they think it will be the same. Now the people do not trust anyone, neither the president nor the governor.
>
> (CH7: 23–24)

And this distrust grew with the arrival of the mining company (see above), which brought more corruption (CH15: 21).

> For example when communal land is divided, the first that the authorities do is to give to their families: uncles, nephews, brothers-in-law, and then the rest. The authority thinks that the people do not notice that, but they do and this created distrust in the people.
>
> (CH13: 23)

Another problem are the political campaigns against certain authorities although the major part of the population still supports them (CH1: 23).[38] The rate for trust is 3.6, much lower than toward families [5.8]. The corn given to the authorities ranks between 0 and 3, to neighbors it is slightly more 0–5.

Almost 90% of the community members state that there are conflicts within the community, mostly about territory. It is significant that formal registration of territory to a certain family member within different programs created a lot of problems because there had only been verbal agreements before. This formal registration is required by the social programs: "These confrontations were created by Cofopri.[39] Many people have children, have chakras, and verbally they give to them 'this is yours' without making a testament. When Cofopri comes they are making an urban plan and visit house after house" (CH14: 34). The juez de paz mentions that most of the conflicts are about domestic violence and maintenance payments. People first try to find a solution in their families, if this does not work they come to see the judge. But he calculates that only 30% come to report the case (CH6: 32). The governor and police mention the same problems. It is hardly possible to sanction anyone because the women do not dare to make reports or withdraw them saying that they reconciled (CH4: 39).

The 33% of the interviewees who stated that there was violence mainly refer to domestic violence: "There is a lot of machismo and alcoholism and it generates problems, like domestic violence with serious injuries" (CH11: 21). There are only few other delinquencies such as robberies, according to the police because people generally abide by the laws: "Now they know about their rights and obligations that they have as a community and as inhabitants" (CH11: 57). The community members state that they would talk to local authorities when they have a conflict.

Another type of conflicts are those with neighboring communities, which are mainly about territory as well. And the mentioned dispute with Quispillacta. These political fights have been ongoing for years and recently a new campaign was launched against the mayor of Chuschi by community members from Quispillacta. Local authorities in Chuschi explained to me that this conflict weakened the whole district. For example there was the case of important negotiations with the state and a company, which wanted to construct high-voltage power lines totaling about 900 km across the district of Chuschi as part of a national project.[40] The local government of Chuschi wanted Quispillacta to join the negotiations about the price for constructing the towers on the property of the two villages. However, in the end, both negotiated separately and their income was likely lower than if they had done it together (Exp38).[41]

When asked regarding current conflicts in the community, many state: "it is quiet today" (CH10: 19; also CH16: 40). Usually younger interviewees who only heard of the violent past answered in this manner. But also older people recognize that life is peaceful today (CH23: 48).

Asked whether such violence could return, opinion is divided, with roughly half of those interviewed thinking it was possible and the other half that is was not likely [7 yes, 9 no]. One interviewee connects the risk to the presumed ongoing presence of rebel groups (CH14: 39–42). Another man explained that new violence in that form could only come from the selva and not the sierra (CH5: 51). Others explain that the people themselves have changed and therefore new violence would be unlikely: "I don't think so anymore. We are more reflected now. We have more capacities now" (CH10: 39). Nevertheless, some do believe that new violence could occur if the state does not provide the community with the necessities:

> Yes, it [the violence] could occur if there are no basic provisions. Desperate people could do anything and this could come back, the situation of the past. But therefore we ask the Peruvian state for its presence here and to provide for our basic needs.
>
> (CH2: 44)

This seems crucial. One of the main reasons behind the violence – according to the TRC and to opinion surveys (Barrantes 2007) – were the poverty and difficult living conditions. And these issues have not yet been successfully addressed; therefore the risk of new violence remains, also in the opinion of some interviewees.

The state has more importance than before but is still not providing all the basics, mainly its presence is seen in the social programs (CH4: 56). These are seen critically as shown earlier, which definitely has an effect on the levels of satisfaction vis-à-vis the state as a whole. Trust in political institutions is very low 1–2.

Fujimori and his presidency are still at the forefront of people's memories. They see Fujimori ("*the chino*") as the one who brought peace (without any participation from the community members) which, nevertheless, did not lead to higher levels of trust in the state. Only one interviewed person mentions the good work of the military in fighting against Shining Path today in the *selva* when asked about new violence. "I don't think so because the government of Fujimori was the one that won everything. They say that over there [selva] it is growing. But thanks to God there are people, the military try to eliminate this" (CH8: 38). All the other people replied that violence was not likely again because people were satisfied now when asked about new violence and they did not credit the military or its ability to prevent or end possible new violence.

Fujimori's legacy is still strong:

> The 'chino' tranquilized everything. The present mayor of Peru, the current president is not doing anything for Chuschi. [...] Because the pavement of the road was made by the 'chino', the secondary school was built by the 'chino'. Now this government, what is it doing? Nothing. This is what troubles us.
>
> (CH21: 23, 73)

Interestingly, the presence of Fujimori in some form seemed to increase the expectations of what the state should do: "The state has to help us all. The 'senor Fujimori', yes, he came, he brought clothes, shoes, clothes for children, notebooks" (CH18: 59). The expectations toward the state are high: villagers expect infrastructure construction that in turn generates employment: "The state should make sustainable projects, in the area of productivity" (CH3: 56). The government should provide higher education in the village:

> [The state] has to continue with the decentralization, most of all in education because it is an opportunity, a door for progress not only for the individuals but also for the population. [...] the state should not oppose this [technical institute] because at least the ones that cannot go to the cities could study here as an alternative.
>
> (CH13: 59)

> For example, we are making 'pachillas' [artesania], decorations, these kinds of things. So [the state] should create a place for that instead of giving presents [Juntos]. This is one idea. From there the state could intervene to create opportunities to build an income.
>
> (CH1: 60)

The people in Chuschi identify strongly with Peru as a nation but do not see themselves as active members of the state with rights or as agents. The narrative that is predominant in Chuschi matches with the perception that it was Fujimori who brought peace and not they themselves who fought for it and against Shining Path.

Political participation is fairly low. Due to compulsory voting, the election turnout was 69% in second round of the last presidential elections in June 2016.[42] Apart from the elections, there is hardly political participation. Interest in national politics is not that high as people are preoccupied with the local situation. People did not ask me about national politics, apart from social programs. Apart from the election time, the political parties are not present in the village. The only political mobilization I observed was when the conflict between Chuschi and Quispillacta was the topic of a meeting of the Ayacuchean government in Cangallo.[43]

As mentioned earlier, the lack of state presence is seen as one cause of the conflict. Others state that it was the violence that brought higher state presence in the form of programs and infrastructure. Moreover, the decentralization brought money and power to the municipalities (CH13: 41). "Thanks to this violence changed everything. [...] Ayacucho was totally forgotten. With this situation, they [the government] noticed us and they are giving support in some form" (CH15: 41). "In recent years I consider that at least it stretched the arms, [the state] is attending in some forms the forgotten communities. [...] but not to all needs, only some" (CH5: 77). The state presence is higher but the community members are not satisfied. They notice the visits of presidents and high ministers but complain that nothing happens afterwards (CH20: 50). Corruption is seen as a major problem (CH5: 27).

One member of the local authorities uses Chuschi's history to make his point:

> Maybe make its presence in a personal way to see how we are living, the situation in which we are in and what our most urgent needs are. [...] many villages have the same needs but the government should give priority to the district of Chuschi because Chuschi suffered from the political violence, too much.
>
> (CH2: 70)

Nevertheless, there is still no agency arising from these claims.

The importance of the state is seen as low to medium. From the point of view of political science, it is a very interesting that nearly all villagers see the state presence only in the form of social programs and some infrastructure construction projects. The state is not seen as an entity that brings a political system with rights and laws establishing a social and political order and providing security.

In Lucanamarca and Chuschi, people believe that they have always been marginalized and the state never did anything for them. This is a perception that is not entirely consistent with reality. There was some awareness of the state – in the local archives of Chuschi and Lucanamarca, there are "demands" for the government to assist with the construction of a school, etc. send to Lima by the local authorities. That means, there was the perception that there was a state entity, which would help communities by providing infrastructure, education, health, and so on – but the state did not comply with this expectation. Nor did it provide security or maintain the state monopoly on violence – one of its main tasks according to state theory – but not in the perception of the people. This is a very interesting concept of the state that has an impact on the perception of reparations.

In objective terms, the state is present in the community in the budget designated to the local government, infrastructure work such as *Trabaja Peru* ("Peru is working"), social programs, the health post, education, the governor, the police, and the *juez de paz letrado* – however, many of these are not perceived as state entities. The reparation program was also not perceived as such by all people. As in Lucanamarca, there it was confused both with other state and NGO programs.

The community members evaluate the situation today as better than the situation some years ago [12]. When asked which entity caused the positive changes in the community, they mention state programs [7], the municipality and local authorities [4], and NGOs working in the agriculture sector [5] but no reference is made to the reparation program. Community members see some effort by the state but are not satisfied with it.

The concept of the state that the villagers have influences the perception of reparation because reparations are not perceived as a right for compensation that affected people have because they were harmed. Reparations, on the contrary, are instead perceived as "presents" from the state that the "right victims" are eligible for. The receivers are therefore perceived as "winners" not as people who received something as a right. This creates new envy within a community.

Summary

I conclude that the level of social cohesion in Chuschi is relatively low at present. As in Lucanamarca, community members constructed a narrative of the "happy time" before the conflict came. However, it was not only the conflict and the violence suffered that weakened the social cohesion in the village. Other issues that were present before the conflict started are the same as in Lucanamarca and concerned: Growing importance of money, less agricultural output, municipality budget and paid work, education and migration to and from the cities, and, to a lesser degree, climate change, and less productive land used for agriculture. Nevertheless, the conflict worsened some of those problems and led to higher migration as well of local leaders. The political and social structure was weakened. Chuschi is also one of the emblematic cases within the Peruvian Andes. As the starting point of the fight of Shining Path, the village was hit by the internal armed conflict and suffers from its social, political, economic, and psychological consequences until today. Yet the whole topic of the violence suffered is not as present as in Lucanamarca. The "victim–narrative" is not that widespread, and it is also the narrative of Fujimori bringing peace to the village that is present here.

With regard to transitional justice, Chuschi also received high levels of attention from the TRC and the reparation program accompanied by different NGOs but less than Lucanamarca. The trial of a case of Chuschi with participation of community members was not mentioned. The exhumation and collection of testimonies carried out by the TRC are seen as important. However, community members state that its work was not concluded and that there are many cases that have not been investigated so far. They also demand further exhumations and for the search for the disappeared to continue. The TRC was also perceived as an entity to bring reparations and is thus evaluated negatively for not fulfilling the high expectation that were created by its presence. The awareness on the TRC is fairly high, the satisfaction rate low.

In theory, the collective reparation project in the form of the communal house implemented in Chuschi was meant to restore infrastructure that was destroyed in the conflict. The house is still there. However, is not perceived at all as the form of reparation. People mentioned to me that they heard of other communities receiving some form of reparations instead, and this lack of knowledge leads to envy although many of those are not working. The communal house serves the community in a practical sense but did not influence social cohesion.

On the individual level, the merely act of giving testimony to the TRC was not described as positive by any of the interview partners. The victims' certificate seemed useless if it did not entitle the bearer to reparations. In theory, individual economic reparations as well as individual scholarships and health insurance aim to improve the situation of the affected people. However, I could not find an individual who had received such economic reparations and only people affected by the conflict that had not received anything up to that point. In addition to the non-fulfillment of their expectations, villagers note an unequal distribution of reparations because all of the people have heard rumors of others receiving something. This leads to more discontent.

Chuschi is one of the emblematic cases within Peru that received a lot of attention by NGOs, the truth and reconciliation commission, and the reparation program. Within my cases, it is the one with the second highest attention. However, the programs were not able to enhance social cohesion as they were meant to by their design. More than half of the interviewed people have only low satisfaction with the reparation program (13), no one evaluates it with high satisfaction and only one uninformed observer with medium satisfaction. Similar as in Lucanamarca, the majority is not rejecting the general idea of reparations but the form of implementation. The theorized aim of reparations to feel attended and satisfied and therefore enhancing trust in the state could not be observed in Chuschi. The village of Chuschi does not feel properly attended. Concluding, I could not find a positive impact of the TRC, and the reparation program had rather negative effects on social cohesion.

Santa Rosa: reparations in the "lost" region of the jungle

The village Santa Rosa is the capital of the **district** Santa Rosa, which includes three *centros poblados* and 34 villages, situated in the La Mar province in Ayacucho.[44] It was created in November 1992 and is geographically located in the VRAEM region at 740 m above sea level. It is about five to six hours' drive from the regional capital of, Ayacucho. Small buses run hourly to the neighbor village of San Francisco (about one hour's drive) and from there to Ayacucho. The road to Ayacucho was recently completed in 2017. In the rainy season, however, the problem of landslides still persists which often block the roads. In the district, there are several villages that still cannot be accessed by car for most of the year. Infrastructure improved in recent years in terms of roads, electricity, water, and drain systems. Projects were carried out by the national, regional, and local government. A peculiarity of Santa Rosa in contrast to the other two communities is the presence of coca and the proximity of the neighboring districts. The district capitals San Francisco, Pichari, and Kimbiri are only about 45–60 minutes by car.

The landscape is characterized by mountains and rivers, which create irregular surface with high slopes and waterfalls. The 372 km^2 have a range from 600 to 4200 m above sea level. The main cultivated products are coca, and to a lesser extent cacao, coffee, yucca, and fruits. Its climate is tropical, typical for the *selva*. Agriculture is the only source of employment, and it is mainly coca. There are few other types of work available similar to Lucanamarca and Chuschi (SR6: 20; SR16: 18). Soil contamination by waste water containing chemicals from the production of the coca paste is a new problem in the area. There have been some projects to promote alternative products such as cacao and coffee but those have a significantly smaller profit margin than coca and are only profitable when the farmer has a large piece of land, which most do not. Santa Rosa is highly dependent on income from coca, a drop in prices for coca has a devastating effect on the population:

> Now the situation in Santa Rosa, here in the selva is low, how is it called, economically going down. There is more poverty, more than ever. To live there is nothing anymore. It was coca nothing else but as coca is going down the cliff. Cacao and coffee is only once a year, you cannot live from it.
>
> (SR15: 17, see also SR14: 54; SR11: 22)

The district Santa Rosa was founded in 1992 and is, therefore a fairly young community. The village formed in the 1960s when people came for road construction works and stayed on after the work was concluded. However, this region was already used for agriculture during the Wari era from AD 500 onwards. The majority of the population originates from the *sierra* of the districts Tambo, San Miguel, and the province of Huanta. Migration to Santa Rosa rose in the 1980s and 1990s due to the violence and poverty. At the same time, the production of coca grew tremendously in the 1980s generating new income possibilities.

Local authorities are the mayor and the council of five members, the district governor, *juez de paz*, and the president of the *CAD – comités de autodefensa* (self-defense committee). This committee does not exist in the communities in the *sierra* but has historical roots in the VRAEM and is, according to some interviewees, even more important than the municipality (SR13: 88). Kimbiri and Santa Rosa are no *comunidades campesinas* and do not have a president or communal board. These authorities and traditions did not develop here or were not brought here by the people coming from the *sierra*. The VRAEM region was established only fairly recently and communities formed for practical reasons. The formal registration or acknowledgement of many communities took place during the time of the conflict and as part of the installation of self-defense committees, which explains their status today (see Chapter 5 on Nuevo Progreso and Zamora Castellares (2014)). The CAD lost some of its power when the municipality was installed and given an annual budget but it is still an important actor in Santa Rosa.

The last census of 2007 counted 11,200 inhabitants of the whole district. The capital has about 3,300 inhabitants.[45] The poverty rate is about 63% with 27% living in extreme poverty. More than 40% of the children are undernourished and 25% of women are illiterate. About 54% of the inhabitants are in the focus of MIDIS programs.[46]

The population mainly migrated from other rural areas of Ayacucho. There is still migration from the cities but many also leave for the cities to study there or look for better jobs. The majority of the population is Catholic (83%) or member of the Evangelical church (16%). Only a small percentage is Jehovah's Witnesses.

The older generation is bilingual (Quechua/Spanish) but the younger ones speak primarily Spanish. Traditional clothing is not that common anymore. Only in the communal festivities traditional clothing, songs, and products are still popular.

There are pre-, primary, and secondary schools in Santa Rosa. The quality of these institutions is often criticized, but this raised awareness of the importance of education. The number of families sending their children to study in the cities has increased. The network of family members living in Ayacucho or Lima is also growing and so is the interchange with the cities. Some studied "professionals" return to Santa Rosa later, but the majority does not come back due to the lack of work opportunities. Interview partners complain about the bad educational situation and about the teachers who would not conduct classes in an appropriate way or who are not able to control the students (SR14: 49; SR15: 18).[47]

There is a health post installed in Santa Rosa. But interviewees state that health care is not good there and that people have to wait a long time and most of the staff do not speak Quechua (SR19: 70). The people are not satisfied and mention health and the high number of children suffering from malnutrition as the main problems in the community that should be addressed by local and national authorities. There is a small police station in Santa Rosa, the main police station is located in the neighboring community of San Francisco. There are also special units present to combat drug trafficking. There is some distrust in the police and claims of abuse (SR19: 48). People don't want the police to enter the community because they fear to lose their coca business. Community members also complain about the way the police work at nighttime and that they are not effective (SR14: 53). The state of emergency was declared in different provinces of Peru, including in Santa Rosa as part of the province La Mar in mid-September 2016. The aim was to combat drug trafficking, criminality, and terrorism. The police and military have extraordinary power, and civil rights are limited.[48]

There are only few institutions such as the social programs and an office of the national bank. Local authorities are trying to improve this. As they state the problem lies in the lack of communal territory, which could be provided for the institutions. This results in competition with San Francisco, which houses more institutions such as the UGEL for education, ATMs, and broader services. According to the local people, the presence of institutions is a sign for more development (SR2: 21). The municipality plans to increase the number of institutions present:

> Now this is an epoch of transformation and reconstruction, in the last years it was postponed. Recently, there is a working plan with the actual administration to bring institutions such as the national bank ('Banco de la Nación'), the civil register ('Reniec'), the police, UGEL, ...
>
> (SR4: 19)[49]

NGOs are hardly present in the community. Human rights organizations have never worked in Santa Rosa, the only organizations that came worked in agriculture projects, mainly anti-coca projects with the aim to cultivate alternative products such as cacao, coffee, or pineapple. There is high distrust toward NGOs because community members think they came to eradicate coca and that they would lose their income.

Attention from social programs is lower than in Lucanamarca and Chuschi: the programs mentioned are *Juntos* [17]; *Pension 65* [7]; and a few mentioned *Beca 18*, *Cuna Más*, and *Qali Warma*. The MIDIS lists for August 2017, the following numbers of beneficiaries of the different programs: 763 families in *Juntos*, 360 people in *Pension 65*, 80 children in three daycare centers run by *Cuna Más*, and 64 children in *Qali Warma* in seven educational institutions.[50]

Pension 65 is seen as positive. There is mainly indifference toward *Juntos*. Five people find it positive, helping the families in their lives and forcing the mothers to take their children to school and health controls (SR1: 78). More than half of the interviewed people criticize the regulations regarding, which families can or cannot receive benefits. People complain that some have enough money and receive benefits regardless, while there are others who are in need but who do not receive anything (SR3: 70). They also say that women get used to receiving money and that the system encourages them to have more children (SR4: 68). One community member complains about her neighbor receiving money from the state and using it to invest in drug trafficking. She does not receive anything and does not understand it. She heard rumors that the reason could be that she has a loan from the bank, but there are others who receive it anyway as she explains. She is very dissatisfied with the situation (SR14: 85).

These are the similar arguments and problems as in the other communities:

> [...] I observe that there is an irregularity, people that receive their money, people that are 'cocaleros', that have a car or people that have only one son, but those who really need it are not in there. There the ones tied up with the workers of the municipality and the promoters, they register their people and their relatives, and not the people that really need it.
>
> (SR7: 75)

While the number of families profiting from social programs is lower than in the other two communities of Lucanamarca and Chuschi, the same problems appear, there is the same lack of information, problems of envy, and dissatisfaction.

There is only little information available on the situation of Santa Rosa before the conflict. The community was almost non-existent before Shining Path entered the area. One interviewee explains the development of Santa Rosa as follows:

> In the beginning it was a centro poblado which depended on the district of Ayna/San Francisco of the La Mar province. Now with all this work we can say it is a district and there are changes. But within this process there was the social problem, in which the life was worthless ['la vida no valia nada'], we could have lost our lives at any time. But there was the organization of

> the self-defense committees, we started to organize ourselves, we received trainings and the 162 Senderistas capitulated here in Santa Rosa. From this moment on we were breathing pure air; we could come back to our land that we had to abandon for 14 years. Later we became a district and we managed to receive budget from the state, to build roads and paths, portable water, there was a change.
>
> (SR1: 21)

When asked about the most important changes, the locals refer to the violence and the fight against terrorism, Santa Rosa becoming a district (and the budget they received as a result of this reclassification) as well as economic development (SR1: 21). Santa Rosa's population has been growing and roads and education improved. However, according to the interviewees, the most important change is the calm situation today without any violence from Shining Path. Interviewees state that there were still assaults but any violence was not of the same magnitude as in the 1980s.

During the internal armed conflict, Santa Rosa was a zone that was strongly affected by the violence. Shining Path, the state forces, and self-defense committees all killed many people. The victims were peasants, members of the local authorities and members of the committees. In 1983, the military base was installed in Louisiana, a few kilometers south of Santa Rosa. Many people lost their lives or disappeared on the military base. There are also testimonies of sexual violations at the base. The history of Santa Rosa during the internal armed conflict shows that the village suffered violence from different sides. In the testimonies, people talk about the rebel group as well as the military coming into the village, searching for people, and taking some with them that were never seen again. The people recount their experience of being trapped between the different forces. Del Pino (1996, 141–42) also describes the dynamics in the village as being between two fires ("dos fuegos") and the development of the law of the jungle ("ley de la jungle") in which all the different actors, the rebel groups, military, and self-defense committees used violence. People killed neighbors out of envy (SR7: 50, 60). One woman narrates that during the conflict, one day Shining Path arrived with 200–300 men, who had to be allocated accommodation and given food, and, the next, the military came and asked for the same. In contrast to the other two villages, in Santa Rosa, the narrative of the community members fighting against Shining Path and creating peace is strong (SR1: 21; SR2: 2). The event mentioned in the quote above was the liberation of families who were in a Shining Path camp by the CAD. The man perceives it as 162 people capitulating, and this is how the narrative formed around the event.

In total, the TRC lists 309 fatalities for the district of Santa Rosa (CVR 2003, Annex 5).

The consequences of the violence are similar to the other communities and affect the social, political, and psychological aspects as well as in health and education. Some interviewees stated that the consequences had still not been overcome in

Santa Rosa (SR9: 20). Many mention the fear that they lived through during those years. Some experienced the violence as children and saw their parents and grandparents suffer, saw dead people and lost family members (SR9: 63). The emotional consequences can be especially debilitating as one interviewed person explains:

> because they have been affected by the terrorism, because there are dysfunctional families. There is the father or mother missing, and the things could not move on in the same way. Therefore, there are their problems, the insecurity, the economic part, the emotional part. Everything is not good. Well. Therefore, everyone seeks to leave from here.
>
> (SR19: 19–20)

These social and psychological consequences of the armed conflict for the families are also mentioned by a health center worker in Santa Rosa, cited in a study undertaken by UNICEF for the region.[51]

The conflict was the important event in recent history of Santa Rosa. The production of coca and development of drug trafficking, however, was another important factor as was its reclassification as a district and its population increase as interviewees report.

The main problems today mentioned by the interview partners are: Violence [11], lack of development/poverty [5], water [5], education [3], and health problems, especially child malnutrition [4].

The implementation of transitional justice in the community

In Santa Rosa only few transitional justice mechanisms have been put in place.

The PAR program did not work in Santa Rosa. The TRC and reparation program did work there but only sporadically. No exhumations were carried out. The TRC came to collect testimonies in Santa Rosa but stayed only for few days in September and October 2002. There were about 150 cases reported across the whole district of Santa Rosa. Some of these cases concern people from other areas that were brought to the village and tortured or disappeared in the military base in Louisiana. The testimonies were not all recorded in Santa Rosa with the majority being collected in Ayacucho or in Lima with Santa Rosa residents living there. For the community of Santa Rosa itself, there were around 25 testimonies collected by the TRC. I reviewed nine testimonies that are available to the public. In all of these people already asked for reparations in the form of some support for the education of their children or housing. Some ask for other forms of psychological and medical support. Some demand justice. One testimony giver demands punishment for the ones who killed his wife and economic support for himself and help with his house (204720). Another man states that his family was still a victim of slander and that his family was being accused of belonging to Shining Path (202732).

There is no victims' association in Santa Rosa itself but there was one on the VRAEM level. It was led by Jorge Gutierrez but the association dissolved because their leader asked the members to support to the association financially and this did not happen. The high expectations created by him regarding the reparations were not fulfilled and members withdrew from the organization. Therefore, nowadays everyone has to complete individual applications to receive reparations (Exp39; Exp40).

In total about 1,540 people from Santa Rosa are registered in the RUV, 1,016 direct victims and 526 family members. This is the highest number in all villages and also in relation to the inhabitants. Of the people interviewed for this study, three people already gave a testimony to the TRC. Of all 20 people interviewed 17 declare themselves as victims but only four are registered in the RUV. Three of them received reparations and four family members of those interviewed. In the whole district of Santa Rosa, CMAN lists 608 beneficiaries of economic reparations. Again, this is the number of potential beneficiaries not those who have received their reparations already.

One woman explains that she heard of the existence of a register on the radio and went to register and finally received reparations (SR15: 66). This is the quickest case that I ever heard of. But there are still many people not registered in the community, which also applies to many of my interviewees. Problems in the registration for the national register of victims occur just as in the other communities. Santa Rosa did not benefit from the assistance of an NGO during the registration process. The municipality does not seem well informed about the topic although there is an office of attention there (Exp39).

Again people speak of the difficulties in meeting the requirements: "[...] there are many that have stayed without reparation, without registering, because of missing documents, they don't have their DNI" (SR13: 76). Many community members explain that there have been many difficulties and distrust as well of being blamed to be a supporter of the rebel groups (SR10: 67). And another person complains about the hierarchy or separation of different victims: "No. [I did not register] and my grandma neither because in the end these reparations are for victims of terrorism and not for victims of the military or the state" (SR9: 72). This idea of not being the "right victim" is widespread throughout all communities.

In July 2010, a ceremony was organized by the *Consejo de Reparaciones* in Santa Rosa to distribute the certificates to the victims with participation from the local authorities and the victims' organization. However, none of my interview partners remembered this event.

In the interviews, only two people mentioned reparations in health, education, or housing. One interviewee explains that there have been collective and individual reparations but that the attention from social programs such as *Beca 18* and *Techo propio* was not satisfactory: "There is no real focus on the victim in social terms in a way that develops these parts, these aspects. Because they should offer a health insurance to the victims but you don't see it" (SR4: 56).

There was a collective reparation project granted to Santa Rosa in 2008 for the construction of a communal house. Information about this process is very confusing. The budget for the project was transferred by the CMAN to the municipality of Santa Rosa in 2008. It seems, however, that the work was never carried out. None of my interview partners referred to the project or knew anything about it, and neither did the local government. The budget was never accounted for or the project finalized so that it remains listed as "ongoing" in the national bank of municipality projects. There are 40 villages of the district Santa Rosa listed in the registry of affected communities by the CMAN, of those 28 have already received collective reparations (CMAN 2017).[52] One of them was the construction of a road, others also in infrastructure of communal houses or schools. Because the project in Santa Rosa was never implemented CMAN has now blocked Santa Rosa from receiving further projects. However, even the responsible person of the municipality in Santa Rosa was unsure about the project's actual status. The administration of the last years did not leave any documents on the matter (Exp39; SR17: 72).

There are no symbolic measures apart from a coat of arms and plaque in the central place with the expression *cuna de la pacificacion* (cradle of the pacification) referring the self-defense committees defeating terrorism. It also refers to the liberation of Shining Path's camp. However, it is still topic of debate between members of the self-defense committee of Pichihuilca, located in Palmapampa, and the one of Santa Rosa who was the winner. The self-defense committees organize a commemoration day on June 21st every year to celebrate the pacification, but, again this is in conflict with Palmapampa, which celebrates the pacification on the same day (Exp40; mentioned as well in SR3: 52). The former military basis Louisiana has not been turned into a memorial site. There is nothing there to indicate its former function or to explain what happened there or to commemorate the people who died there.

As mentioned earlier, no exhumations were carried out in Santa Rosa, and there are not so many graves as in other conflict zones because the majority of bodies were thrown into the river.

The awareness and perception of transitional justice

In Santa Rosa, I find surprisingly high awareness of the TRC and very high awareness of the reparation program. As many as 14 people state they know the TRC, and all the 20 people interviewed have heard of the reparation program. Nevertheless, half of them confuse the work of the commission with the reparation program [7]. Real knowledge of the commission is very low. Only very few people, three of them member of the authorities, are well informed [3 med, 1 high]. One person explained that he read some parts of the commission's final report (SR9: 65). Others state that the TRC's first task was to investigate: "[The TRC] came to collect all the histories of the people to the degree in which it was feasible to do. Registering the degree of violence suffered" (SR2: 62). Many of the interviewed people refer to the commission as the entity to "give money to the victims" (SR10: 63). The knowledge is not high, the same applies to members of the authorities: "They called for a reunion and visited the communities and I think they gave certificates to the victims. I was not part of it" (SR1: 65). This man knows only a little about the work of the TRC even though the case of his disappeared brother was investigated and appears in the commission's report. This case demonstrates the low levels of knowledge regarding the work of the commission in Santa Rosa and how it is mistaken for the reparation program.

Regarding the reparation program, I found surprisingly high awareness, all of the interviewees have heard of the program. However, as in the other two communities, real knowledge is low [15] and there are mainly rumors surrounding the program and a lack of information: "Yes, I think the people registered are in this [program]" (SR8: 68) and another women states: "Yes, I heard that some affected people received something. But further away" (SR3: 60). One community member explained that her sister did not receive anything although she has been affected due to the high requirements:

> No, she [her sister] did not apply, she did not present any document. But there are people here that received, 30,000, 25,000, something like that. My sister did not apply these documents. What things did they require? They asked for a lot of documents.
>
> (SR14: 68)

This uncertainty about who received how much and how to receive it once again shows the many rumors surrounding the reparation program.

As in Lucanamarca and Chuschi, I found confusion with other social programs, even within the authorities: "This consists of this, that the state is giving an incentive to the victims, no? This refers to the Pension 65, no?" (SR1: 67). Only few people have higher levels of knowledge [2 high, 3 med]; these are again members of the local authorities. Only two people mention collective reparations at all referring to other communities. This is less than in the other two communities.

Only three of the people interviewed have received reparations, and a further four have family members that received reparations. As in the other two communities, there is hardly any knowledge about the different areas of reparations in health, education, or housing or about the collective reparations program.

The work of the TRC is not well known by the community members. Although 14 people know the commission, only one person knows its work well, three have only medium, and the rest have low knowledge. As already mentioned, people do not remember the different types of work the commission did, they remember that they spoke to the victims – but with the aim to provide some form of reparations [7]. So, the TRC is perceived by half of the people as an entity formed to give support to the victims of the conflict. The commission is not very present in local memory, and the TRC's connection with the reparation program has again an impact on the satisfaction with its work.

A strikingly high number of interviewees (SR1, SR2, SR5, SR7, SR9, SR17, SR19) commented that the work of the TRC has not been concluded: "It investigated some cases but not all of them" (SR5: 63). The same person, therefore, demands that the commission should investigate more, and not only the cases involving Shining Path but also those involving the military (SR5: 64). One interviewee demands that the commission should pass from house to house to register all the people:

> They [the TRC] should register, at least in the affected zones, place to place, house to house. Find out who was responsible, e.g. they could ask me in that time who was it and I could tell them, [...] they should broaden their investigation.
>
> (SR7: 67)

Especially interviewees who are still searching for their disappeared family members complain that the investigation was so limited: "The truth is that here they did a superficial job. Very quickly and without staying in the communities as they maybe did for the 'sierra'. Finally you don't know some things. For example what happened with my uncles" (SR9: 67). Another authority states that the work of the commission was important but is still not concluded: "At least like this the Peruvian people should know how many deaths there were, to let our children know what happened" (SR2: 63).

One interviewee reports that the people working for the commission lacked awareness and did not speak Quechua:

> In a way, my grandmother told me that she withdrew from it [the TRC] because the people collecting the information were insensitive. Because when you remember this, you need a person that is patient and listens to you. My grandmother speaks more in Quechua, me too. So, if the person that listens to you does not speak Quechua, which truth will he receive? What will he write if it is not in Quechua? And they did not record it either. Where will we arrive like this? To which truth will we arrive? [...] is this ethical? The minimum of respect is the language.
>
> (SR19: 64)

Another member of the authorities is also very critical and explains that the commission did an important job but created conflicts in the communities as well. He elaborates on how the reparation program caused conflicts because some received something and others not (SR17: 67). This shows again the confusion or connection of the work of the commission and the reparation program in the perception of the people as well as the problems arising of the victims' definitions.

The overall perception or satisfaction with the TRC is rather negative [0 high, 3 med, 6 low].

The perception of reparations is, as in the other communities, mainly focused on individual economic reparations. A collective project was not carried out in Santa Rosa and only two interviewees have heard of projects in other communities. Regarding individual reparations I divide the people interviewed into the three groups again: observers, non-receivers, and receivers (see Chapter 3). Of the people interviewed in Santa Rosa, there were three receivers, 14 non-receivers (of those only one registered in RUV), and three observers. Everyone knew of the program.

The observers evaluated the reparation program positively [1 med, 2 high]. Their judgement is the most positive of all interviewed people: "Yes, it [the reparations] is good. Because they compensate the people for the dead ones in their family" (SR6: 63). And another perceives them as justified as well: "Yes, it [the reparations] is good, because my uncle was in the military and was fighting in the armed forces. My uncle received reparations" (SR12: 64). It is important to mention that their knowledge about the program is very low.

The non-receivers judged the program mostly negatively. There were only two people who saw the reparations positively: "Yes, it is good, there are many families that need it" (SR1: 70). Another one states that it was very good for the people who really deserved it, but not for others (SR8: 73).

Other interviewees welcome the idea of reparations but not the form of the implementation of the program. They hint to the problem of defining victims:

> But the people started to misjudge themselves [...] They said that one who was fighting for Shining Path was receiving. The truth is that here in Santa Rosa it is complicated because many people in this time in the community itself were fighting for Shining Path before the self-defense committees forced them to join them instead.
>
> (SR9: 70)

This man refers to the complex identities that were created but not discussed in Peru, in the TRC and especially not in the reparation program. There was no room for mixed roles.

> I am aware that there is a program that grants as a benefit, grants money to the victims. But as I have seen, this has generated more conflict because in communities what happens is that they give the money to someone and the neighbor says 'why have they given to them if their relative was a 'terruco' (terrorist)?' Then people don't like that, the state simply gives money in a discriminating form. Yes, it [the TRC] did some research but the investigation is not very rigorous, profound.
>
> (SR17: 69)

In Santa Rosa, the same problem occurs as in the other communities, defining who should or should not receive reparations is very difficult. Another community member states that reparations, as well as the social program Juntos, are given to people that are not in need but who are rich thanks to their coca and chakra:

> I think this money instead of this reparation, this Juntos, instead of [giving it] to people that have coca, that have their chakra, that have their car; Juntos as well, they don't need this money. I think from my part that they should give it to the elderly and disabled people. They should receive the money but the healthy people, we work, so.
>
> (SR14: 71)

Many people perceive the distribution of the reparations to be unjust.

There is disappointment and people do not understand why some people received something when they did not although they perceive themselves as victims in need of reparations. There is a lack of information and transparency. One woman explains that her father went and registered the family because her mother died but they did not receive anything:

> Yes, they registered but nothing came out of it. [...] when he [her father] was here others told him that there was some money, civil reparations for the violence affected people. My father traveled and went there [the CMAN office], there they told him, why did you not come, why have you not been there. Now it is over, so we left it like this. It is exhausting.
>
> (SR7: 64)

As this woman reports many families gave up, disillusioned.

Another interviewee explains that her grandma did not receive reparations although she lost her husband and three sons. She has got the health insurance, but it remains unclear whether this is via the reparation program or the program for poor people. Nevertheless, even with this insurance, she did not receive enough attention. The woman states:

> I think economic reparation no, because the money what will it do? What we want is education. Why are there no NGOs that educate and support? There are no therapies, things that could help more, that would be useful. [...] that would restore the hope into your life. I think that the part of the psychology could be a lot, the emotional part.
>
> (SR19: 72)

She points to the possible positive effects of reparations when applied in an adequate manner.

Some commented that they appreciated the idea of reparations and pointed to the state's duty to give reparations and to take care of the affected people but were not satisfied at all with the way in which the program had been applied:

> How can they repair with an illusory sum practically. They told me they would give 10,000 Soles for his mother's, his wife's and his sister's lives, for all of them 10,000 Soles. One life does not count ['Una vida no vale']. But these people, how many lives have they been defending? [Q: What should the program do?] The government should make the children of the victims study, education for free, because the government does not care about the education. Now with the Beca 18, but the people are complaining already. They say that they are being tempted by illusions but in reality they do not receive the things promised to them.
>
> (SR11: 64)

Another woman whose cousin received reparations approves the general idea of reparations but states that it is not enough what they are giving. Her cousin was kept for in a camp of Shining Path with her whole family for nine years. Her husband was killed there. She only received a very small amount of reparations. The interviewed person points out as well that many affected people have not received anything yet:

> With this topic of reparation what is missing is that they register all of the affected people of the terrorism, those whose husbands were killed, that they register his family and with this educate their children. The state should educate their children, make them professionals. [...] Now the ones most worried are the self-defense [committees] because they lived through all of that. Including several of them have traveled to Lima to claim that they are compensated. Those of the self-defense [committees] they have not been compensated at all.
>
> (SR18: 64, 67)

Both interviewees refer to the responsibility of the state to educate the children of those who have been killed in the violence.

One calls for the program to be halted and completely reevaluated:

> I think what they should do is to stop the project and maybe evaluate a bit, what they have been doing. Like an evaluation, see a bit the panorama, what is it that is happening, what has been the impact that it had.
>
> (SR17: 77)

There is a lot of criticism and some community members are totally against reparations: "I don't know, I assume it is a way of consolation for the mothers. But it is difficult for the state to satisfy all, so it would have been better not to give anything because always creates resentment" (SR5: 70). Another woman also describes her disappointment: "No, it [the reparations] was all in vain, deceit. It should be that they acknowledge all of those who have passed through this [violence]" (SR20: 72).

The overall perception of the non-receivers is negative [11 low, 3 med, 0 high]. This might not be surprising because these people see themselves as victims who would deserve reparations as compensation for the harm suffered. Knowing that some people, for reasons they cannot understand or that are not transparent, received some form of reparations when they did not leads to dissatisfaction.

The three *receivers* who were interviewed, however, did not have a very positive perception either [2 med, 1 low]. One woman received reparations because her husband was among the disappeared. She states that the money provided some help but "very cheap what they gave us". She heard of the program on the radio, registered, and received the money. While the registration was comparatively easy for her, she is also not satisfied because her husband's body has still not been found. She mentions that only the people who had a lawyer were able to receive their loved one's bodies for re-burial. She mentions that her grandchild received a scholarship, but it remains unclear whether this was via the Repared or the Beca 18 program. This woman states she would have preferred more concrete help such as a scholarship for her son at the time of the conflict. Now, the money was only a little help for her (SR15: 69–72).

Another person who received the amount of 2,500 Soles for the death of his father expresses his anger that "guilty people" were now receiving reparations:

> there were groups of Shining Path or groups of people that were fighting with their neighbors and killed many people. Now they are the first beneficiaries. And they are been paid up to 5,000 Soles, like a reward for murder. Maybe this hurts a bit. But finally all of us have been affected.
>
> (SR2: 69)

The third person is not satisfied at all:

> No, it is not good. It is not just what they are giving, it is not even enough for the children. I received 10,000, 5,000 for the children and 5,000 for me. [Q: You don't agree?] No, I don't agree. It should not be that a life is worth 10,000 Soles. [Q: You feel compensated?] No, not at all. [Q: What should the state have done?] It [the state] should give more for the children. And there should be reparations for the displacement, something, but there is nothing.
>
> (SR16: 73)

The 10,000 PEN did not help a lot, and she does not feel repaired. She says her husband was killed by the police and what would help her most is to find his body. She prefers collective to individual reparations and suggests a hospital for the victims or family members.

In summary, the perception of the collective reparation program in Santa Rosa is very limited because the planned project was not carried out. Individual reparations are perceived as negative because they were not implemented in the form the people had hoped for. Furthermore, the requirements, conditions, and amounts are criticized as they were in Lucanamarca and Chuschi. Both non-receivers and receivers were discontent. The majority of the people interviewed have very low satisfaction levels with the reparations overall [12 low, 6 med, 2 high]. The observers were the most satisfied group. The results of my study are confirmed by the impression of the responsible person for reparations in the municipality (Exp26; Exp39). There is hardly any positive impact on social cohesion to be expected.

The impact on social cohesion

The level of social cohesion is relatively low. I find similar patterns as in the communities of Chuschi and Lucanamarca. However, differences occur because Santa Rosa is a relatively new community and because of the presence of coca. The situation in the community is perceived as having improved in terms of economic development and infrastructure [18]. Solidarity is still present according to 55% of the interviewed people and improving rather than decreasing as in the other two communities. It is important to bear in mind that the community was only recently formed and does not have a long tradition. In the memory of the people, they refer to the time "before" ("antes") as the time of the conflict. They hardly ever refer to the time before the violence came because the formation of the community occurred in the time of the conflict.

On the horizontal level, I observe that the community lacks trust and solidarity, communal organization and participation are low. General trust is the lowest of all communities I researched for this project. The factor of solidarity is interesting in Santa Rosa. Interviewees state that the solidarity was increasing. This is a difference to the other two communities. Some explained that before the people lived only for themselves but nowadays there was solidary. Before people had been concerned with the fight with or against Shining Path: "Now yes, the envy, the egoism is changing in some form. Before, there were not so much, recently solidarity is growing between neighbors" (SR5: 30–31). Some are very firm: "Yes, there is solidarity, for everything, people help each other" (SR13: 32). The perception is split, however, with one half stating that there was solidarity and the other half saying that there was not. Of the latter some say that there is less solidarity or that there has never been solidarity in the first place. Coca, money and paid work, and the growing size of the community are given as reasons: "As the village is growing, the people don't have interest anymore and when they have more money they are more individualistic" (SR12: 31; SR6: 29; SR9: 32). One local authority who was raised in a different part of Ayacucho explained:

> I have seen in other regions that the people always help each other, in the faenas. Here more or less. As well because many people came from the sierra, there we are a bit more with the neighbors, we help each other.
>
> (SR17: 29)

People coming from the sierra did not establish the customs of ayni and faena in Santa Rosa in the same form as in the other two communities. The same person continues that the social programs had a negative influence on solidarity:

> I think that the people are only waiting for their money, money from the state and they do not worry about work anymore, about progress, maybe have their house, their car. They adjust themselves, now there is no more this spirit of support of the neighbors anymore.
>
> (SR17: 30)

Although some interview partners are skeptical about the solidarity of their fellow community members, they all state that they would help their neighbors if they had problems and even lend them money. With the exception of Lucanamarca, I find this in all communities. Envy is very high in all communities and all interviewees confirm it to be high in Santa Rosa but they also perceived that was even higher during the time of the conflict (SR18: 38; SR15: 45). Today envy is connected with economic progress and the money some make with coca: "Sometimes when you have a better economy and when you work more, the people are envious" (SR6: 42; also SR9: 45).Trust seems to be lower in Santa Rosa than in the other communities. One interviewee explains the low trust levels by referring to their experience of the violence:

> The people here in Santa Rosa after what happened in times of terrorism have changed, have become violent. The neighbor of long ago was like your brother, however, after having lived through those hard times, no one trusts anyone anymore.
>
> (SR9: 27)

Others state that the distrust comes from drug trafficking (SR17: 23). Trust within the family is about the same as in the other communities.

Trust is said to have diminished, but the sense of belonging and identity is still high among the community members. In comparison to the other two communities, however, it is less. This is interesting because of the suspected unifying narrative. Traditional clothes, dances, and music are not so present. The above-mentioned narrative of the past of Santa Rosa as being the place of pacification and defeat of Shining Path is connected to this sense of identity:

> Santa Rosa was one of the places where people were fighting against the terrorists and thanks to this fight and the sacrifice of the people, men as well

> as women, we won the peace. Thanks to this, 162 senderistas surrendered. Since this day we have calm.
>
> (SR2: 21)

I also heard the narrative of Fujimori pacifying the country but not as often as in the other communities: "I don't think these things [the violence] will come back. Thanks to God and to Fujimori, he pacified these things" (SR15: 53). Here people highlight the role of the self-defense committees: "I say that here in the valley the self-defense committees fought the terrorists but at the national level, it was the government of Alberto Fujimori fighting" (SR11: 41).

People state that the violence suffered in the past still has importance but do not agree whether they prefer to remember or to forget [40% remember, 55% forget]. Some state that it is important to remember so that such violence is not repeated: "To speak about those problems of Shining Path, the self-defense committees, is important. To know this is very important, maybe for the young people, to know this and don't get involved, the new generation" (SR7: 54; also SR2: 54). Others prefer to forget about the past and look toward the future and development (SR3; SR4; SR13; SR15; SR16). Notably, two women who received reparations explained they would now rather forget what happened while the third one expressed it would be important to remember the past. So the opinion is split as well.

Overall, I found medium solidarity, which is mainly focused on extreme situations, egoism and individual economic well-being are the main focus and not others or the community. Trust is very low. People still seem strongly affected by the violence, all agree that the past plays an important role. They do not agree on whether to remember or to forget the past. In contrast to the other two communities, the memory of the past focuses on the self-defense committee's fight in Santa Rosa and how peace was a result of local engagement.

Participation in the local assemblies and in communal work is less than before. In the past, the community was more organized, participation was very high, even obligatory in the times of the conflict. This development is described by many interview partners. Those who do not participate today were those with businesses, especially transport businesses (SR1: 41). *Faenas*, the communal work, only take place in smaller communities or sectors. "There are fewer and fewer faenas in the district capital, they are not participating anymore but expecting the municipality to do so. 10 years ago there was participation in the faenas" (SR2: 40). This expectation toward the municipality is the same as in the other villages. The same interviewee continues:

> There are always people that show only little interest or are not interested at all. For them it is only their money, their particular life. [...] 30 years ago, in 1984, 85 and until 92, or 95 people participated a lot more. But it was radical, obligatory. Let's say there was an order in the population, let's say

> an authority said we had to assemble in three minutes, they assembled in this time, an order.
>
> (SR2: 41; also SR13: 42–45)

Another person explained that nowadays there were still participation and sometimes the assemblies resulted in conflicts: "The participation is a lot. Always the assemblies are full. But nearly always they end in conflicts. In particular reunions with the cocaleros" (SR9: 41).

The relationship with local authorities is weak, trust is only at a medium level [3.9] and less compared to trust within families [5.8]. Those willing to give authorities a little of their corn harvest would only do so if it is for a good reason [1.3]. People talk about the huge problem of corruption (SR7: 28). As authorities that care the most about the community people named the municipality [12] and to a lesser extent the governor [4], *juez de paz*, the president and the self-defense committee. One interview partner claims that all the authorities should work together: "They should work all together but in reality, everyone goes his way, this does not have power" (SR11: 77). As in the other communities, people criticize the authorities would not do what they promise: "There is hardly any confidence because in the campaign they promise things to you and then they don't fulfill it" (SR11: 28). One interviewee explains that it is very difficult for authorities to gain the population's trust:

> In Santa Rosa always when a mayor's term in government ends they call him thief. To the last mayor everyone said thief with such a certainty but without any proof and it was always like this. It seems like they have huge expectations. These are difficult to fulfill, even for the best administration that there could be.
>
> (SR9: 29)

People blame experiences of the past for this low confidence:

> They have low confidence because of the consequences of the past, in past years it was land of no one [without rules] and the people did not trust in 100% of their authorities. Recently we are strengthening this confidence between the authorities and the people.
>
> (SR4: 24)

Three-quarters of the interviewed people in Santa Rosa state that there are conflicts today. Conflicts between community members arise because of envy or territory disputes, sometimes because people fled and left their land during the conflict time and when they returned it had been taken by someone else (SR18: 40). In case of conflict, people rely on the local authorities, the *juez de paz* or, as a last resort, to higher legal institutions.

Violence is present in Santa Rosa: "Yes, there is physical, sexual, and domestic violence" (SR1: 49). According to my interviews, there are a lot of fights and violence ongoing because of alcohol and the bars. One woman reports that the violence already started in the secondary school. She, as others as well, state that many conflicts and violence are connected to coca and drug trafficking (SR14: 49). However, the violence is present in another form than during the conflict:

> I speak about the years from 83 to 94, the life had a superior order led by the self-defense committees. The people lived under someone's orders. Now it is very different, we are living in a democracy with a state under the rule of law.
>
> (SR2: 48)

This is the only person in all the interviews conducted who refers to the rule of law and democratic constitution.

People explain that in the past, the violence had a different character: "Yes, sure, before the violence was a daily thing, the killings were cruel, people died every day" (SR5: 49). Many community members report this cruelty: "One thing is when you get killed with a weapon, with a bullet but here the people were getting killed with machetes, the women were killed with sticks. To know this and have seen this is very hard" (SR9: 51). The majority of community members do not expect this kind of violence to occur again [6 yes; 13 no]. Another interviewee states: "I don't think that those actions will occur another time because the people are more conscious, they know about it. Similar things repeating does not seem very probable to me" (SR17: 53; also testimony 202732).

Those stating that the violence of the past could occur another time believe that it would be because of coca: "But the drug trafficking causes terror as well and it is terrorism. But they don't intervene with the civil society but only with those that interfere in their business. We are calm now" (SR12: 49). And another community member refers to the high level of envy present in the community when stating that the violence could come back: "I think for the movement itself, for the envy itself, I think that Shining Path, what I have noted, did not kill because of double faces or other parties but because of envy" (SR7: 50). Others state that the violence could come back because of the ongoing lack of the presence of the state: "If the state stays absent, these acts could come back, above all because of the problem of the coca" (SR5: 51).

The trust rate for congress is fairly low. Interviewed people state that they have low or no confidence in congress: "I don't trust a lot. The politics are dirty. In the end no one believes in no one. But I still trust a bit" (SR2: 76–77).

> No, the truth is that I don't trust in congress. They are only thinking of themselves, of their salaries. In the last years there were congressmen from La Mar, but they did not do anything. They don't care, only about their own lives.
>
> (SR18: 72–73)

"I don't trust them at all. Now they are doing their campaign, they make promises but do not keep them" (SR11: 73–74).

The results on the importance of the state in Santa Rosa are differentiated with high [4], medium [10], and low [6]. But people would barely give the state some of their corn harvest. In contrast to the other communities, the state is not only perceived in social programs and infrastructure but also because of coca. Some are rather positive about its presence: "Yes because it is investing a lot here. In the end the state understands the VRAEM and it is giving us special attention" (SR2: 75). Others observe as well that the level of state involvement is increasing: "Here the government has been growing in importance recently but nearly always the governments are absent" (SR9: 76). "The state is very important, the state intervention, because Ayacucho in general has been abandoned for 20 years and because of the sociopolitical violence the development of those villages was delayed" (SR4: 66).

Expectations toward the state are very high. First and foremost people expect state functionaries to visit the community to get to know their reality and learn about their lives and problems. They expect the state to provide them with infrastructure and good education and a higher budget as the one in neighbor communities for the development of the village: "What we are expecting is that there is more budget because without budget one cannot develop. Because this is one of the first communities that was formed without the budget in comparison to Kimbiri and Pichari" (SR4: 67). Only one interview partner refers to the political system: "That it applies democracy. That it is respectful in its acts and there are no lies" (SR2: 78). Another professional who went to study to Ayacucho and came back to Santa Rosa observes: "In Santa Rosa they don't believe in the state, it does not have much importance. In my faculty, I heard my mates, I have always been a leader, and they do not have any hope in the state" (SR19: 76). The people in Santa Rosa, similar as in the other two communities, show high levels of identification with Peru as a nation but not with its state institutions.

The importance of the state is rated in the form of the development the state does or does not provide. The state is only rarely seen as institution with laws and rights establishing a social and political order. Security is a more important topic than in the other two villages but not mentioned as often as one would expect in view of the problems with drug trafficking. But all interview partners agree that the state should more for Santa Rosa.

Political participation is rather low. People are voting because it is obligatory. The turnout in the second round of the presidential elections in June 2016 was 75%.[53] As mentioned earlier, the community members and authorities are demanding a higher state presence. Hardly any politicians visit Santa Rosa. The state presence is mainly perceived in infrastructure projects, social programs, the police, or the military. People are demanding more institutions in Santa Rosa [SR3; SR2], they want a higher state presence: No, it is not present. If the government would be interested they would come to see how the population is doing. What does it require for them to come here?" (SR11: 72).

They are aware of the problem of corruption, also in the program *Juntos*. According to a community member, people paid to join the program (SR7: 75). In Santa Rosa, as in the other two communities, the memory of Fujimori prevails as he came to visit with presents:

> We are expecting like the 'señor Fujimori', that they send us a bit more help for the poor people, more of the communal canteen for the orphans, children's canteen, these things. In the past, with Fujimori, there was a children's canteen, it supported the children a lot. When there was the 'señor Fujimori', when another government entered, they cut it down.
>
> (SR15: 81)

Nevertheless, the community members evaluate the situation today as being better than some years ago [18]. When asked which entity helped bring about this positive change, 14 mention the state, which is more than in the other villages, followed by local authorities [8], but no reference is made to the reparation program. It is not present in the mind of the people as a helpful program. The state is seen as doing something, in the form of infrastructure improvements and social programs, but it is not enough. They demand more attention, budget, and projects. When asked about their expectations toward the state, no one referred to reparations either. As in the other two communities, reparations are not really perceived as a state duty. The theorized aim of reparations to make the population feel that their needs have been attended to and satisfied and thus enhancing trust in the state, could not be observed in Santa Rosa.

Summary

The level of social cohesion in Santa Rosa is relatively low today. The most important factors for the low social cohesion according to my analysis are migration to the cities and the influence of new residents from other places combined with the introduction of money and paid work. Another important factor, and a point of difference with the other two communities, is the coca trade and its resulting problems such as illegal economic actors, crime, money flows, addicted people, fewer farm products, water contamination, and economic dependency. Violence is also seen as a consequence of coca farming and not only of the conflict. Nevertheless, it is obvious that the conflict reinforced some of these developments as it led to higher migration, loss of social and political structures, and experienced leaders. Development in terms of education, housing, infrastructure, agriculture, and income opportunities was interrupted. The psychological consequences of the violence further weakened social cohesion. Another difference exists in the prevailing local narratives. Only some interviewees refer to the "happy time" before the conflict in Santa Rosa because it is a relatively new settlement. People speak of their village as being the birthplace of peace and the place where Shining Path was defeated thanks to their efforts. They remember the members of the self-defense committee as heroes and victims at the same time. The village was strongly affected by violence from different sides. Still, cohesion was not totally high in conflict time. It was the order that was high and forced participation but trust and solidarity were low during the conflict.

I found that there are still conflicts prevalent in Santa Rosa, mostly for territory as in the other cases. During the time of the conflict, violence was very common, but other conflicts were regulated by the "hard control" of the self-defense committees. A lack of control and rule by local authorities does give way to more conflicts and violence nowadays. The violence, however, today has another form than in the 80s and 90s. The conflict does, therefore, have consequences in this regard but is not the main reason. The reparations program does not seem to play an important role in this regard but does lead to new conflicts than helping settle existing ones. New violence at the level seen in the 1980s seems not very likely because people have learnt something, although some refer to the problem of high envy, coca, and the state actions against it, which could lead to new unrest. In comparison with the other two villages of Chuschi and Lucanamarca, the level of violence and incidents is higher in Santa Rosa. Drug trafficking seems to be the main reason for that.

With regard to transitional justice, Santa Rosa did not receive as much attention as Chuschi in Lucanamarca, but the TRC was also present there, if only for a few days. However, the awareness of the TRC is nearly as high as in the other two villages and its presence generated expectations, mainly of receiving reparations or help in the search for the disappeared. Satisfaction is low, however, because community members state that the TRC's work, the investigations, have not been concluded and the expectations not been fulfilled. On the individual level, the mere act of testimony giving was not described as positive by any interview partner. On the contrary, those whose family members gave testimonies criticized the procedures for the re-telling of these harmful stories, and of the staff who did not speak Quechua and the high expectations and promises created.

Regarding reparations on the community level, the idea behind the collective project in Santa Rosa was the same as in Chuschi, namely to create a house, which serves the community. It did, however, never come to be. The money from CMAN was transferred, but the house never constructed and the funds lost, probably through corruption. Symbolic measures have been implemented by local authorities in the form of a memorial plaque in the central square and the design of a coat of arms for Santa Rosa. The past and the narrative of the heroes of the past are still important within the village.

As far as individual reparations are concerned, the municipality created an office for registering people in 2014. Possibly due to this office, many people are registered today but many are still not on the list. People fear that they might be accused of being terrorists and not granted reparations. While the introduction of the office is an advance for the affected people, the person in charge was not well trained and received no clear instructions on how to register people, and so she relied on her intuition and discretion. While registration might be easier now in Santa Rosa, there are still only a few people who have received their reparations. And the victim certificate alone is seen as useless here too if it does not entitle to reparations. With individual scholarships and health insurance policies, the reparation program seeks to improve the situation of the affected people. Economic reparations should provide support for their lives as well. But, as analyzed, only few people benefited from these programs until today, and they are not totally satisfied with it, either. The reparations were not able to further enhance solidarity but the contrary. Non-transparency surrounding the distribution of reparations caused more envy and conflict in the community. More than half of the people interviewed describe low levels of satisfaction with the reparation program (12), two observers evaluate it with high satisfaction. Receivers and observers are fairly satisfied with the program in Santa Rosa, many of them know someone personally who received reparations, which might influence their opinion because it is not only rumors that they heard. Also the communal narrative could be a factor in this the perception. In Chapter 6, I analyze these individuals' responses in more detail to understand why they have a positive attitude toward reparation. Here it is important to mention again that the general idea of reparation is not rejected, it is their implementation that is being criticized by those with low levels of satisfaction. The TRC's work is rated by some as important but not fulfilled. Expectations were not fulfilled, and opportunities for positive change that the program brought were not taken advantage of. Despite both the TRC and the reparation program working there, the village of Santa Rosa does not feel that its needs have been attended to. Satisfaction with the TRC and reparations is very low; therefore, no positive impact followed and social cohesion was not affected positively. Quite the opposite, some comments show that the unfulfilled expectations and the envy and distrust caused by sporadic reparations had a rather negative effect on the community.

Kimbiri: transitional justice and its non-importance

In Kimbiri and Santa Rosa, I was confronted by the fact that there was less information and hardly any academic literature available. The existing publications focus on the topic of coca, the anti-coca politics, or the current situation regarding Shining Path.[54] In the press, Kimbiri appears only in connection to the security situation and drug trafficking.[55]

Kimbiri (formerly Quimbiri) is the capital of the district Kimbiri, which consists of a total of five *centros poblados* and 75 villages, situated in the province La Convención in the department of Cusco, but it is part of the VRAEM region and, therefore, more strongly connected to the region of Ayacucho than that of Cusco. It is located in the jungle region at about 739 m above sea level and still marginalized. From Ayacucho, it takes about four to five hours and from Cusco eight to nine hours after construction works were finished in 2017.

Infrastructure improved in the last years in terms of roads, electricity, water, and drain systems. Projects were mainly carried out within the budget of the *Canon Gasifero*, which was introduced in 2009 to distribute money gained from gas exploitation to the local authorities, which permits them to implement projects with higher budgets. Its importance is mentioned by many interviewed community members [12]. Four aspects are unique to Kimbiri, namely its urban surrounding, the presence of the *Canon*, the presence of coca, and the proximity of the neighboring districts. The district capitals San Francisco, Pichari, and Santa Rosa are only about 5–60 minutes by car. Kimbiri depends highly on income from coca and *Canon*, according to the interviewees it would be in severe crisis without it (K13: 85). The *Canon* budget of Kimbiri in 2012 was about 90 million PEN.[56] The people interviewed were disturbed by the prejudice that the VRAEM was living in luxury because of the money from coca and state: "But it is not like that" (K17: 89). The main economic activity is still agriculture at more than 90% including coca farming. Apart from that there are only few work opportunities in local institutions and to some degree tourism. For educated women, there are hardly any opportunities apart from work in the municipality (K20: 26).

The landscape is characterized by mountains and rivers, which makes for a rugged terrain with high slopes and waterfalls. The 1134.69 km^2 are across an area ranging from 560 m to 4200 m above sea level. Coca takes up about 35% of the cultivated soil. There are hardly any farmers that do not grow coca at all because, as they explain, cacao alone does not give them an income. There are many that are growing both, coca and legal crops (K12: 23). Half of the agriculture production such as cacao, coffee, yucca, banana, beans, and citrus fruits is sold at markets. According to the community members, the land is not as fruitful as it was and the years of coca plantation have destroyed many soils. According to them, coca is both a blessing and a curse. It brings economic profit for the families (K13: 20) and some improvements in road access but also problems with drug trafficking. Another problem caused by coca is the water pollution due to the chemicals used for the production of the coca paste. There have been some projects promoting different crops such as cacao and coffee. But those have a very much lower profit margin than coca and are only profitable for peasants with larger plots of land, which most of them do not have (K11: 23; K18: 24). Instead farm land is getting smaller due to a growing population (same as in Chuschi and Lucanamarca). As in Santa Rosa, coca production has not diminished in spite of anti-coca campaigns. According to the interviewees, the agricultural practices need to be modernized, and the area is in need of economic and scientific development. Furthermore, the growing population makes the need for a land plan more pressing (K5: 21). The inhabitants hope that with the recently constructed road, there will be new opportunities to sell fruits and other products in Ayacucho (K8: 22). According to the community members, it would be good for Kimbiri to be able to not only export raw materials but developed goods with higher profit margins.

A huge problem in Kimbiri is the lack of land titles. A major part of the land in Kimbiri was owned by one landlord, Señor Risco. The fight with him has been ongoing for years. After he died, the municipality is still seeking a solution with his family in 2017. A related problem is that the community is not acknowledged as *comunidad campesina*, which would regulate land property. The national agency in charge of registering land titles, *Cofopri*, is trying to make progress in Kimbiri. The problem of land titles is also connected to the registration of people in the *Sisfoh*, which is necessary for state attendance in the form of social programs.[57]

People state that there are more and more tenants and fewer landowners in Kimbiri, which changes the social structures. Tenants were not as interested in community issues and did not assist with communal activities: "Now the majority are tenants, only very few no more we are landowners, we are the only ones attending [assemblies]" (K9: 38).

Kimbiri was founded as a district in 1990, the community was recognized in 1980 and is a fairly young community. Interviewees explain that the community formed to concentrate business there, to sell and buy fruits and other products. It was formed by a small number of people from the surrounding area (K3: 16). The first settlers in the valley had come during the age of the Incas who already used coca leafs for medical purposes. But no long-term settlement was installed. The *Ashánicas* and *Machiguengas* are the most traditional groups living in the valley. Different church missions arrived, and, in 1910, a Franciscan mission was installed permanently. The colonization of this part of the *selva* started in the 1920s with the aim to export different goods. In 1955, a small airport was built. The boom in coffee, cacao, and barbasco led to further population growth. The importance of coca grew in the 1980s, and today it is the most important source of income for the locals. Up to now, Kimbiri has grown steadily and has become a little city, it is the most urban area of all communities investigated.

The district is organized into the capital and more than 70 villages. Local authorities are the mayor and municipality with the council of five members, the district governor, *juez de paz*, the *juzgado penal* (a form of local court), the president of the self-defense committee, and the president for the interests and development of Kimbiri. These two committees do not exist in the communities in the sierra. As already explained in the case of Santa Rosa, in the VRAEM region, the leaders of the self-defense committees (*CAD – comités de autodefensa*) are local authorities as well and, for some issues, they play a more important role than the municipality (K12: 78). The *Frente de Defensa de los Intereses de Kimbiri* (committee to defend the interests of Kimbiri) is very active in the community. Its main task is to observe and inspect the projects carried out by the municipality with different budgets but mainly the *Canon*. So the development of this new institution is due to the economic structure of the *Canon*, and they are powerful as they forced the former mayor to resign in 2013 after accusations of nepotism. In 2016, there was a campaign against one of the council members.[58] There are several other active committees in Kimbiri, the most important the

Comité de seguridad ciudadana concerned with providing security in the district.[59] Kimbiri and Santa Rosa do not have a president or communal board, and they do not have the status as *comunidad campesina*. The formal registration or acknowledgement of Kimbiri as of many other communities took place during the time of the conflict and as part of the installation of self-defense committees (see 4.5 on Nuevo Progreso; also Zamora Castellares (2014)). This explains the importance of the CADs within the communities.

The municipality appears well organized. Its vision is to increase tourism and income through improved production, they want: "development in conditions of security and healthy environment. The inhabitants reach to social peace, ordinary and healthy environment, with leaders of the society in the strengthened organizations".[60] Community members, however, accuse the municipality of being corrupt and linked to drug trafficking.

The last census 2007 counted 16.434 inhabitants in the whole district, the National Health Service about 20,000 inhabitants in 2012. The capital has about 4,300 inhabitants.[61] The index of poverty was 58%, of which 23% lived in extreme poverty and the rate of malnutrition was 35% in 2009. About 69% of the inhabitants are in the focus of MIDIS programs.[62]

The population mainly migrated from rural, the areas of Ayacucho and Cusco, and is made up of colonies of Ayacuchanos (90%) and native populations of *Ashanincas* y *Machiguengas* (10%). There is still migration both to and from the cities. With regard to the religion, the population practices the Catholic and Evangelical faiths, and there are a small percentage of Jehovah's Witnesses. The older generation is bilingual (mainly Quechua) but the younger people speak Spanish only. Traditional clothing is not that common anymore. But during the communal festivities traditional clothing, singing, and products are still seen.

There are pre-, primary, and secondary schools in Kimbiri. While the quality of these institutions is criticized, the importance placed on education has grown. Therefore, the number of families sending their children to study in the cities has increased as well. The network of family members living in Ayacucho, Cusco, or Lima is also growing as is the interchange with the cities. Some studied "professionals" return to Kimbiri later, but the majority does not come back due to a lack of opportunities. Interviewees complained about the bad situation with education, the loss of respect and values, and that it was difficult to find staff for the health posts and schools (K8: 18; K17: 19).[63]

Kimbiri also has a hospital. The most common diseases treated there are malaria and bacterial infections, 2005 about 98% of the children had parasites according to a report.[64] The problem of malnutrition was not mentioned as often as in the other communities although rates are still high. Some interviewees criticized that the health sector was still not that good (K17: 19) but that it had improved (K12: 19). People demand better medical attention.

There is no police station in Kimbiri, but there is one in San Francisco. The *Serenazgo* and special units are present to combat drug trafficking and terrorism. As in Santa Rosa, there is some distrust against the police and claims of abuse of authority during the state of emergency. The state of emergency was declared in different provinces of Peru, in Kimbiri as part of the province La Convención in mid-September 2016. The aim is to combat drug trafficking, criminality, and terrorism. This grants the police and military extraordinary powers, and civil rights are limited.[65] According to one interviewee, people did not complain more about this status because they did not know their rights (K17: 67).

There are some institutions present in Kimbiri, and the local authorities are trying to enhance these by providing infrastructure. As interviewees state the problem lies in the missing territory and land titles which need to be provided for the institutions (see above). This results in a strong competition with Pichari, which has more institutions such as the UGEL for education issues. The presence of institutions is perceived as an indicator for development (K4: 75; K7: 20; K14: 19). Importantly, in Kimbiri there are also ATMs and a bank branch, an office of the MIDIS, of the judicial power, and of the district attorney. Social programs such as *Juntos, Cuna Mas*, and *Pensión 65* operate there, too.

NGOs are hardly present in the community. Human rights organizations never worked there, and the only organizations that did come undertook agricultural projects, mainly trying to promote anti-coca alternative crops such as cacao, coffee, or pineapple. There is high distrust toward NGOs because community members think they would eradicate coca and thereby cut their economic income. Furthermore, NGOs are seen as paternalistic (K11: 23–24) and blamed for misusing money (K18: 23). The population does not let new organizations enter the community as one interviewee reports (K12: 24). One community member has a very bad opinion of the NGOs connected to the TRC and claims that they were only enriching themselves through this work (K1: 62).

Attention by the social programs is lower than in the other districts: The programs mentioned in the interviews are *Juntos* and *Pension 65*. *Beca 18* is mentioned by one person, *Cuna más* by one and *Vaso de leche* by two people. The MIDIS lists, for September 2017, the following numbers of beneficiaries of the different programs: 739 families in *Juntos*, 286 people in *Pension 65*, 269 children attending centers of *Cuna Más*, and 3,205 children in *Qali Warma* in 67 educational institutions.[66]

Pension 65 is seen as positive support for elderly community members who had helped build the community and who do not have an income now (K5: 81; K15: 79). But others stated that *Pension 65* would face similar problems in the implementation because some people received help even though they did not need it and others in need could not receive it (K17: 87). The opinion on *Juntos* was as divided as in Chuschi, Lucanamarca, and Santa Rosa. The receivers saw it in a positive light because it allowed them buy things that the children wanted, shoes and reported what a happy day the payday was for them: “This day is happy, we go shopping, we cook, huh, it is wonderful. Yes, it is pretty” (K8: 75). But people mentioned as well that sometimes the requirements were difficult to fulfill and that there was not enough information available (K12: 77). Others stated that the use of the money should be better controlled because some parents used the money to buy clothes for themselves. Moreover, the program was an incentive to have more children (K4: 72; K17: 86). "Program Juntos what for? Young ones full of strengths with children, others are failing, they have three, four children and receive and eat calmly. They don't even think about working, more idleness. The people don't want to work anymore" (K9: 70). This woman pointed out as well that people of the sierra would not come to work anymore because of this program. Another person suggests that the families who benefitted from the program should do some community work (K16: 85).

Before the conflict started the region had experienced a boom of coffee, cacao, and barbasco in the 1960s and a growth in population. In the 1980s came the boom of coca, which replaced the other crops and drug trafficking grew parallel to Shining Path. The people refer to the most important changes of the last years as the increasing population and improving economy, the increase in coca farming and the loss of other products such as cacao and coffee. And as a positive development, they see the introduction of the *Canon* budget that allowed advances in infrastructure such as roads, water supply, education, and health. But the *Canon* also reinforced the importance of economy and money as well, which led to a further loss of solidarity and interest in the common good.

During the internal armed conflict, Shining Path used the VRAEM as a basis for its development. Ayacucho was the region were the rebel group evolved. At the beginning, the focus did not lie on the VRAEM, however. In 1982, the federation of small farmers started initiatives to sell products directly without any middlemen to enhance their profit margins. This created conflicts of interest during which people became more open toward the ideas of a revolution of Shining Path. The group began to spread its ideas via teachers and "popular schools", they installed camps and recruited men, women, and children, sometimes whole families. Often times this was not entirely voluntary. Coca played an important role as a financial resource for Shining Path but also for the self-defense committees (CVR 2003, Vol. V, Ch. 2.23: 739).

In 1983, the armed forces entered the region, in the VRAEM, it was the infantry units of the Marine Corps. They divided the population in *centros poblados* and organized them in self-defense committees if they had not done so already themselves. Initially, the population was reluctant to join. In some places, military repression generated renewed support for Shining Path. In 1983, a military base was installed in Louisiana, south of Santa Rosa, where many people were tortured and disappeared, and sexual abuses were also recorded. Several incidents were reported to the TRC in testimonies such as the following: On November 10th of 1984, the military assembled everyone in the airport of Kimbiri. A captured member of Shining Path identified other people suspected of being supporters of the rebel group within the population. Those identified people were transferred to the base in Louisiana, many of those were killed and thrown into the river on the way there. More and more self-defense committees organized themselves to fight against Shining Path. The TRC found that they played an important role in the victory over Shining Path. Nevertheless, there are some critics of the committees and some uncertainty about their actions as well. When the TRC collected testimonies, many people were still not willing to talk about the committees in their ambitious role. Another point is the link of some committees with drug trafficking. They used the income from the rising price of coca to buy weapons – which was much faster than waiting for the government to give them some. Some *ronderos* seemed to use the committees to settle old fights with neighbors by denouncing them as supporters of Shining Path. The committees posed a threat to Shining Path as many villages had supported them before. These CADs controlled the roads and made it difficult for Shining Path to move in the region. Until 1999, the committees specialized even further and community members, mostly young people, were paid to dedicate themselves totally to the fight in the committee. The committees played an active part and were often fighting instead of the armed forces, which took the position of observers. The TRC (CVR 2010: 101) stated that the *ronderos* were proud to fight on behalf of the state. I did, however, not find this interpretation in the interviews but rather complaints about the state leaving them fighting alone against Shining Path.

This narrative of the *ronderos* (member of the self-defense committees) fighting is very important in Kimbiri: "My father was in the pacification of the villages" (K8: 61). In all the communities, interviewees mention that the situation of the political violence was misused for "solving" other old conflicts, blaming people of being members of Shining Path, knowing that they would be arrested or killed by the military (K12: 42). People tell about the fear they had, hiding in holes under the ground or in the mountains. Children grew up with this fear and many lost their parents and had to get by on their own (K8: 52; K12: 57). It was a hard time for the people, with little to eat because working on the land was difficult, many people were displaced through the violence, some survived by fishing and complained that there had been no state support in that time (K17: 62). There are less burial sites in the VRAEM because dead people were mainly thrown into the river to hide killings. This brought serious health problems such as cholera because people were consuming the water from the river, as one woman explains, hundreds of children died because of this (K9: 50).

The consequences of the violence in Kimbiri are very similar to those in the other villages and are related to education, health, social, political as well as psychological factors. The same woman who was proud of her father being part of the *ronderos* explained that this was the reason she did not receive a better education (K8: 61). Another man commented: "Because of the violence I stayed in the selva, enclosed for the political violence" (K14: 72). Another community member described the negative consequences such as the many deaths and the separation of families. On the other hand, he mentions that the violence caused the organization of communities and attention from the state:

> For example the disunion of the families, many families have inserted a movement and until now they do not return, it is not known where they are.

> Mothers, fathers, children were lost and this would be the downside. The positive side is the strengthening of the organization, the origin of the communities. Also that the state now has a look at the whole VRAEM, which was not considered, was not on the map, before.
>
> (K12: 53)

The TRC counted 51 fatalities in the district of Kimbiri (CVR 2003, Annex 5). There were probably many more cases that were not reported to the TRC because of reluctance and fear (see 5.4.1).

Apart from the conflict, it was the spread of coca, the drug trafficking and presence of the police and military combined with the introduction of the *Canon* that had a lasting influence on the development of the community of Kimbiri. Today Kimbiri has the dynamic of a small, modern city, and also problems of modern cities such as delinquencies and assaults. The problems mentioned by the people are different from the other communities I studied. In Cusco, they have a higher budget due to the above-mentioned *Canon* program. The people I interviewed mentioned that the situation improved thanks to the improvements in infrastructure. No reference is made to poverty or malnutrition although numbers are still high in Kimbiri as well. People only lament the slow progress in development. The predominant problem of land titles has been going on for decades (see above), and people complain about the lack of a communal hall and lack of institutions. The problems mentioned include: Land titles [11], education [7], violence [4], malnutrition, and lack of organization and participation. One interview partner also mentioned the distrust within the community and toward authorities in general as a major problem (K20: 18).

The implementation of transitional justice in the community

In Kimbiri, only some transitional justice mechanisms have been applied but the attention has been higher than I expected based on the information that I had collected before the interviews were conducted. The PAR did not work there. The TRC came to the VRAEM and collected testimonies but only for three days and only in the main villages (Exp32; Exp36). For Kimbiri, about 40 cases were registered for the whole district, but those were not collected in Kimbiri but in other places where the victims live today or where they went to give the testimony at the time. The TRC did not come to Kimbiri itself. There were no exhumations or public audiences carried out by the TRC in the VRAEM. Only as recently as 2015 exhumations were carried out in some parts of the district.[67] As mentioned, there are fewer graves in Kimbiri as in other regions because so many bodies were thrown into the river. The seven testimonies I had access to were recorded in May 2002 in Ayna-San Francisco (201910, 201907) and in September and October 2002 in Santa Rosa (205105; 204644) or other places further away where people lived then.

In the testimonies collected by the TRC, the participants demanded economic reparations and support for the children for their education or for houses to be build and food (204644; 201910; 201907; 205105; 204065). One victim explains that her daughter who had been deterred in the SL camp as well, died as a consequence of a sickness she got while deterred. And she expresses the wish to see the dead body of her son that was never found (205105). A widow of a community leader demanded support with the education of their children – one of whom was interviewed for this study (201907). One man deterred for fighting for Shining Path demands a lawyer as he did not have access to one before his conviction (732006). Those detained suspected members of Shining Path were convicted at military trials and without any legal assistance.

There is no victims' association in Kimbiri itself but as mentioned, there was one on the VRAEM level as mentioned above which dissolved due problems with its leadership and disappointed members. There is no support for affected people in Kimbiri from any organizations and they have to organize their own applications to receive reparations by themselves (Exp39; Exp40).

According to CMAN, 1,367 people are registered in the RUV in the whole district of Kimbiri, 837 direct victims, and 530 relatives. Of the 20 interview partners, 12 declare themselves to be victims of the internal armed conflict but only those two people are registered in the RUV that also have received reparations.

In Kimbiri, like in other communities, there are still many people who are not registered. As mentioned, there was no human rights organization working there and instead the municipality supported in the registration of people. However, the person in charge for the registration in the municipality from 2013 to 2014 said she did not receive any training or information at the beginning of her task but tried to find information on the internet. After a while, she was invited for training by the *Consejo de Reparaciones.* Again it becomes obvious that it depends highly on the municipality whether there is a person in charge of reparations and whether this person is sent to receive training. The woman in charge in Kimbiri estimated that she registered about 200 people for the RUV in 2013–2014. She reported there was a "boom of reparations" when the people heard that they were going to pay something. But, there was misleading information from the leader of the association of the displaced in the VRAEM zone who told its members that they would receive huge amounts of money – which they did not. Still many people came to ask for their reparations (Exp39).

This lack of information was observed in various places. But at least the municipality offered the possibility to register in the RUV. The person responsible explained that there were three different types of cases to register: Those who were victims because of dead or disappeared family member; torture victims and the displaced. The majority of people whom she registered fell in the last category, and the majority of cases were caused by Shining Path, which is probably because others still dare to tell their story. It was only her who took notes and the history of the people – without any investigations taking place or any training on how to do so before sending the cases to Lima. This certainly influenced how these cases were recorded. (Exp39).

One man reported:

> There are many people that were strongly affected, whose family members died, but they are not in the victim's register. The information gathered is only superficial, and many do not now [about how to register], it is not well spread and many are not registered.
>
> (K5: 68)

Another problem again lies with formal requirements. One woman said that her parents died but she could not provide the birth certificate because they were born in Huancavelica and she did not know where the village is and could not afford to travel there. In the end, she did not register (K8: 64). Others reported that there are affected people who cannot do all the paperwork themselves and asked other people do it, sometimes ending up with less money:

> There was a woman who told me that her husband died and they gave her civil reparations via another person, because she is illiterate. She gave the letter to another person that made all the formalities and received 3,000 Soles in the end.
>
> (K12: 61)

Normally, it would be 5,000 PEN for her and 5,000 PEN for the children.

The person in charge of the reparation program and the interviews was not well informed and confused the program with other governmental social programs such as *techo propio*. She did not understand the regulations of the recently started program, in which registered victims are supposed to receive special conditions within the program *techo propio* (K4: 63; K16: 73). Still, more than 1,300 people were listed in the RUV for the district of Kimbiri.

According to the yearly report by the *Consejo de Reparaciones*, a ceremony was organized in Kimbiri to distribute the certificates to the victims with participation of the municipality, the *Organización de Afectados del VRAEM* in May 2010. However, none of my interview partners remembered this event and neither did the local authority members.

As far as healthcare is concerned, the person responsible explains that nearly 80% of the population of Kimbiri would had the SIS, the free integral medical insurance, so that the registered people had no additional needs. But under new regulations only poor people registered in *Sisfoh* will be able to get insurance and therefore, the victim certification could become more important (K16: 74). According to CMAN, there could be more than 1,200 beneficiaries of these programs, as well as in education. For the area of education, she stated at the time of the interview she was still awaiting the announcement for the new *Repared* program (K16: 75). I could not get information about whether someone of Kimbiri already gained such a scholarship meanwhile.

In collective reparations, there were projects executed in the neighboring villages (Limatambo, Palestina, Chirumpiari, Santuari) but not in capital of Kimbiri. There was only one project in guinea-pig farming for the organization of displaced, but not in Kimbiri itself, implemented in 2015. None of the interview partners mentioned this project. Kimbiri itself and 48 of its *anexos* are registered in the list of affected communities and CMAN lists 13 finalized projects in the district (CMAN 2017).[68] The projects implemented were all livestock projects.[69] But again these projects were not connected to reparations nor did they have a symbolic part. And, at least in two cases, the aim of setting up viable businesses failed. Furthermore, the community members did not work together. Only in one community, the number of cattle was growing (K16: 71; also Exp39).

Another problem may be that the district has a higher budget from the *Canon* so that the collective reparations do not matter that much. In some of the collective projects realized CMAN contributed 100,000 PEN and the municipality 265,000 PEN, which shows that it is more a symbolic contribution. Furthermore, in the information about the project, the fact that these are reparation projects is not even mentioned and even this symbolic contribution is not recognized. It can be assumed that their reparatory impact will be non-existent. Apart from the person responsible at the municipality, only one of the interview partners mentioned the collective program at all, the smallest number in all villages (K4: 63).

In terms of symbolic reparations, only a few things were implemented. Exhumations and a re-burial were only done in 2015. There is a memorial statue at the central square, which is called the *plaza de la pacificación* – the square of pacification. The memorial has different parts, a fighter, a *rondero*, appears on top and the plaque reads: “in honor of the men that fought for our peace, and that continue day after day to fight for the greatness of Kimbiri”. It was constructed by the municipality in 2013 with the *Canon* budget within the rebuilding of the whole park to highlight the discourse of the VRAEM being at the core of the pacification and the importance of the self-defense committees in the fight against Shining Path. Neither CMAN nor any NGOs were part of the process. The park is frequently used by community members but whether the memorial matters to them could not be assessed. I observed some families taking photos there, but no one mentioned it in the interviews.

The awareness and perception of transitional justice

In Kimbiri, I find high awareness of the TRC and of the reparation program, which I had not anticipated. In total, 15 people stated that they knew the TRC but only three people knew more about its work, the rest confused it with reparations, and this was true for members of the authorities as well as for community members: "They came to recognize some heroes and those who have fallen. They gave compensation to those who lost people, but they gave very little. And they did not do it well because many have been forgotten" (K7: 60). Some interviewees stated that the commission came to the region to register the victims. But others complain that the commission did not reach all the villages:

> Nothing, you could no see what they were doing. Commissions simply were calling to come but for a farmer or settler it was difficult to come to the offices, taking the time to give the testimony. They did not come to the communities, they were calling no more.
>
> (K14: 64; also K17: 69)

As mentioned already, some thought the commission only worked in the sierra: "But I know that the truth commission focused more on the 'altoandine' region, on the communities 'altoandinas', here in the selva you do not hear a lot" (K13: 66; also K5: 67). Others are not sure about the work of the TRC and confuse it with others:

> Yes, they came to interview. I think they gave some training on how to exhume bodies. But here in the selva, when the people – the terrorists and the military – killed the peasants, they did not bury them, but they threw them into the river. This is why, there is nothing to find.
>
> (K18: 67)

The reparation program is known by nearly all interviewed people [19] and most of them state that there were reparations in the community [15], but they only referred to the individual economic reparations. Collective reparations were only mentioned by four interviewed people, one of those was the person responsible at the municipality office, and the others were members of the authorities as well.

The awareness was high, but the real knowledge is low – as in the other communities. It was mostly just based on rumors about people having received something. "Yeah, but only for a few people, few people know about this" (K18: 72; also K15: 67; K14: 68). Some even said that there have not been any reparations: "My father and grandparents told me that there were no reparations. The family members were left somewhere, without being able to bury them, nothing" (K20: 71). Only the person in charge at the municipality knows about the whole program, the others are only speculating about what they heard. There is hardly any information about the reparation program in general and even less about the programs in education, health, or housing (K11: 81).

As explained in the other cases, the perception of the TRC has several different dimensions. First, its work is not known that well by the community members. In my study, 15 people knew the commission but only three knew details, the rest confuses it with reparations. The TRC is not very present in the memory of the people. They did not see its work apart from registering people for the reparation program [10]. There is no need to explain again that the perception and judgment of the commission's work is strongly connected with the satisfaction about the reparation program.

Regarding the specific work of the TRC, one interviewee demanded that the cases investigated by the TRC should be made public to the local authorities. She is a local authority herself (K2: 61). There is the perception that the TRC did not leave anything, similar to Lucanamarca:

> The majority of the communities do not know the work of the TRC. They did not leave reports or information with the institutions. They did not leave anything. When a person comes to investigate, they should come back and leave their report, at least a history so that the young people, the children, can see how it happened, how they lived in this era and that thanks to this we are here.
>
> (K12: 62)

Some people have a lot of distrust toward the work of the commission, which only came to register for reparations in their opinion:

> I think in something it [the TRC] helped but I think that many people abused it to sell their services to the investigation, the NGOs. For example, many NGOs care for the delinquents, saying that this young man could recover and they fight for those delinquents but not for the peaceful people. I don't know. The NGOs use some conflicting spaces to generate money. How much does a friend of the TRC gain? They get a lot of money. Finally, when there is a war, people die on both sides. Maybe the TRC brought a bit of truth and reconciliation but they have extended it to gain more money. Finally: What is the aim of the TRC? Only to say what had happened in Peru, there was this and we forgive and it won't happen again. What else?
>
> (K1: 62)

He is against further investigations and says they would be a waste of money:

> This money could be better used directly and not in contracting professionals that force you to remember things you do not want to remember. I don't want to put myself in the shoes of those who lost their parents in a violent act.
>
> (K1: 63)

Interestingly, this statement comes from a person who does not identify as a victim. This is one of the interviews that I would have liked to conduct myself to find out more about his opinion and mistrust toward the TRC and NGOs.

Some other community members also complained that the commission did not work properly and did not collect all the histories properly and many cases have been forgotten (K7: 60). Others said that it was only the first step and that the people who told the commission about the deaths of their family members and were waiting for reparations now (K18: 68). Others stated that the work was good but that it was not concluded. They demand a second truth commission that continues to investigate, especially for all the disappeared people: "There are still many people that are looking for their family members, for the disappeared" (K13: 67). These expectations such as a continued search for the disappeared and the reparation program to come into force, were not fulfilled, therefore satisfaction levels with the TRC are low [11 low, 2 med, 0 high].

The perception of the reparation program is rather negative as well and only focused on the individual reparations. Again, I divide the community population in three groups: receivers, non-receivers, and observers. In Kimbiri, there are eight observers (non-victims), two receivers, and ten non-receivers, none of the latter are registered in the RUV. Only one of the observers did not know the program.

The eight observers have different opinions. Some think that the reparations are good because they are an acknowledgement for the families that lost everything (K6: 67). Others are not satisfied because there were many people who were still not registered but who needed reparations, and they demanded that this should be arranged with the municipalities (K15: 70). One young woman explained: "Look, it is certain that money cannot compensate these pains but it can be a help with burial costs or, if a father was killed, it can be a consolidation to support his family, his sons" (K20: 75). The person in charge at the municipality office explained: "The reparations that they gave do not compensate the damage that they suffered, absolutely not. But it is a way to let them know that, yes, we are with them, that it won't happen another time, acknowledging, motivating" (K18: 68).

The ten non-receivers, half of my interview partners, are victims who did not receive reparations and are not registered in the RUV either. Many people state that they did not know about the program:

> No, I had no knowledge about this, nor had my family members. For example, I have uncles that have been kidnapped, innocent and they could flee, they have been displaced, my other uncle died already, they were displaced and in many cases tortured. But there was no training or information for them.
>
> (K12: 68; also K7: 63)

Others criticize that the authorities do not know enough either. That those responsible for the program only came to look for the victims and that they did not involve the authorities, which is an significant statement from a member of the authorities: "They are commenting but I don't know if they will give something or not, I hear commentaries no more" (K2: 61). The lack of information remains a recurring theme:

> Yes, we heard something, when they came, they have to register but they have not done their job well because they say they evaluate and, for example, my parents have suffered this but saying 'I don't think you need this' because my father constructed his house by his own efforts and already improved his situation. And according to this they come and see this and say 'he does not need it', [...] I don't know, who they considered. What outrages me is that there are people who really need it and they are not being considered, I don't know which excuse they give.
>
> (K17: 73)

The same woman explains that a friend received reparations but that it seemed

> a joke because it was very little and does not help with anything, everything they lived through in those times, it does not compensate for anything. I think it would have been a good option to send people, psychologists or sociologists, and intend to investigate how a person feels today after living through these experiences.
>
> (K17: 75)

The program is perceived as unjust and not benefitting the real victims: "There are people that benefitted but never have been in action" (K7: 61). Interviewees assume that people told different stories to benefit from the program:

> The people in important positions benefitted. They considered themselves to have been victims, commanders. Many people exploited the system, however, those have not been the 'pacificadores'. Maybe they did not know very well. But those who were really the fighters, the 'pacificadores', we did not even benefit.
>
> (K14: 65)

These people would be left with the feeling of being a victim of the conflict but not receiving any acknowledgement, even worse because they know that others received something. This man states: "Reparations would be good, to feel acknowledged at least" (K14: 73). Others question the whole concept of economic reparations:

> Well, I don't know whether it is the right way to compensate the harm with this money [...] I don't know whether they could give money to you for the death of your mother and this would make you satisfied, contented? I don't know, this topic should be discussed. Because life is not

> money. […] instead of very particular reparations there should be more integral reparations, for the whole community. Maybe invest in a good college for the sons, where good teachers teach, including to building a university only for them.
>
> (K18: 76)

Another person argues as well that there should not be economic reparations:

> Money will not give someone back. Well, in some way it helps economically. I think they should build a museum where the people can go to, a register with photographs, to get informed. Or they should implement a special school or college or a hospital for mental health that helps them. There are people that have been affected that do not know, they do not have access. An institution in mental health could go, assist them, in some form it would be a benefit.
>
> (K12: 69)

There was another person demanding mental health provision:

> I think it [the reparations] are in some way an incentive but they are maybe not proportional to the damage that a family has suffered. Because, for example, there is a woman that has received, who is widow, her husband worked as authority, he gave his life for the community and the damned ones ['malditos'] killed him. I think these reparations should see how much harm was caused, how much loss a family has had. An in accordance to that should be the amount of reparation […] And the question is not only to give money but to give psychological attention, an attention more personalized.
>
> (K13: 74–75)

Interestingly, not all of these people who identified as victims of the conflict expect reparations for themselves but for those that have been affected even more.

The two receivers interviewed both received reparations for the death of their fathers. One is satisfied that there are reparations but not with the amount. The other one is not satisfied at all:

> Yes, we received, brothers and sisters, 2,000 Soles. I think they gave 10,000 to my mother, but it was separated for the sons. Even though the support came very late it is a way of the state to compensate everything, well, not compensate, in some way acknowledge the pain of those years. Even though with the highest amount of money they give you, they can never bring back your family member.
>
> (K19: 69–70)

But she complains as well about the lack of organization and the inaccessibility of the program:

> What we observed when my mother made all the formalities, there is a lack on behalf of the state, they should send some qualified people that do a good investigation, to discover the incidents because it is sure that there are people that have benefitted from this reparation and there are people that have not received anything, that are waiting until today, a way of justice like they say.
>
> (K19: 71)

This woman criticizes the way in which reparations are implemented and states that many were missing out on this part of receiving justice. She is the only one that draws this link to justice that is very strong in the literature.

In the second case, the mother of the interviewed person gave a testimony to the TRC, already demanding support with the education of their children because she was their father and mother at the same time (201907). But after the death of her husband, it nearly took 30 years until she and her children received reparations. The family is not at all satisfied:

> They [the TRC] told us that they would support the affected people, that they would give us a house at least, that they give you 5,000 Soles, it is a joke, 5,000 for the widow and 5,000 for the children, in total it was 10,000 Soles I think. As we are seven siblings we shared the 5,000, I think I got 700. What can I say – does this shit ['huevado'] equal my father? I think that the whole world is not satisfied with this stupidity they made. But it would be good if there were support for the affected people, for the sons not anymore but a house for the widow. Take your house, ready. Or take your piece of land or flat. This helps at least. The state, hmm, 10,000 equals the death of my father?
>
> (K11: 77)

The interviewed person expected more:

> I expected some more, not only 5,000 Soles, a house for my mother. I had a brother who was studying that time [of the testimony] and they said with this document they will give us a scholarship, but it was a lie, nothing.
>
> (K11: 80)

He does not feel compensated: "No, not at all!" (K11: 82).

In summary, the perception of the reparation program is rather negative in all groups: observers, non-receivers, and receivers. No one is really satisfied with the program, more specifically, with the implementation of the program. As in Lucanamarca, Chuschi, and Santa Rosa, the requirements, conditions, and the amounts paid are all criticized. The majority of the interviewed people have very low satisfaction with the reparations [13 low, 4 med, 0 high]. The results of my study are confirmed by people responsible for reparations in the municipality (Exp39; K16).

The impact on social cohesion

The social cohesion indicator for the community of Kimbiri shows that the overall level is relatively low. I find similar patterns as in the communities of Santa Rosa, Chuschi, and Lucanamarca. However, differences occur because the community of Kimbiri was not as settled before the conflict arose and also because of the presence of coca and the *Canon*. The situation in the community is perceived as having improved in terms of development and infrastructure [16]. Solidarity is still present according to 70% of the interviewed people but to a lesser extent than before [15].

On the subjective horizontal level, I observed that the community lack trust and solidarity, which is still present but mainly in extreme situations such as severe problems, accidents, or deaths. The traditional mutual help *ayni* is barely practiced anymore, and working for the community is not common anymore either. Today, everyone works for money and acts more egoistically as these interviewees report: "In my times, when I was young, we all helped each other in communal projects, people expressed solidarity, there were ceremonies and we all participated. But now, as there is money in the community, they do not participate anymore" (K3: 24). And he explains further: "In the past, there was more solidarity. We made a lot of things without money, in the past we did faenas for everything. [...] nowadays the 'fiesta patronal' is only to fill their pockets. They don't even invite us" (K3: 29).

> Solidarity has changed, it is a value that has been lost. [...] now we are in the economy, these changes make the human a bit more egoistic. Egoism loses the idea [of solidarity]. In the past, the communities were more cohesive.
>
> (K13: 33)

As in these statements, money is mentioned as one factor influencing the reduction in social cohesion in Kimbiri: "money destroys the human heart" (K20: 35). People are no longer working for the well-being of the community:

> In the past there was more solidarity but now we have the municipality and the money. With this the people have forgotten the solidarity a little bit. [...] In the past we constructed bridges to pass and we did not wait for the municipality. Rather the people have forgotten about it, now when we want to make faenas people say that the municipality should do it, they don't want to work anymore.
>
> (K8: 31)

The budget of the municipality and the paid authorities changed people's behavior: "[Solidarity] has changed because of economic interests. In the past someone became mayor and nothing happened, peaceful. Nowadays when someone wins and somebody else loses, they get armed, it is lost, there is a feeling of separation now" (K1: 32).

Another factor is the migration into the community:

> In the past there was more [solidarity] because now new neighbors came that we do not know. When a village grows its problems grow as well. In the past we were fewer but we did know each other better. [...] the problems have grown, assaults and robberies that you could not see before.
>
> (K7: 29)

The Canon is seen as having a negative influence: "Now, as there is the Canon the people are focused on accumulating money. And they overlook the responsibility one human being has to another human being" (K4: 32).

The influence of the conflict on solidarity is judged differently by the interview partners. One stated that the fight against Shining Path was a unifying factor: "In the past there were no [violent conflicts], we were more united because there was a 'public good' which was the fight" (K7: 47). And another man also confirmed:

> Before the sociopolitical problem, there was more [solidarity], this mutual help, more organization. But because this is not there anymore and because of the communication ways it has diminished a lot. There is not this view of the development of others or the community anymore. Everyone sees their own interests. It's a topic of disorganization. In the past, well, it was not good this problem, but it helped that the community was more organized.
>
> (K5: 33)

Before the conflict, there was also more solidarity as this man describes. During the conflict, the community was organized but not trusting. Other people also stated that nowadays, there is more solidarity, people are more communicative, and that there was no solidarity in the past because of the terrorism, they did not know whom to trust: "You did not have confidence, you did not have anyone you could trust" (K19: 31). Since then, solidarity was growing again according to some (K11: 34; also K14: 33). All the interview partners stated that they would help neighbors in case they had severe problems, most of them would even lend them money. And most of them said that they would share a huge part of their harvest with their neighbors in the imaginary corn question [4.5], the highest in all communities.

Interviewed people mention a lack of solidarity and interest in the common good. In the past, people were more attentive on each other's needs. Envy is very high today, 90% of the interviewed people stated that there was a lot of envy in the community. People see the economy and the *Canon* as having caused higher levels of envy: "The Canon brought us some conflicts of economic interests and these are connected to political conflicts" (K4: 44). There are more mayoral candidates today because the increased budget brought more power and made the position more lucrative. As discussed before the local elections are now very hard fights.

In the past, during the conflict, envy led to murders:

> in the epoch of the violence envy was more evident, when in this time of the political violence they pulled the people out, they said 'yes, he participated', they did everything. They killed just because they were envious, some territorial conflicts from before and they used this moment.
>
> (K12: 42)

There are people nowadays that suspect a connection to drug trafficking when someone's economic situation improves: "One person buys a car, starts to improve, his economy, his house, changes, and there are others people that feel that this person must have illicit money, that he is involved in whatever, they are speculating" (K17: 42; also K13: 47). Community members feel that this egoism is bad for the community: "There is a lot of egoism. And in those communities there is no development, it is not growing, there is a delay. The division weakens the population" (K14: 42). Envy is also problematic in the topic of reparations as mentioned earlier because only some victims received benefits, and therefore this led to more envy rather than any positive impact on social cohesion.

Trust and solidarity have diminished but the sense of belonging and identity of the community members is still high. Traditional clothes, dances, and music are not that popular but are still present. The problem of stigmatization as a region of terrorists, violence, and drug trafficking is mentioned by many community members. They stress that it is quiet nowadays:

> As you can see Kimbiri is a quiet zone, there is nothing. But those from outside think that it is not like that, they demonize it. But Kimbiri is a paradisiacal place, with its wood, parks, rivers and it is quiet.
>
> (K1: 22; also K17: 79; K19: 75)

This stigmatization is connected with the perception of the past in other parts of the country. Kimbiri is still seen as the region with a lot of coca and connected with the drug trafficking. In the village itself, the perception of the past is slightly different than in Chuschi and Lucanamarca. In comparison to the other communities, Kimbiri and Santa Rosa are the only ones that mention "heroes" in the interviews. In Kimbiri, the narrative of "how our parents were fighting in the self-defense committees" is very strong (K2: 49), and this is reflected in the memorial as well.

The community members believe that it was Shining Path [9] if not all, Shining Path and state forces [7], and the self-defense committees that committed violent acts:

> In reality as it was a war, it was a conflict between all, the terrorists, the military, the rondas campesinas were involved as well, confused, you did not know who to support because if you supported one side you could be killed by the other. It was a total confusion, the people living in the rural areas were living in fear, there was no good food. There was no support from the state.
> (K8: 61–62)

There is one interviewee who justifies the violence of the armed groups:

> The terrorism has caused more deaths but in a war there are always cases of innocents. I don't want to say that the marine did not cause [deaths], yes there were deaths of innocent people but they were fewer and it was necessary to pacify because we were getting murdered.
> (K11: 67)

His father was killed by Shining Path, which might influence his perception. According to him, the armed forces used intelligent strategies: "They knew that this man there was proof that he was a leader, so the militaries would go there and kill him. It was necessary" (K11: 68).

Most people state the violence of the past is still important today. They are undecided whether it would be better to forget about the past or to remember it to prevent it from happening again [9 forget, 7 remember, 4 both]. Victims of the violence declared that "it would be better but is impossible to forget [...] for anything there is resentment, I am bad" (K8: 54; K10: 49). And another man said: "Forget it, not remember, because we would remember the feelings that happened in these years" (K15: 54). Others state that it was important for the younger people to learn from the past. And that it would always be in the memory of those who lived through the past anyway. Peru would have the right that its history exists, and it should be taught to the children. This could serve as well as comparison: "When my parents, uncles, cousins have resolved this problem, why can I not resolve my problem right now which is small?" (K11: 62–65). Another authority states as well that

> it is good to remember. Because it allows us to realize the situation we live in and to start to appreciate [...] We have learned that life is worth a lot and that now our lives are better than in those years.
> (K4: 53)

"We always have to remember, the society today forgot about its heroes" (K7: 51). This man complains that the authorities do not give importance to and do not remember the heroes and martyrs who died. People should know about what happened (L7: 53). The narrative is widespread: "the ronderos were the ones that saved us, it was them who reached the pacification" (K8: 57). It is important to them as well that the self-defense committees were the ones who did the real fighting and that the military played a supporting role and nothing more (K14: 62). I do not find the narrative of Fujimori bringing peace that I heard in the other communities.

Overall, I find medium solidarity, which is restricted to extreme situations. Individualism and a focus on individual economic success are on the rise, caring for the community is only important to some people. Community members still feel the consequences of the past but interpret them differently and do not agree whether to forget or remember the past. In this community, the narrative of the heroes is very strong, nevertheless only few people want to remember the violent past.

Participation in the local assemblies and communal works is lower than before. In the past, the community was more organized, participation was very high, obligatory even in times of the conflict. This development is described by many interview partners: "In the past we were all united, they did not speak of 'individuals'. Now it is very different, they say 'I don't belong to Kimbiri'" (K8: 41). Another community member supposes that participation rates have changed because only a few people are still landowners:

> Nowadays the majority are tenants, only a few we are still landowners, it's only us going. In the past, when there was the Junta de Vecinas, Defensa Civil, we all had to be present, obligatory, women and men. Now there is no discipline anymore, they do not take note of the authorities, they don't want to collaborate, in the past it was not like that.
>
> (K9: 38)

The people who do not participate are the ones with micro businesses and who do not care much about the community according to the interviewees. Inhabitants of the surrounding villages are the ones with the highest motivation to participate (K4: 42). Now, there is even transport provided that takes the villagers from remote areas to the assemblies (K20: 46). Membership in associations is rare, only some producers for cacao or coffee (or coca) form associations. Faenas are still taking place occasionally but only in the single barrios, minkas are not practiced anymore: "When I was young, we all participated in communal works, there was solidarity, there were ceremonies and everyone was participating. But now, as there is money in the municipality, they don't participate anymore. The barrios are not organized" (K3: 24; also K11: 49; K5: 42). Another man reports the same:

> Now the people have more envy. In the past, we did our minka, to clean the streets, the college, the airport, this doesn't exist anymore, the whole population participated but today it does not happen anymore [...] it is because of their interests, their children are studying at universities, they have other priorities.
>
> (K18: 33–34)

The migration to and from the cities and the changing priorities are given as reasons for lower participation as well (K17: 49). Others state that those who do not participate would not know about their rights and mechanisms of participation, they would say "for this we elected him" (K13: 45). People would only come to activities when there are incentives: "they ask: 'What will they give us? Snacks, vests, polo shirts?'" (K14: 44). The decrease in participation is connected to the lack of trust and lack of respect for local authorities.

The relationship with local authorities is weak; trust is only medium [4] and significantly less than levels of trust within families [6.5]. Those willing to give some of their corn harvest to authorities would only do so if it is for a good reason [1.4]. As the authorities that cared the most about the community people mentioned the municipality [14], the governor [1], and self-defense committee [2]. Community members complain that there are many new types of authorities that are not known in the population, with members who "buy" votes and trust and who do not connect with or value the population (K3: 26; also K7: 35). Furthermore, they are in charge of executing the *Canon* and other projects and do so very slowly and in an ineffective manner. Moreover, authorities are seen as corrupt and working for their own benefit only. As in the other communities, villagers complain that they do not employ people from Kimbiri: "Because there are only few authorities that really work for their village, some only work for their pockets and are millionaires, they bring people from other places and forget about the Kimbirinos" (K8: 26; also K7: 38). There are rumors of the actual mayor bribing other authorities such as the president of the *Frente de Defensa de Intereses*, the committee in place to observe the administration (K20: 85). In 2013, the mayor was forced to step down from his position because of reproaches of corruption. The case was fought by the *Frente de Defensa de Intereses.*[70] In Kimbiri as in the other villages, "good governance" is judged by the amount of projects or investments that the authorities managed to get from diverse funding institutions. The villagers demand more of those projects. Interestingly, the problems of drug trafficking, terrorism, or security are not mentioned at all when referring to the village organization or authorities.

Nearly all interviewed people state that there are conflicts prevalent in the community [90%]. These are mostly disputes over territory between neighbors or with other communities. One community member explained that nowadays there were more conflicts of envy because in the past it was regulated by the CAD and people were scared of terrorism: "When you had a conflict with a neighbor 'just shut up' and that was it. They were scared, everything went well. Now not anymore, the authority is filthy, the one that has more money, the authority looks after them" (K9: 40). According to the person formerly responsible for the reparation program in Kimbiri, reparations caused conflicts within families that received financial benefits. More and more people came to register because they heard of a potential benefit but she said that the program caused more disappointment than it solved. The people became disappointed and disagreed because there were so many rumors and expectations of receiving a large amount of money (Exp39).

Others mentioned social conflicts or fights arising due to drunkenness. But people describe these conflicts as "normal conflicts": "Here are no conflicts that destabilize the political order, the society, they are not like those mine conflicts. Here the conflicts are more domestic and can be solved in the community" (K13: 49). The people also state that when there were conflicts they would appeal to local authorities such as the self-defense committee, *juez de paz*, or higher legal instances.

Nevertheless, there is a lot of violence in the community [85%] that is not a consequence of the conflicts above but rather of the problems with drug trafficking as community members explain in the interviews:

> There are groups of young people organized in gang groups, they brought alcohol, bars and cantinas with the drug trafficking. Prostitution has increased a lot. And, obviously, with the alcohol the number of assaults has gone up. Yes, there is a lot of violence. It is a product of the drug trafficking.
>
> (K4: 48)

Domestic violence is also still very common, even increasing according to one authority: "There is a lot of domestic violence. It is increasing. Daily new cases are reported" (K15: 50). This is connected to problems with alcohol consumption as well. Local and national governments and institutions do not care enough or only if it is too late and they do very little work on the prevention of domestic violence (K5: 51; K18: 51). There are also cases of students bringing weapons to school and one student got shot last year because of an internal fight: an incident that shook parents (K8: 49).

According to the community members, the violence has changed:

> In the 1990s the violence was needed to protect your life against attacks of Shining Path or against the militaries of the Ronderos. Today this violence is linked to crime and prostitution as well, that was not here before, but now it is normal.
>
> (K4: 49)

Nowadays, it is more crime-related violence as one man observes (K6: 50). The past violence was "more cruel, more inhumane, unreasonable. This type of violence we don't have anymore" (K13: 53).

But before the conflict, there was less violence according to the interview partners. There were higher values:

> They lived with good values, they were responsible for all the problems within the community. But now, as it does not interest them, they are in

> conflicts, sometimes some take drugs or get drunk, the alcoholism and after getting drunk they create problems. It's more the young ones than the adults.
>
> (K17: 48)

It is surprising how the interview partners reported about assaults, robberies, and accidents but still claimed that it was be peaceful to live there today similar as in Chuschi: "They always say that in the VRAEM there is terrorism but it is not like that. It happened in the past, but today it is quiet" (K8: 18; also K11: 57; K18: 52; K15: 20). This was the same woman who reported about the boy, who was killed with a gun in the local school. To her and the other interviewees, it nevertheless seems as though it was very peaceful nowadays. Peru's image of the VRAEM as a center for drug trafficking and terrorism remains, and this is why people of Kimbiri talk even less about the past – they want it to be quiet and peaceful (K17: 59).

Regarding the question whether the violence of the 1980s could be repeated the majority of the interviewed people do not think that it was likely [only 25% yes]: "Nowadays the people are more aware" (K7: 49). New institutions would also not allow a reoccurrence of violence: "I don't think so anymore. Not in this era because there are institutions that are in the middle" (K16: 52; also K12: 49; K13: 55). Only one person interviewed refers explicitly to the state as providing security but still believes that terrorism could come back but in another form (K18: 54). As did some interviewees, who thought that violence could still reoccur because of coca, as there was drug trafficking on one side and the anti-coca-programs on the other:

> The state promotes alternative programs to coca in but the farmers do not see their needs satisfied. Therefore they or another sector of the valley could opt to join Shining Path and this would be a strengthening and it would come back a horrible episode for Peru.
>
> (K4: 51)

Interviewees make the state programs responsible for creating unrest (K5: 53). One interviewee explains that the military or the state might behave so badly that violence could reoccur (K9: 48). Furthermore, the reasons for the conflict of the 1980s are not solved yet, as another interviewee describes: "As long as there is poverty, and big differences in the income of the people, there will be people with envy and resentments, this is latent. Poverty brings social conflicts" (K1: 52).

So, there are conflicts prevalent in Kimbiri, mostly for territory as in the other cases or related to drug trafficking. When combined with alcohol consumption they are often violent. During the 1980s, violence was everywhere but the self-defense committees regulated other conflicts using their "hard control". A lack of control and rule on the part of the local authorities does permit more conflicts and violence nowadays. The conflict does, therefore, have consequences in this regard, but it is not the main reason. The reparation program seems to lead to new conflicts rather than helping settle existing ones. New violence such as that of the 1980s seems not very likely although some refer to the anti-coca-programs which would create unrest and the unattended needs of the people as causes of the conflict of the 1980s already. In comparison with the first villages of Chuschi and Lucanamarca, the level of violence and incidents is higher in Kimbiri as in Santa Rosa. Drug trafficking seems to be the main reason for that.

Interviewed people state that they have low or no confidence in congress: "In the news they are only fighting" (K8: 73). I also observed a gap in information and communication: "We don't see what they are doing" (K15: 78) and another women: "you don't notice what they are doing, they don't come, the projects do not reach to certain areas" (K17: 85). Again, the "good governance" is measured in projects arriving or not arriving in the corresponding area. A sign of the problems in this area is that the elected congressperson representing the VRAEM, Joaquién Dipas, was involved in three juridical investigations in 2016.[71]

The importance of the state for Kimbiri is rated as high [12], medium [3], and low [3]. In contrast to the other communities, it is not only present in state programs but mainly through the military and the Canon budget: "A lot of importance. It depends on the state that our budget arrives here, moreover, it is the state that finally intervenes directly in the development of the villages" (K6: 71). Another interviewee confirmed:

> in the last years a shift towards the state could be observed. Because any claim they make towards the state, goes through the municipality, through the governor. Yes, it took an importance but it is still not covering it totally, for example all of the necessities, we still need to talk about citizen security. (K12: 24, 73)

One community member states that the state is more important today because of the scholarship program *Beca 18* because her family benefitted from it (K10: 64). Social programs are mentioned only once in this question as a form of the state being closer than before (K16: 81). Another woman explained that the state would now take notice of Kimbiri because it was put in emergency zone but still with the wrong image of the VRAEM, demonizing the area as haven for terrorists (K19: 18; 75).

Finally, all interviewees believed that the state should do more for Kimbiri.

Expectations are very high and mostly related to education, infrastructure, and development: "I expect of the state as I said that it sends good teachers. And the food, at least one nutritionist for the valley and good teachers so that our children will not be as we are" (K8: 74). "Well, simply taking responsibility and attending to our basic needs. I think the VRAEM has always been organized, knocked the door of the state for the necessities that we have" (K14: 82). Many community members demanded a stronger focus on development and on helping the poor and mentioned social programs: "In fact the social programs are a relief but they don't eradicate poverty. I think a different methodology is necessary, create work, teach them to earn their own money with their own effort" (K16: 83). Others are so disappointed that they don't have any expectations anymore: "Nothing, there is no hope anymore. It did not do anything" (K3: 61).

The people in Kimbiri have a high identification with Peru as a nation: "The importance that it [the state] has is that it forms an identity of being Peruvians, this is the important thing for us" (K18: 82). But they do not feel that they are a part of this state.

Interestingly, the state importance in Kimbiri is evaluated mainly by the *Canon* budget and projects and not in the social programs as was the case in Chuschi and Lucanamarca. But also here is the state only rarely seen as an institution with laws and rights that establishes a social and political order. Security is a more important topic than in the first two villages.

Political participation is rather low. People only vote because it is obligatory. The turnout was 71% in the second round of the presidential elections in June 2016.[72] Several interviewees explained that there was no education in civil rights, and this was one of the reasons for the misuses of police power (K17: 67; K12: 21).

The level of corruption is very high. One mayor had to leave office because of substantial accusations of corruption. One of the elders faced the same in 2015/2016 as did the congressman for the VRAEM. Many interview partners complain about the high levels of corruption, reinforced as well by the *Canon* and present in institutions and state programs (K7: 38; K14: 22).

The state is not very present. Also the memory of Fujimori visiting the community and building roads and schools is not that present as in the other villages. He came to visit twice as one interviewee remembered (K7: 22).

> No one comes, nor the regional government nor a president has come here, I think. The only president who came was Fujimori, I think. After him, nobody, I think they are scared. But as you can see, it is quiet.
>
> (K11: 87)

Another one explained: "we don't see its presence. The state hardly reaches here" (K2: 67). The politicians would only arrive to gather votes and not know the reality of the VRAEM, would only talk about it, nothing else (K17: 83). The state was still largely absent said another man (K7: 69). A community member explains: "It is like a pact between the drug trafficking and the peasant who does not allow the state to enter here" (K12: 73). He refers to the reluctance of the population to accept the anti-coca-actions undertaken by state forces. So while people demand more presence in the form of visits and attention with development projects and social programs, they are at the same time against the strategy of the state to combat the cultivation of coca and this poses a challenge for both sides. The reparation program was not mentioned in this context.

The community members evaluate the situation today as being better than some years ago [16]. When asked which entity helped bring about this positive change, 12 people mention the state, followed by local authorities [11] and the mayor [4] but again no reference is made to the reparation program. It is simply not present in the mind of the people as a helpful program. The state is seen as doing something, mainly in the form of infrastructure improvements and via the *Canon* budget, but it is not enough. The people demand more attention, budget, and projects.

Summary

In summary, the level of social cohesion in Kimbiri is low but slightly higher as in the other communities. The most important factors for the low social cohesion according to the interviewees are migration to the cities and from other places which led to an overall population growth as well as the introduction of money and paid work. Money seems to be even more important in Kimbiri because of the *Canon* budget. Just as in Santa Rosa, the presence of coca is another important factor and causes problems such as illegal economic actors, crime, money flows, addiction, fewer farm products, water contamination, and economic dependency. Violence is also seen as a consequence of coca and not only of the conflict. Nevertheless, it is obvious that the conflict reinforced some of these developments as it led to higher migration, loss of social, and political order and experienced leaders. The psychological consequences of the violence further weakened social cohesion.

Kimbiri is also a relatively new community with few traditions. The narrative of the "happy time" before the conflict does not dominate as it does in Lucanamarca and Chuschi. In Kimbiri, I also found the hero-narrative, which is very noticeable thanks to the memorial in the central park, the "park of the pacification". The local people perceive the VRAEM as the place of the pacification where Shining Path was defeated by them. Members of the self-defense committees are heroes and victims at the same time. Kimbiri's affectedness by the violence from different sides is very high.

As far as transitional justice is concerned Kimbiri only received low attention. The TRC was not present in Kimbiri, and only some Kimbirinos gave their testimony in other places such as Santa Rosa. However, awareness of the TRC is as high as in the other two villages, although again it was mostly perceived as an entity tasked with bringing reparations to the affected people. It is evaluated accordingly for fulfilling this expectation. The interviewees said that the commission did not conclude its work and that many cases have not been investigated and disappeared people have not been found.

In Kimbiri, there was also distrust toward the TRC and the reparation program. Many did not know that the registration in the RUV was necessary in order to receive reparations – this is a difference to Lucanamarca where this was known, maybe because of the work of COMISEDH. Another difference to the first villages is that in the VRAEM more people were linked to Shining Path, and they were not eligible for reparations, feared that they would be accused of being terrorists and so they did not register. Nowadays, more people are registered because of the new office in the municipality. However, this office also still lacks information.

On the community level, the community of Kimbiri itself did not receive a collective reparation project. Projects were only carried out in neighboring communities but those projects are also not widely known. It is important to note that compared to the other communities Kimbiri's *Canon* budget allows for larger scale projects to be implemented here. Once again we see problems of corruption and the decline in voluntary work because people expect the municipality to complete works. This leads to lower communal participation. This is why collective reparations are given low importance, as there is other funding available for projects. In one neighboring community, the collective project was supplemented with high municipal co-funding.

Symbolic measures have been implemented by the municipality in the form of the memorial of the hero *rondero* in the central "park of the pacification". The past and the narrative of the heroes are very important within the village.

Although more people are registered in the RUV in Kimbiri, only few have received their reparations, and the majority is still waiting for it. The people of Kimbiri mainly want scholarships and healthcare. As in the other communities, the mere act of testimony giving was not mentioned positively by any interview partner. The victim certificate alone seems useless if it does not entitle the bearer to reparations. The reparation program seeks to improve the situation of the affected people with individual scholarships and health insurances. Economic reparations are another form of support. However, as mentioned earlier, only very few people have benefited from these programs so far and they are not fully satisfied with it either.

As for the other villages, I have to conclude that the reparation program suffers from shortcomings in the implementation, awareness, and perception within the village. Kimbiri has not seen as many transitional justice measures as the first two villages and even less than Santa Rosa. I observed unfulfilled high expectations leading to further envy, distrust in the authorities and neighbors and more conflicts. The obscure methods of distributing reparations caused more envy and conflict in the community. More than half of the interviewed people have only low satisfaction with the reparation program (13), only four people assessed it with medium satisfaction. Here it is important to emphasize again that the general idea of reparations is not rejected, it is their implementation that is being criticized. Expectations and possibilities of the program for a positive impact were not fulfilled. The village of Kimbiri does not feel that its needs have been met. Satisfaction with the reparations is very low, therefore no positive impact follows and social cohesion is not affected positively. Quite the opposite, the analysis shows that the unfulfilled expectations and the envy and distrust caused by sporadic reparations have a negative effect.

Comparison of four post-conflict communities

In this chapter, I investigated the transitional justice processes in four post-conflict communities. The idea of the research design was to compare two communities with high levels of attention from the TRC and reparation program and two with low levels. The case selection was based on the information available at the time (see Chapter 3). The interviews later revealed that the reality was different. In the first two villages, I knew that there was high objective exposure to the TRC and both individual and collective reparations. However, there were only few people with individual reparations and regarding the collective project not all the people were aware of it and so subjective exposure was very much lower than expected. In Santa Rosa and Kimbiri, the attention of the TRC was low but of the reparation program still medium-high and the awareness also very high, which I did not anticipate. As mentioned, there were no previous studies on the VRAEM area, which would have indicated that before. My study brings new insights here. So, I did not find what I expected in terms of the level of the TJ measures and the awareness of the measures. These are very important and surprising results.

All four communities are situated in the rural part of Peru and have high levels of poverty and malnutrition. The main occupation is agriculture – in form of coca in Kimbiri and Santa Rosa.

The life in the communities before the conflict is described as "happy time" in Lucanamarca and Chuschi. As relatively new settlements Kimbiri and Santa Rosa do not have this strong communal memory of the time before the conflict began. It is certain that the conflict had tremendous negative effects on the social cohesion in the communities but also in terms of economic and political conditions. However, there were other influencing factors already present before the conflict started such as the increase in paid work and improvements education as well as cultural and economic interchange with the cities and temporal and permanent migration. Rural communities all over the world face these developments today or have faced them in the past. The conflict and violence experienced within the villages sped up some of these processes such as more migration from and to the villages, the loss of leaders and with them the loss of political and social structures. The social, political, economic, and psychological consequences are visible until today. As far as the link between social cohesion and conflict elaborated in Chapter 2 is concerned I did not find that the violence as external threat caused inner cohesion but rather divided the communities in my study. What people do mention is that in Santa Rosa and Kimbiri the self-defense committees were in charge for the communal order to organize the fight against Shining Path. In that time, meetings and communal work projects were attended by everyone because of fear and threat. Communal order might have been high but levels of trust and solidarity and therefore an important part of social cohesion was very low as interviewees explained. They did not trust neighbors or community members because they did not know who supported whom. Moreover, it was not "one" external threat, but various actors were involved. First, the people supported Shining Path before fighting against them in self-defense committees and then the military was another actor that also posed a threat and committed violent acts. In the communities, there are complex victim, perpetrator, and mixed roles. These, however, do not appear in the official debate or in the TRC report or the reparation program. The conflict affected all four communities severely and their communities suffered violence from Shining Path, state forces, and self-defense committees.

The central research question of this book is how the attention from the TRC and reparation program affected social cohesion. The background of the development of weaker social cohesion and the influencing factors is important when judging the effects of the TRC and the reparation program. It would definitely be too much to expect transitional measures to turn back this development that had already begun before the conflict. Nevertheless, I expected to find some positive impact of the TRC and reparations on social cohesion – at least on a small scale. However, in none of the four communities could any positive impact be observed. As main reasons, I identified problems in the implementation and with the perception of the reparation program.

Regarding the implementation of the TRC and reparation program on the local level, I made clear that Lucanamarca received the highest attention while Chuschi was also in the focus, Santa Rosa only had a short visit and Kimbiri did not have any at all. These different levels of attention in the communities were due to political and practical considerations. With regard to the reparation program, I made clear in the analysis that it depended highly on the information, initiative, and capacities of local authorities whether a collective project was implemented and how many individuals were registered and had a chance of receiving individual reparations. Without the support of the authorities or an NGO, it is very difficult for the affected people to manage the administrative process. But even in the communities with registration offices, there were problems and a lack of information as found by Ulfe, Ríos, and Málaga (2015). So, in the implementation of the reparation program already became clear that the Peruvian program did not fulfill de Greiff and Roht-Arriaza's criteria (see Chapter 2).

With regard to the awareness and knowledge of the TRC and reparation program, I conclude that as the first national transitional measure to reach the communities, the TRC had a huge problem with awareness and information. Interestingly, the awareness was very high in all communities. About three-quarters of the interviewed people stated they had heard of the TRC and more than 90% had heard of the reparation program. This is surprisingly high in all communities regardless of the levels of attention they received. In Lucanamarca and Chuschi, however, people knew slightly more about what the TRC did than in the other two villages where the TRC was less or not present.

However, most of the respondents reduce it to the paying of money to victims. Yezer (2008, 281–82) also describes the suspicion of some village members toward the TRC when they came to collect testimonies in that village of Ayacucho. And she also hints to the problem that the TRC "promised" reparations. My interviews point in the same direction. Most people associated the commission only with the reparation program and disregarded other measures such as the testimony giving, exhumations, and the publication of its final report. The gathering of testimonies is seen by some as an important step but the majority perceives it as a means to an end – the end being reparations. In Chuschi and Lucanamarca, they remember the exhumations and that the commission collected testimonies. The public audiences were not mentioned and neither were the trials against Guzmán and others with the participation and testimonies of community members from Chuschi and Lucanamarca. And there is confusion about the commission as an entity: according to a former TRC employee "people did not understand what the TRC was until the end" (Exp19). The TRC was not perceived as state entity but as something connected to the NGOs. This was most apparent in Lucanamarca and was partly due to the fact that the TRC employed people who had formerly worked with human rights associations in the same area. The creation of two further institutions, the *Consejo de Reparaciones* and CMAN created even more confusion. People did not understand why three or more entities were needed to bring them reparations and why they had to tell the same harmful story several times.

In the testimonies that the TRC collected in the villages, many victims already mentioned that they expected reparations, they referred not only to economic payments but also to support with housing, education, and health.[73] I do not find regional differences in the expectations mentioned in the testimonies given to the TRC. Because the TRC is so closely connected to the reparation program in the minds of the people and promises or expectations also for the search for disappeared were not fulfilled, the evaluation of the TRC is negative in all four communities. The lowest approval rate was observed in Kimbiri, where the TRC did not even arrive to work there. That caused disappointment as interviewees were aware of its work in other places.

As stated, awareness of the reparation program is even higher than that of the commission. Knowledge about the reparation program is, however, very low with the exception of Lucanamarca and Chuschi. In all communities, people stated that reparations had been paid in their village, however, people generally do not know any details or who received it. Besides, this only applies to economic reparations and other parts of the program referring to education, health, and housing are hardly known. Detailed information about the reparation program and the registration process is scarce even in those communities with special offices in the municipality. And again, it varies considerably from one local authority to another. Some municipalities are well-informed and engaged and share information with the affected people – and others do not. Even the professionals in the health departments sometimes do not know about the reparations in the healthcare sector. CMAN does not have the capacity (or is not given the capacity by the state) to visit all districts and to inform people. Only recently the CMAN is visiting intensively remote areas. As a result, rumors are rife about who received reparations and who did not within the communities. Envy and a hierarchy of victims are the result of missing information and a lack of transparency. Even in Chuschi and Lucanamarca awareness of the implemented collective reparation project is very low. In Kimbiri and Santa Rosa, people barely knew that there was a collective program.

I observed incidences of bad or wrong information and high expectations in different places. In the first two villages, I assumed that the high expectations had been raised by NGOs; no human rights organizations worked in Kimbiri or in Santa Rosa but the association of displaced people who informed the people in a way that was difficult to comprehend. Maybe the authorities also played a role in generating high expectations (Exp39).

For the perception of the transitional justice measures the biggest problem for all collective reparations projects was that they were not really perceived as such. The report by the APRODEH and the ICTJ (Paredes and Correa 2011)[74] has similar findings and in Columbia Firchow (2013) reports parallel results. Within my communities, in Chuschi, a communal storehouse was constructed but only one of the interviewed people referred to this as a form of reparation. In Lucanamarca, the fish farm was perceived as reparation project by some, but because it was not successful, it did not have compensatory effect. Furthermore, the symbolic part was missing. There was objective exposure in both communities but there was almost no subjective exposure to the collective reparation program. The confusion with development programs is so high because the local authorities attempted to harness the positive effect for their appreciation within the community. Even ex-president Toledo saw reparations as a kind of development program. Here comes together that the victims are not only victims of the internal armed conflict but also poor, with indigenous roots in the rural marginalized parts of the country. This ambiguous relationship between reparations and development projects is also highlighted by Dixon (2016) in a recent article and Firchow (2014) finds the same confusion in Colombian collective reparation projects. For those reasons, the compensative effect, even for the successful house construction project, is very low.

Regarding the individual reparations, it was also interesting to see that even community members, who judged themselves as not having been directly affected by the violence knew about the reparation program for individuals. The awareness as at nearly 100% in my interviews, 76 out of 80 people have heard of the reparations. The news of the reparation program had created high expectations.

I already elaborated on the late and incomplete implementation and the lack of information about the program. This had the following effects on its reception in the three different groups:

First, the receivers: those who received economic individual reparations were not satisfied with the amount, with the late payment and that it would just cover one loss even if a family had lost several members. Furthermore, they do not perceive the reparation as a right and compensation but rather as a "gift" or "assistance" given to them because of their socio-economic status. This is connected to a lack of understanding of civil rights and the obligations of the state in general. The beneficiaries I interviewed did not feel "repaired" while only some said that the money represented at least a little support. Satisfaction with the collective projects was also low as most of them are not working.

Second, those who did not receive economic individual reparations (non-receivers) but considered themselves victims perceive the program as "unjust". This applies also to people not affected by the violence (observers). Envy is a huge problem in the communities and seeing some people receiving a benefit when others do not creates new conflicts. In Lucanamarca, for example, family members who lost their relatives in the massacre received other forms of support than victims not affected by the massacre but who had been affected just at different points in time. These different victims' categories created a rift between affected people. Also in the VRAEM people answered repeatedly that they did not belong in the "right victim group". More disappointment was created by unfulfilled expectations than satisfaction resulting from reparations. Only very few people had a positive opinion. Some higher satisfaction can only be observed in Santa Rosa, but these are not the individual receivers but observers who evaluated the program positively. In Chapter 6, I focus on these individuals in more detail.

Interestingly, in all the four communities similar problems arise and similarly high unfulfilled expectations lead to discontent with the transitional justice process. This was observed regardless of the levels of attention received or whether coca or the *Canon* budget were present in the community in question. The perception of reparations is mainly negative in all four communities as well. The TRC was perceived by some as an unnecessary re-telling and re-living of the violent past. Others saw the commission as the starting point of a project, which was not concluded. Satisfaction is especially low because both expectations of finding the disappeared people and reparations was largely unfulfilled. I can only conclude that the TRC and reparations had no positive impact in the villages. The level of social cohesion is rather low as analyzed. Social programs and development programs implemented by the state, that are seen both positively as negatively; migration to and from the cities; money and paid work play a more important role in the social development of the villages

On the basis of the interviews, I assume that in order to have a positive impact, the commission would have had to work through cases in much more detail, investigating more cases and carrying out more exhumations. Furthermore, people demanded for the results to be distributed and expected more information from the commission. For reparations to have a positive effect, a fully implemented program would be required with no hierarchy of victims, easy access, and transparency. Collective projects would need to be successful and not hindered by technical problems as well as include a symbolic part and reinforce cooperation within the community. In the design, these criteria were met but in the implementation not anymore.

Notes

1 The *Canon Gasifero* is a fund which is generated from profits of mineral exploitation projects and distributed to regional and local municipals: www.loshidrocarburosenelperu.org/2014/08/canon-gasifero/.
2 www.inei.gob.pe.
3 www.midis.gob.pe/mapas/BaseLineamientosDCI.xlsx.
4 There was an initiative of COMISEDH in 2015 to build up a little food market in the central place. However, the women had only customers on some days and did not earn any money on other days.
5 As "white elefant" are projects called, mainly in infrastructure or specific programs, financed by the state or NGOs, which are not working. Because they are mainly works with concrete in an often green surrounding they appear as white elephants. Interestingly, the term is used by four interviewees in Lucanamarca, and it seems that there was a discourse about it.
6 http://infomidis.midis.gob.pe/formatos/documentos/05_20170914_F3_AYACUCHO.pdf.
7 This activism was mentioned to me by leaders of those associations in Lima and Ica. They are very present in the celebration of the anniversary and other festivities. Their actions are e.g. documented in facebook: www.facebook.com/photo.php?fbid=773858169435018&set=t.100004072897544&type=3&theater; www.facebook.com/photo.php?fbid=381685622181095&set=rpd.100004072897544&type=3&theater.
8 Own data is cited in brackets [ ]. These numbers refer to the 20 people interviewed and used for the analysis and indicate the number of interviewees, percentage or mean. The gap to 20 results from missing answers or indecisive answers.
9 Observation in a speech at the anniversary in January 2015 and in a communal assembly in November 2014.
10 "Lucanamarca" is a film by Carlos Cardenas & Hector Galvez, see: http://icarusfilms.com/if-luca.
11 The influence of human rights and victims organizations on expectations and perception of transitional justice measures by the affected people is a factor that needs to be investigated more thoroughly (see also Waardt 2014; Yezer 2008).
12 The transitional justice process forced victims to organize themselves because the requirement for receiving a benefit or reparation is the formation of an organization. In Lucanamarca the *Asociación de Familiares Víctimas de la Violencia Política Distrito de Santiago de Lucanamarca* was formed and united about 25 affected families (Exp1; Exp10).
13 www.ruv.gob.pe/RUV/ConsultasLinea/Libro02/Listado_Web02.aspx.

14 www.facebook.com/photo.php?fbid=558335227680244&set=a.550706551776445.107 3741826.100005113146157&type=3&theater; www.facebook.com/photo.php?fbid=558329864347447&set=a.550706551776445.1073741826.100005113146157&type=3&theater.
15 In two construction works of the last two years the rests of human bodies were found. There was, however, no investigation made of the judicial instances informed but people decided to continue with the works (Exp8).
16 For a description of the project and problems see also Ulfe (2013).
17 A few days before the visit an authority complained in an interview that collective reparations were not just and demanded more attention for the district of Lucanamarca (Zenitagoya 2012).
18 Informal talk with a woman whose father was entitled to receive economic reparations but died before receiving them, Lucanamarca, March 2015.
19 Observation at a carnival celebration in March 2015.
20 Observation in faenas in February and November 2015.
21 www.web.onpe.gob.pe/modElecciones/elecciones/elecciones2016/PRP2V2016/participacion-ciudadana-Nacional-050803-Pie.html.
22 This project of COMISEDH to inform about civil rights and enhance political participation was in place during my first stay in the village in 2009. The theoretical workshops were sometimes difficult to understand for the people. However, one interviewee stated that workshops with women were successful (L12).
23 End of September 2017, CMAN organized an information workshop in Lucanamarca, also in reaction to the results of this study, to inform the people about their status of inscription in the RUV and the possibilities of the reparation program: www.facebook.com/permalink.php?story_fbid=1558745084147333&id=276556615699526.
24 www.munichuschi.gob.pe/municipalidad/vm.html, translation by the author.
25 www.inei.gob.pe.
26 www.midis.gob.pe/mapas/BaseLineamientosDCI.xlsx.
27 This could be observed especially in the debate about the possibility of Quispillacta becoming a district. The organizations in Ayacucho and Lima were mobilizing people and trying to influence local politics. In the meeting of the regional government in Cangallo, where the topic was debated, many functionaries were present (observation March 2015).
28 http://infomidis.midis.gob.pe/formatos/documentos/05_20170914_F3_AYACUCHO.pdf.
29 www.andina.com.pe/agencia/noticia-programa-juntos-promueve-acceso-a-los-servicios-salud-y-educacion-575650.aspx.
30 http://sellomunicipal.midis.gob.pe/; www.facebook.com/386878784743028/videos/1342259892538241/?h c_ref=ARRG33XPt_lIouS3r7xr-9pSA8B8QljTr1fJxByszP5f9twWOKDBum0PmHillxKxyOQ.
31 The presence of the American researcher and her family and team in the community was perceived by the community members in a differentiated way. Some were getting friends with her but others suspected Isbell of being a spy of the CIA or the government to observe subversive actions. She left Chuschi after a conflict escalated. She describes that the problem was the filming of her team in several occasions (Isbell 1985, 221–37). The other version which I still heard many times is that she and her team were getting drunk with young male community members and having sexual encounters with them.
32 (Municipalidad Distrital de Chuschi 2007).
33 http://lum.cultura.pe/cdi/foto/exhumacion-de-restos-en-chuschi.

34 https://caminantesdelamemoria.wordpress.com/.
35 www.ruv.gob.pe/RUV/ConsultasLinea/Libro02/Listado_Web02.aspx.
36 www.youtube.com/watch?v=XJJ9xo5ikxY.
37 I could also observe it in the communal activity of shearing vicuñas (similar to Alpacas) in the upper part of Chuschi in July 2015.
38 The attempts by Quispillacta to be considered as district and their "dirty" campaign against the local government to reach this aim is one example.
39 Cofopri (Organismo de Formalización de la Propiedad Informal) is the state entity in charge of registering informal properties: www.cofopri.gob.pe/.
40 www.proyectosapp.pe/modulos/JER/PlantillaProyecto.aspx?ARE=0&PFL=2&JER=5640 http://busquedas.elperuano.com.pe/normaslegales/otorgan-concesion-definitiva-a-favor-de-consorcio-transmanta-resolucion-ministerial-no-136-2017-memdm-1508850-1/, www.osinergmin.gob.pe/seccion/centro_documental/electricidad/Documentos/PROYECTOS%20GFE/Acorde%C3%B3n/Transmisi%C3%B3n/2.1.1.pdf.
41 It is interesting to see that Lucanamarca within the same project did not negotiate at all but accepted the company's first offer.
42 www.web.onpe.gob.pe/modElecciones/elecciones/elecciones2016/PRP2V2016/participacion-ciudadana-Nacional-050204-Pie.html.
43 Both sides mobilized community members in Chuschi and in the neighboring community of Quispillacta for the session of the regional government in Cangallo, March 25, 2015.
44 In contrast to the last two villages there was little information and hardly any academic literature available about Santa Rosa and Kimbiri. The existing reports focus on the topic of coca only apart from one book chapter on the self-defense committees in the area of Santa Rosa (Del Pino 1996). Existing literature focuses on the topic of coca and/or security (Díaz 2015; Ipince and Salazar 2016; López and Castillo 2012; López Villanes 2014; Villagaray Yanqui 2014). General information about the community is based on interviews and two project reports: *Mejoramiento y aplicación de los servicios limpieza pública, recolección y disposición final de los residuos sólidos de las localidades de Santa Rosa, Marintari y Comumpiari del distrito de Santa Rosa, Provincia La Mar, Ayacucho*, 2011; and: *Paz y Desarrollo. Plan de Desarrollo Urbano. Santa Rosa 2006–2015*, Ministerio de vivienda, Construcción y Saneamiento, 2006: http://eudora.vivienda.gob.pe/OBSERVATORIO/PAZYDESARROLLO/2006/AYACUCHO_LAMAR/PDU_SANTA_ROSA.pdf.
45 www.inei.gob.pe.
46 www.midis.gob.pe/mapas/BaseLineamientosDCI.xlsx.
47 See also an article of Mariano Aronés Palomino concerning the difficulties of teachers in the VRAEM: https://redaccion.lamula.pe/2015/11/11/a-que-se-enfrenta-diariamente-un-docente-en-el-vraem-un-antropologo-te-lo-cuenta/danielavila/ and a presentation of Aronés: Ensenar y educar en una zona de conflicto: El caso de los profesores/as del Valle de los ríos Apurímac, Ene y Mantaro, Ayacucho, November 2015: http://seminarioanual.cies.org.pe/2015/sites/default/files/mesas/ARONES%20FORGE.pdf.
48 http://elcomercio.pe/sociedad/peru/declaran-estado-emergencia-distritos-huancavelica-y-cusco-noticia-1930834.
49 www.noticiasser.pe/04/02/2015/ayacucho/autoridades-de-santa-rosa-insiste-que-ugel-vraem-se-instale-en-su-jurisdiccion.
50 http://infomidis.midis.gob.pe/formatos/documentos/05_20170914_F3_AYACUCHO.pdf.
51 NIÑOS EN ZONAS COCALERAS. Un estudio en los valles de los ríos Apurímac y Alto Huallaga. Fondo de las Naciones Unidas para la Infancia (UNICEF), Lima, 2006, p. 31: http://repositorio.minedu.gob.pe/handle/123456789/509.

52 www.ruv.gob.pe/RUV/ConsultasLinea/Libro02/Listado_Web02.aspx.
53 www.web.onpe.gob.pe/modElecciones/elecciones/elecciones2016/PRP2V2016/participacion-ciudadana-Nacional-050408-Pie.html.
54 Existing literature focuses on the topic of coca and/or security (Díaz 2015; Ipince and Salazar 2016; López and Castillo 2012; López Villanes 2014; Villagaray Yanqui 2014). General information on Kimbiri is based upon interviews and several reports: Plan de Organización de la Municipalidad Distrital de Kimbiri: www.peru.gob.pe/docs/PLANES/11021/PLAN_11021_ROF%20MDK_2011.doc.

Paz y Desarrollo. Plan de Desarrollo Urbano del Distrito de Kimbiri 2007–2016. Ministerio de Vivienda, Construcción y Saneamiento, Lima, 2007: http://eudora.vivienda.gob.pe/OBSERVATORIO/PAZYDESARROLLO/2007/CUSCO_LACONVENCION/PDU_KIMBIRI.pdf.

Proyecto de Inversión Publica: Mejoramiento de la competitividad en la cadenas productivas de mango, palto, papaya y frutales nativos en el distrito de Kimbiri: https://de.scribd.com/document/225548434.
55 http://larepublica.pe/sociedad/708268-caen-12-narcotraficantes-con-armas-y-350-kilos-de-droga-en-el-vraemhttp://larepublica.pe/impresa/politica/16889-cocaleros-exigen-suspension-del-programa-de-reconversion.
56 https://issuu.com/sociedadmineroenergetica/docs/reporte_canon_gas__fero_2012.
57 www.inforegion.pe/30823/cofopri-entrego-3-mil-619-titulos-de-propiedad-a-pobladores-de-tres-distritos-del-vrae/.

www.sisfoh.gob.pe/.
58 http://diariocorreo.pe/ciudad/declaran-vacancia-de-alcaldia-en-kimbiri-vr-208314/.
59 http://eudora.vivienda.gob.pe/OBSERVATORIO/PAZYDESARROLLO/2007/CUSCO_LACONVENCION/PDU_KIMBIRI.pdf, www.inforegion.pe/202114/juramentan-integrantes-del-comite-de-seguridad-ciudadana-de-kimbiri/.
60 www.munikimbiri.gob.pe/index.php/municipalidad/mision-y-vision, translation by the author.
61 www.inei.gob.pe.
62 www.midis.gob.pe/mapas/BaseLineamientosDCI.xlsx.
63 See also an article by Mariano Aronés Palomino concerning the difficulties of teachers in the VRAEM: https://redaccion.lamula.pe/2015/11/11/a-que-se-enfrenta-diariamente-un-docente-en-el-vraem-un-antropologo-te-lo-cuenta/danielavila/ and a presentation of Aronés: Ensenar y educar en una zona de conflicto: El caso de los profesores/as del Valle de los ríos Apurímac, Ene y Mantaro, Ayacucho, November 2015: http://seminarioanual.cies.org.pe/2015/sites/default/files/mesas/ARONES%20FORGE.pdf.
64 http://eudora.vivienda.gob.pe/OBSERVATORIO/PAZYDESARROLLO/2007/CUSCO_LACONVENCION/ PDU_KIMBIRI.pdf page 21.
65 http://elcomercio.pe/sociedad/peru/declaran-estado-emergencia-distritos-huancavelica-y-cusco-noticia-1930834.
66 http://sdv.midis.gob.pe/Infomidis/#/.
67 http://elcomercio.pe/sociedad/cusco/acusaron-terroristas-y-mataron-hoy-vuelven-casa-noticia-1864809.
68 www.ruv.gob.pe/RUV/ConsultasLinea/Libro02/Listado_Web02.aspx.
69 www.inforegion.pe/208937/entregan-ganado-vacuno-a-pobladores-de-kimbiri/.
70 www.inforegion.pe/146155/vacan-a-alcalde-de-kimbiri-humberto-pelayo-chavez-nunez/comment-page-1/ www.inforegion.pe/146628/vacado-alcalde-de-kimbiri-presenta-recurso-extraordinario-ante-jne/.
71 http://larepublica.pe/impresa/politica/767665-piden-11-anos-de-carcel-para-electo-congresista-fujimorista-dipas.

72 www.web.onpe.gob.pe/modElecciones/elecciones/elecciones2016/PRP2V2016/participacion-ciudadana-Nacional-070909-Pie.html.

73 This analysis refers to 42 testimonies reviewed that are available in the electronic archive based at the *Defensoria del Pueblo* for the communities of Chuschi, Lucanamarca, Kimbiri and Santa Rosa.

74 Paredes and Correa (2011) investigated 15 communities in six departments of Peru, in which collective reparation projects were implemented in 2007/2008. They also found technical problems with the implementation of the projects and a missing link to the reparation program leading to medium levels of satisfaction. Only 42% of their interviewees knew that the project was a form of reparation.

References

APRODEH. 2008. *Chuschi, 16 Años de Lucha Hasta Alcanzar Justicia*. Lima. https://de.scribd.com/document/342654567/Chuschi-16-anos-de-lucha-pdf.

Barrantes, Rafael. 2007. "Memoria y Justicia En La Opinión Pública Peruana. Reflexiones a Partir de La Encuesta Nacional Sobre Percepciones de Memoria y Reconciliación." *Memoria. Revista Sobre Cultura, Democracia y Derechos Humanos*, Lima: IDEHPUCP, 2: 29–38.

CMAN (Comisión Multisectorial de Alto Nivel). 2017. Balance del Nivel de Cumplimiento del Programa de Reparaciones. Lima. CMAN.

CVR (Comisión de la Verdad y Reconciliación). 2003. "Informe Final." Lima.

CVR (Comisión de la Verdad y Reconciliación). 2010. "Hatun Willakuy: Abbreviated Version of the Final Report of the Truth and Reconciliation Commission." Lima.

Del Pino, Ponciano. 1996. "Tiempos de Guerra y de Dioses: Ronderos, Evangélicos y Senderistas En El Valle Del Río Apurímac." In *Las Rondas Campesinas y La Derrota de Sendero Luminoso*, edited by Carlos Iván Degregori, Orin Starn, José Coronel and Ponciano Del Pino, 117–188. Estudios de La Sociedad Rural, 15. Lima: IEP.

Díaz, Fernanda Daniela. 2015. "El Neosenderismo y El Tráfico Ilícito de Drogas En El Perú." *ESD. Estudios de Seguridad y Defensa* 5: 123–146.

Dixon, Peter J. 2016. "Reparations, Assistance and the Experience of Justice: Lessons from Colombia and the Democratic Republic of the Congo." *International Journal of Transitional Justice* 10 (1): 88–107.

Falconí, Carola, Edilberto Jímenez, and Giovanni Alfaro. 2007. *Lluqanamarka: Llaqtanchikpa Yuyariynin. Lucanamarca: Memorias de Nuestro Pueblo*. Lima: Asociación de Familiares Víctimas de la Violencia Política del Distrito de Santiago de Lucanamarca, Municipalidad Distrital de Santiago de Lucanamarca, COMISEDH.

Firchow, Pamina. 2013. "Must Our Communities Bleed to Receive Social Services? Development Projects and Collective Reparations Schemes in Colombia." *Journal of Peacebuilding & Development* 8 (3): 50–63.

———. 2014. "The Implementation of the Institutional Programme of Collective Reparations in Colombia." *Journal of Human Rights Practice* 6 (2): 356–375.

Flórez Salcedo, Gustvo. 2012. "Rivalidades Comunales y Contiendas Electorales: Micropolítica En Las Elecciones Distritales de Chuschi. El Caso de Las Comunidades Campesinas de Chuschi y Quispillaccta." In *Tensiones y Tranformaciones En Comunidades Campesinas*, edited by Alejandro Diez Hurtado, 225–261. Lima: Pontificia Universidad Católica del Perú.

Huaycha Cayllahua, Fredy S. 2013. "Batallas Comunales: Reconocimiento Legal, Conflictos Territoriales y Violencia Política En La Comunidad Campesina de Quispillaccta. Caso Cuchoquesera (1941–1983)." Thesis. Ayacucho, Peru: Universidad Nacional de San Cristóbal de Huamanga.

Ipince, Yasmin Calmet, and Diego Salazar. 2016. "Política Antisubversiva En El Perú: VRAEM Una Nueva Era de Violaciones de Derechos Humanos?".

Isbell, Billie Jean. 1985. *To Defend Ourselves: Ecology and Ritual in an Andean Village*. Prospect Heights, IL: Waveland Press.

López, Noam, and Sofía Vizcarra Castillo. 2012. "La Cadena de Valor de La Cocaína: Un Análisis Georreferenciado Del Vrae." *Politai: Revista de Ciencia Política* 3 (4): 79–92.

López Villanes, Noam. 2014. "Political speeches from local authorities about the coca leaf in the districts of Kimbir and Pichari 2006–2010." *Revista de Ciencia Política y Gobierno* 1 (1): 157–178.

Mendoza, Rafael Ramírez. 2016. "Una Lectura Crítica de La Memoria Emblemática de La CVR Desde Los Testimonios de La Masacre de Lucanamarca." In *Dando Cuenta: Estudios Sobre El Testimonio de La Violencia Política En El Perú (1980–2000)*, edited by Francesca Denegri and Alexandra Hibbett, 211–236. Lima: Pontifica Universidad católica del Perú.

Municipalidad Distrital de Chuschi. 2007. "Plan Integral de Reparaciones Del Distrito de Chuschi 2008–2015."

Paredes, Sonia, and Cristián Correa. 2011. "Perú: ¿Cuánto Se Ha Reparado En Nuestras Comunidades?" ICTJ. www.ictj.org/publication/per%C3%BA-%C2%BFcu%C3%A1nto-se-ha-reparado-en-nuestras-comunidades.

Ramirez Castillo, Nora. 2007. "Erinnern Für Ein Neues Leben Die Peruanische Kommission Für Wahrheit Und Versöhnung Aus Der Sicht Der Betroffenen Am Beispiel Des Andendorfes Lucanamarca." Diplomarbeit. Klagenfurt: Alpen-Adria-University.

Rojas-Perez, Isaias. 2017. *Mourning Remains: State Atrocity, Exhumations, and Governing the Disappeared in Peru's Postwar Andes*. Stanford, CA: Stanford University Press.

Root, Rebecca K. 2012. *Transitional Justice in Peru*. New York: Palgrave Macmillan.

Theidon, Kimberly. 2013. *Intimate Enemies: Violence and Reconciliation in Peru*. Pennsylvania Studies in Human Rights. Philadelphia: University of Pennsylvania Press.

Ulfe, María Eugenia. 2013. *¿Y Después de la Violencia Que Queda ?: Víctimas, Ciudadanos y Reparaciones en el Contexto Post-CVR en el Perú*. Buenos Aires: CLACSO.

Ulfe, María Eugenia, Vera Lucía Ríos, and Ximena Málaga. 2015. "Una Mirada Etnográfica al Programa Integral de Reparaciones." Revista Argumentos. Lima: IEP.

Villagaray Yanqui, Sixto Marcelino. 2014. "Recovery of Degraded Land for Coca Cultivation (Erythroxylon Coca) in Vraem, Peru, with Application of Agroforestry Technology." *Acta Nova* 6: 210.

Waardt, Mijke de. 2014. "In the Name of the Victims?: Victim-Survivor Associations Negotiating for Recognition in Post-Conflict Peru." Dissertation. Amsterdam: VU University.

Weissert, Markus. 2016. "Memories of Violence Dreams of Development – Memorialisation Initiatives in the Peruvian Andes." Dissertation. Berlin: Free University.

Yezer, Caroline. 2008. "Who Wants to Know? Rumors, Suspicions, and Opposition to Truth-Telling in Ayacucho." *Latin American and Caribbean Ethnic Studies* 3 (3): 271–289.

Zamora Castellares, Gabriela. 2014. *La Constitución de Comunidades En El Contexto de Violencia Política En El Valle Del Rio Apurímac, Ene y Mantaro 1980–2000. Informe de Proyecto de Tesis Para Optar El Grado de Bachiller En Historia.* Thesis. Ayacucho: Universidad Nacional de San Cristóbal de Huamanga.

Zenitagoya, Mario. 2012. "Ayacucho: Denuncian Que Reparaciones Colectivas No Son Equitativas En Lucanamarca." *Ideele Radio* (blog). April 3. http://redideeleradio.blogspot.com/2012/04/denuncian-que-reparaciones-colectivas.html.

Chapter 5

Ten villages, truth, reparations, and social cohesion

Analysis of six further post-conflict communities

I will expand the analysis to a comparison of ten post-conflict communities to determine whether the patterns found in the four communities appear in other communities as well. The following table summarizes the attention from the TRC and reparations, indicating where exhumations took place, testimonies were collected and used in trials as well as whether there were collective and individual reparations in the village (Table 5.1).

I chose two villages near the high-attention cases Lucanamarca (Julo and Alanya) and Chuschi (Uchuyri and Quispillacta) and one of Kimbiri's neighboring villages (Nuevo Progreso). Querobamba is a district capital in another area of Ayacucho with medium attention. The TRC only went to Querobamba, Quispillacta, and Uchuyri. In three communities, a collective reparation project

Table 5.1 Transitional justice attention in ten post-conflict communities

	TRC		*Reparations*		*Coll. project*
Lucanamarca	high	exh. + test. + trial	high	coll. + ind.	fish (not working)
Chuschi	high	exh. + test. + trial	high	coll. + ind.	house (working)
Santa Rosa	med	test.	med	ind.	
Kimbiri	low		med	ind.	
Julo	low		high	coll. + ind.	cows (half working)
Alanya	low		high	coll. + ind.	cows (half working)
Quispillacta	med	exh. + test.	med	ind.	
Uchuyri	med	exh. + test.	high	coll. + ind.	water (not working)
Nuevo Progreso	low		med	ind.	
Querobamba	med	test.	med	ind.	

Source: Own elaboration and data.

was implemented (Julo, Alanya, and Uchuyri) while the other three did not have such a project. In all six communities, there are people registered in the RUV but only very few received individual economic reparations. In Quispillacta, Nuevo Progreso, and Querobamba, none of the interviewed people received reparations.

San Antonio de Julo (district of Lucanamarca)[1]

San Antonio de Julo (Julo from now on) is one of the *anexos* of Lucanamarca and shares its geographical and social characteristics. The population is completely dependent on agriculture and the poverty index and malnutrition in children are very high. About 40 families live here. According to the interviewees, the main problem in Julo today is the lack of water leading to problems with the food supply and in agriculture. Some added that the community was not well organized. Social cohesion is low, and the same patterns appear as in Lucanamarca. Solidarity has diminished in the last years. The traditions such as *ayni* have become unpopular and people got used to working for money. Envy is high as in the other cases. Conflicts are present and are mainly about territory or water. Violence and domestic violence are still present but crime rates are falling due to the recent ban of alcohol in the community (J7: 37; J9: 36).

New political violence could occur, according to the community members, and some mention that there are still rebels in the area. The community has high expectations toward the state that have not been fulfilled. They demand projects, mainly to help with the water supply and education. Some community members receive state attention in the form of social programs but information is not extensive, and there is confusion about the requirements and critics state that these programs would lead to fewer incentives for women to work (J1: 77).

During the internal armed conflict, the inhabitants of Julo suffered from the violence as well but not to the same extent as in the village of Lucanamarca. There was no road access to Julo during that time and when groups were passing the community treated Shining Path in the same way as they did the military and did not declare themselves to be on either side. However, of course, the violence still had important consequences and continues to affect the community both physically and mentally.

Concerning transitional justice in Julo, the TRC did not come to the village itself and the awareness is very low. Only three interviewed community members state that they have heard of the commission. They took notice of the work in the district capital Lucanamarca, but knowledge is low and people here confuse the TRC with the reparation program.

Regarding reparations, the awareness is very high though. The village received a collective reparation project in 2013. They chose a cattle project although some community members voted for a water project. The idea of the communal project was that families could improve their food supply as well as their economic situation with the consumption and commercialization of milk products.

However, it was not successful. Some of the milk cows given were not of the quality promised and did not deliver any milk or less than promised (J1: 52; J8: 47). In 2015, only eight or nine of the 40 cows were still alive, the others died due to the lack of food because they were not suitable for Andean conditions and their feed had not been planned accordingly before the cows were given to them. Emotions ran high when the cows were received but the disappointment afterwards was even higher.

In summary, the collective reparation project implemented in the form of milk cows has led to medium satisfaction in some community members, who managed their cows thanks to their experience and suitable land (J8: 47). But the majority was not satisfied because the cows were not of high quality and many died rapidly: "I received a cow but it died because of the grass, alfalfa. Only two month no more, it died immediately. I ate the meat no more, many people's cows died, some sold them" (J7: 48). The project did not enhance communal work or social relations within the community, everyone had their own cow and so the project did not have a communal character. Of the interview partners, only four said that they received reparations although the others received a cow as well – I observed again the problem that they did not perceive the reparations as such, especially as this project was carried out by the municipality with funding from the CMAN. The perceived subjective exposure is very low. The compensatory effect is also very low if not negative because people remained discontent.

Community members also stated that someone may have received individual reparations, but I did not find anyone or even someone who was registered in the RUV. The seven self-classified victims are still awaiting their individual reparations but have not even registered yet. One woman explains her difficulty with the reparations that she would be entitled to because her husband was killed by Shining Path:

> I cannot receive anything, I could not do the process. They told me, you have to get this and that paper and I could not do so. Later they took my papers to Ayacucho and Lima but afterwards I did not hear anything of it. (J10: 49)

Just like this woman, many people in Julo are not satisfied because their expectations were not fulfilled.

Carmen de Alanya (district of Lucanamarca)

Carmen de Alanya (Alanya hereafter) is another *anexo* of Lucanamarca, formally acknowledged in 2012. It shares geographical and social characteristics with Lucanamarca. The population relies entirely on agriculture, and the indexes of poverty and malnutrition in children are very high. Inhabitants are about 120, of those 70 are adults (A2: 63).

The main problems in Alanya are the lack of water and fertile territory and resulting problems in agriculture. The relatively new village is well organized, and there are many young authorities and women participating as well. The village was chosen because it was supposed to have a high level of social cohesion according to local experts consulted before. Nevertheless, Alanya also experiences the influence of migration and paid work as well as the violence, and the overall level of social cohesion is also low. The traditional *ayni* and *minka* are not practiced anymore (A2: 28; A4: 37). According to the interviewees, the village's development depends highly on local authorities and whether those are concerned or not (A3: 67). Solidarity is present only when severe problems or deaths occur. An exception to this, however, was the construction of the new pre-school, where all community members contributed (A9: 29). Conflicts arise mainly because of territory disputes. According to one authority member, new conflicts and violence in the district could arise when those who did not have land protested. Overall, there is less violence today because the community prohibited alcohol as well (A2: 34; A1: 21). One interviewee suggested forming new *rondas campesinas* to be prepared in case of future unrest (A2: 39). Some people in Alanya receive state attention in the form of social programs. Only a few are satisfied (A5: 81). Others complained that there was not enough information about the programs and that it was not clear what the regulations were and who could receive something. Furthermore, the amount given was not sufficient (A2: 63; A9: 65). The people of Juno expected more attention and more projects from the state.

During the internal armed conflict, inhabitants of Alanya suffered from the violence as well but not as much as the village of Lucanamarca. As in Julo, one of the authorities explained that the violent groups had only passed through Alanya, and did not commit massacres there, but still entered the houses and asking for food. If the villagers provided this, they could keep out of trouble (A1: 29). However, there are still about 10 families in Alanya that were severely affected.

In terms of the implementation of transitional justice, the TRC did not come to the village of Alanya but six interviewed community members have heard of the commission and one woman talked about the exhumations carried out in Lucanamarca. Nearly all the people interviewed thought that the commission came to give reparations.

Regarding reparations, the awareness was very high. The village received a collective reparation project in 2013. They received the same milk cows as the community of Julo (6.1.1.). Two people explained to me that they had wanted a tractor but that CMAN decided to give them milk cows instead (A1: 39; A3: 52). Others stated that they had chosen the cattle themselves. The idea of the communal project was the same as in Julo that families would improve their food supply and their economic situation with the consumption and commercialization of milk products. However, here too it was not successful. Some of the 35 milk cows were not of the high quality as promised and did not deliver any milk or not the amount that was promised. Only 3–5 liters of milk would be not a viable business according to the interviewees. When sold the cows only fetched

1,000 PEN and not the 3,500 PEN promised. One authority states that the mayor mismanaged the money (A4: 68). Here I find the problem of widespread corruption and problems in the technical implementation again. Only very few community members are happy with their cows, which are giving some milk. Others are not at all satisfied (A8: 55).

> I did not receive anything, [Q: You did not receive cows?] A cow yes, we received it, some have died, some don't have milk, nothing. They brought cows that were discarded. This is bad, some, only 4 or 5 people have them, but others not.
>
> (A2: 47)

As this statement makes clear another time, the cows are not perceived as reparations. As in Julo, the municipality carried out the project, and the mayor used it to promote himself. In summary, the collective project has barely led to any higher satisfaction in the community members. The attempt to form an association to commercialize milk products failed because the majority of community members was not interested and the cows simply did not give enough milk (A3: 50).[2] The project did not enhance communal work or social cohesion and the compensatory effect was very low.

With regard to individual reparations, there were rumors that someone had received something but I could not find anyone. One of the authorities calculates that there were about 10 people who would be entitled to reparations (A1: 38–40). Three of my interviewees were registered in the RUV but also still waiting for their reparations. Community members were not well informed about the program and reported about problems with the registration process and payment of the reparations (A5: 64). An elderly man, nearly killed by Shining Path, has been waiting for his reparation for years. He demands support for his health because he is suffering from the consequences of the violence and does not understand why he did not receive anything. He claims that they have been promising him reparations for years and that he has submitted more and more documents but that there was no information and no response: "If I would have this reparation I would maybe get healthy again but they are asking more documents, what would that be. I would not want cattle but I would want to cure my health" (A6: 43–44). One woman concludes very critically: "It would have been better if they would have been given nothing, now they made them remember and caused more pain" (A8: 61).

Quispillacta (district of Chuschi)

Quispillacta is a very traditional indigenous village. It was recognized as a *comunidad de indígenas* in 1935 already and as *comunidad campesina* in 1944. During all of its existence, there have been conflicts with its neighboring community of Chuschi (Chapter 5.2). The two villages are only divided by a small river and Quispillacta belongs to the district of Chuschi. There are 13 smaller villages belonging to Quispillacta and a large area of land. It has been fighting to become a district for some years now, causing further conflicts not only with the neighboring community but also within the community. Quispillacta has a strong basis in Lima where people have been fighting for the interests of the village for centuries.[3] Therefore, it seemed a very interesting village to assess the process of transitional justice and social cohesion there.

Quispillacta is known in Peru as an indigenous community with its own traditions in social and political order, culture, and clothing. One example is that the *varayoc* still play an important role, as in Chuschi, they are traditional voluntary authorities that meet and work every day for the village (Q1: 14). However, surprisingly, I observed that trust in local authorities is not higher than in other villages (Q6: 28). This is also connected to its attempts of becoming a district in which, according to my interviews and observations, the local authorities were not always transparent and seemed to manipulate people (see also Chapter 5).

The statute of the community Quispillacta is very rigid as it demands participation in communal works with a high fee and sanctions for non-participation. These communal practices and solidarity work are more common than in the other communities. One example is the *Yarca Aspiy*, celebrated at the beginning of September that begins the planting season, in which local traditional and governmental authorities gather together to discuss the water situation, as it is also tradition in other communities. The whole community then is then gathered to clean irrigation canals a process that is accompanied by music and dances (Marcos 2010, 29–35). These spiritual Andean traditions were challenged by Shining Path and by the Evangelical church, which has been growing since the 1960s. A high percentage of community members belongs to them and follows their strong rules. However, Quispillacta experiences the same developments and influences as other villages. One authority explains that nowadays people had less interest in the community and agriculture because they study other things, some are professionals earning money and do not want to work for free anymore (Q3: 22). Solidarity is in decline. As important positive changes interviewees mentioned more gender equality, especially the participation of women in assemblies and authority positions as well as less domestic violence. The risk of new political violence is quite high according to many community members. The state is important for the people of Quispillacta but does not fulfill the expectations, although attention in form of social programs is evaluated very positively. Surprisingly, I find lower social cohesion in Quispillacta than in the other villages.

During the conflict, Quispillacta suffered many fatalities as well. The village found itself between Shining Path and the military. Chuschi first supported Shining Path, then changed sides and also fought against Quispillacta (Q1: 39). People told me that the Chuschinos used the situation to seek revenge for older conflicts and that they accused people of belonging to Shining Path. Many people reported the fear they lived through and that they had to sleep in the mountains hiding (Q9: 56). Consequences of the violence suffered are still present.

The TRC came to Chuschi and collected testimonies. In Quispillacta, they were inviting for testimonies as well. The bodies exhumed in Chuschi/Uchuyri were mainly from Quispillacta. But people are not satisfied with the TRC and some state the commission did not collect the histories properly and call it: "a commission of lies" (Q1: 49). One woman states: "To me it seems like they have not done a good job, maybe they did it for money. Because they make those families remember instead of giving them consolation. It would have been better to give them money directly" (Q5: 71). As in the other villages, the TRC is judged in connection with the reparations, and it is perceived as entity to bring reparations by nearly all people. NGOs have been very active in the upper part of Quispillacta but not in the village itself and they also did not work in the area of human rights or transitional justice but agriculture and housing.

The awareness of the reparation program is lower in Quispillacta than in all the other communities. CMAN lists a collective reparation project in the village of Quispillacta. However, according to the community members and authorities, there have not been any collective reparations in the village itself. The awareness and knowledge of the collective projects in other neighboring communities is also low. The same applies to individual reparations. This makes sense when the low levels of attention by the reparation program are taken into account. There were only very few individual reparations being paid in Quispillacta. I did not find any receiver and only one person registered in the RUV. The problems in Quispillacta are very similar to those in the other communities. One woman explains that she could not provide necessary documents and witnesses (Q6: 65). Community members do not understand why some people received something while others got nothing. Furthermore, there is a lack of understanding why different amounts were paid to families, which leads to further discontent:

> In regard to the reparations, it is minimal, very cheap. To others they gave 5,000 for their husbands, 5,000 is he worth? To others they gave 8,000, this makes the community wonder, how can it be that a "campesino" from here values 5,000, 8,000, 10,000, but in Lima, those of the case of Barrios Altos, I don't know which other affected persons, it seems that they have received 30,000 or more in the Inter-American Human Rights system, they appealed to other nations and the state is paying a check. But for a community member here? What a difference in reparations! We are bad.
>
> (Q1: 51)

He refers to another case in Lima that was treated in the Inter-American Court of Human Rights and the rumors surrounding the case. The same man tells of the people's distrust of the registration process. And again, interviewees refer to the lack of information and disappointment:

> I did not know that the tortured ones will receive a benefit. But my husband said that for being tortured I will get something. But when I am asking people they say, he himself can receive but he already died and I did not receive anything
>
> (Q9: 78)

San Juan de Uchuyri (district of Chuschi)

San Juan de Uchuyri (Uchuyri from here onwards) is another *anexo* of Chuschi. Uchuyri is officially recognized as *centro poblado* and *comunidad campesina*. There are about 300 inhabitants. It shares the geographical and social characteristics of Chuschi. Only three kilometers separate the two villages. With regard to basic services, the situation in Uchuyri has improved but further improvements in water supply, education, and health attendance are necessary. Community members currently have to use Chuschi's facilities. At the time of the study, the authorities were judged very critically, as not caring and not prepared for the positions (U5: 26). In terms of social cohesion, Uchuyri experienced the same dynamics than the other communities. The conflict reinforced migration to the cities and mainly young people left the community. The increase in paid work led to a decrease of mutual help and voluntary work. There is still solidarity but less than before and only in severe situations (U1: 29). The state is present mainly via its social programs or infrastructure works but not to the degree the people expect. The social programs, however, are mainly seen positively. There were different NGO programs mentioned positively as well that organized training or gave out seeds. Some said they had helped more than the state (U3: 65; U4: 58; U8: 23; U9: 22–24).

During the internal armed conflict, Uchuyri suffered from violence on the part of both Shining Path and the state forces. People slept in the mountains to hide, and many were tortured. Some people were killed in Uchuyri, along the road. They were not originally from Uchuyri but community members decided in one night to bury them all together in a mass grave (U1: 55; U6: 47). In Uchuyri, the narrative of Fujimori as the bringer of peace is also present, although community members were tortured or harmed by state forces as well (U4: 22; U6: 63).

The TRC is known by most interview partners because they exhumed the mass grave, however, under the name of Chuschi although it was on territory belonging to Uchuyri. Community members state that this is not right, that the history was changed and say that the TRC was mistaken (U1: 54). Confusion with the reparation program is high, and satisfaction with the commission low. Awareness of the reparation program is even lower than of the TRC. Despite the fact that Uchuyri received a collective project, not all community members know the reparation program and the knowledge is limited. Only members of the authorities who were directly involved with the collective project know more about it. In 2009, a water drain system was installed. It was supposed to benefit 25 families and their land directly and 55 families indirectly, increase agricultural production and therefore the income of the families, combat malnutrition, create work possibilities, and stop migration. In the official description of the project, no reference is made to social life in the community. The project was meant to "improve the quality of life" of the affected people.[4] However, the water system does not work because it is not connected to the water reservoir. As in the cases of Julo and Alanya, technical problems hinder the positive impact of the collective reparation project.

Concerning individual reparations, I found only one community member who has received economic reparations for his mother, who was killed in the conflict. He bought cattle with the 5,000 PEN and said that it helped his father. However, he is not satisfied because he was told by the TRC that he would get a health insurance:

> I wanted that they give me reparations in health, we are waiting for that. But, it changed something because they give 5.000 Soles to my father, with this we made a change, we bought high-quality cows and my father's situation is a bit better now.
>
> (U9: 74–75)

Others stated as well that they were still waiting for their reparations. Three of the interviewees are registered in the RUV but complain about the regulations:

> I have my certificate. [...] Until today there is nothing. They said they would help but nothing, they only gave for the disappeared and the dead ones, for no one else. There are many people in Uchuyri that are registered as victims, there are many of us. In collective reparations we demanded, when we went to the inauguration in Cancha Cancha [neighboring community]. The mayor helped us. But it is not working, the water system that was constructed.
>
> (U4: 49–50)

This interview makes clear that it was the initiative of the local authorities and the support of the district mayor that made the collective project possible. However, the expectations of the community members were not fulfilled. Another authority expressed his discontent:

> The government does not comply with the reparations. How many have been affected? Some got it, others died already in the whole process. These are not reparations to me. What it did is to make them remember another time, open the wounds and make them cry, live this moment again emotionally. [...] in education, health, living, these exist on the paper, no more. Only those who are close to the government receive reparations and certificates – those most closely to the government receive something. [...] But it does not reach those who were really affected.
>
> (U1: 61)

Nuevo Progreso (district of Kimbiri)

Nuevo Progreso (Progreso hereafter) is an *anexo* of the district of Kimbiri. It was newly created during the internal armed conflict and evolved out of a self-defense committee. Before the conflict, there were hardly any fixed communities in the

VRAEM, settlements developed parallel, and organized themselves to combat Shining Path as explained already. In the case of Nuevo Progreso, the founders decided to leave the neighboring community because of internal conflicts and created a new one in 1983. They installed a self-defense committee and community at the same time and sought recognition from the navy and the organization of self-defense committees. In 1999, it was finally recognized as a *centro poblado.* The community was created to provide security and to encourage development and social cohesion (Zamora Castellares 2014). Progreso has grown fast and today it has about 3,000 inhabitants and consists of 13 villages. The main problem is the regulation of territory followed by a lack of water, health, and education. As far as social cohesion in Progreso is concerned, it is a mixed picture. Trust is relatively high as is solidarity. But, as in the other communities, mutual work and helping others are in decline. The community developed in infrastructure and basic services. Like Kimbiri, it benefits from the *Canon* budget but authorities and community members complain about corruption. Coca has brought development as well as many problems (NP2: 22). Some people are against the state because they do not want the eradication programs of the coca. They are scared of losing their income (NP6: 69). All of the community members said that the central government was far away and did not know the reality of the village. The *Canon* is seen as the state's only presence (NP10: 73).

During the internal armed conflict, there were fights between rebel groups, state forces, and self-defense committees in Nuevo Progreso. The TRC investigated one case of simultaneous attacks in Tulumayo, Nuevo Progreso, and Tocache, when ten rebels and seven soldiers died in 1989. People talk about the discrimination they suffered, after being accused of being "terrorists" when they went to the cities to study or work there (NP1: 57). As in Santa Rosa, the locals see themselves as the ones who brought peace to the country. However, they still feel the social, political, and psychological consequences of the violence suffered.

The TRC did not have any presence in Nuevo Progreso: "They [the TRC] existed only in name, no more. I never saw their results for the VRAEM, They only worked from the cabinets in Ayacucho and Lima" (NP2: 61). A community member said that the TRC should come to all places and investigate all cases to deserve the "truth" in its name (NP10: 63). Four people stated that they had heard about the commission but their knowledge is very low.The people of Progreso are very critical of reparations. Although the awareness is high, information is low and they only have heard rumors surrounding the reparation program. People did not show a lot of interest in collective reparations because they have the *Canon* budget. Nuevo Progreso made no attempts to apply for a collective project. And as far as individual reparations are concerned, there is no RUV office there but some community members are registered. One member of the authorities explained that they had recently started to register people and that there were more in the *sierra* (NP5: 65). There is distrust toward people coming from the cities to register for programs, not least because they do not speak Quechua as one woman explained. She confuses reparations with social programs but her distrust is obvious: "Nothing, I never received anything. What is this collaboration? When they came I did not let them into my house. What is this, I said" (NP8: 58). Another community member who lost his mother because of Shining Path and is registered in the RUV stated: "Until today nothing, it is in process. But I don't think they will give it to me" (NP10: 68). The locals do not understand why some people profited and others did not and who was the "right victim". They express discontent as this man: "If the government wants to bring forward this reparation, it has to be for all and with true information, because many of the real fighters and pacificators are not the beneficiaries" (NP1: 67).

Querobamba

Querobamba was created as *comunidad indigena* in 1943; in 1957, the district was created, and, in 1986, the province Sucre with Querobamba as its capital. The authorities include the communal president and communal board, the mayor and council, governor and *juez de paz*. As a district capital, Querobamba has various institutions, which makes it stand apart from the other five cases. In the 1980s, the road was constructed to improve the connection to Ayacucho. The district Querobamba has about 2,200 inhabitants, in the capital itself live about 80 families. Poverty is at 40%, and, for August 2017, the MIDIS lists the following numbers of beneficiaries of the different programs in the district: 155 families in *Juntos*, 231 people in *Pension 65*, and 14 children in *Qali Warma* in two educational institutions.[5]

In terms of social cohesion, there is still some solidarity in Querobamba, but solidarity and trust have diminished. Local authorities are not seen as trustworthy either (QB7: 20; 26). Many of the interview partners complained about the acting president as well as about people's decreasing interest in the community and lack of participation in communal activities. The acting president herself mentioned that social values and traditions such as solidarity and trust have been lost, also because of the conflict (QB13: 15). Trust in local authorities is the lowest in all communities. Trust in fellow community members, however, is fairly high.

During the internal armed conflict, Shining Path started working in the local schools and some community members joined their fight. However, in the mid-1980s, the community decided in to stand up against Shining Path and asked the military for help and the military arrived in the community. During these years, about 80 people died or disappeared in the district of Querobamba. The people, however, aim to close this chapter of the past and only two interview partners said that they wanted to remember the past as history. There are no communal memory projects. CMAN organized a public ceremony during which certificates were giving to victims in April 2010, but none of my interview partners mentioned this event.

The TRC did come to Querobamba to collect testimonies. However, only five people have heard of the commission, connecting it directly to reparations. They complain that the commission did not do a proper job and demand: "That they investigate the reality" (QB2: 49). One person mentioned exhumations: "It [the TRC] came these days, many people, they have exhumed, they said that reparations will come but until today I have not seen anything. My wife's father and grandfather were killed but she did not receive reparations" (QB12: 52). This man must be confusing the commission with another entity because the TRC did not carry out exhumations in Querobamba, they only registered burial sites. This is another example of an interview that I would have liked to conduct myself to find out more about this exhumation.

Other community members are also unsatisfied with the TRC:

> Well, there is an injustice, the one that tells 'I was a victim', but us those that have been there, are not recognized, [...], many times the TRC did not ask who was a victim. [...] I demand that the real victims are recognized and not those that fled and came back, we are living with this trauma, we have seen people getting killed. The others left and now say they are victims, those who have been here, the old ones have to be recognized.
>
> (QB6: 55–57)

The question of who is a victim arises in Querobamba just as it does in the other communities. And TCR's success is measured based on reparations received and so just as in other communities the ratings are low.

Two of my interview partners said that there had been reparations within the community, but none of the interviewees had received anything and only one is registered in the RUV. Only one had heard about collective reparations but not in Querobamba itself. One of the municipality functionaries mentioned that they were about to open an office for registering more affected people and providing information about the reparation program at the end of 2015 (Exp6). The people who were affected by the violence, are disappointed because reparations are only for dead victims: "Well, yes, only for the dead ones, other people, victims of different kind, no" (QB6: 60). They also complain about the perceived unjust distribution of reparations: "People who have never been here have received reparations" (QB2: 51). This registered person was still waiting for his reparations: "They came here, I have it registered. They acknowledged us for reparations, they said they will pay something" (QB7: 55). Others state that reparations would not be able to compensate for the social consequences of the violence suffered (QB13: 46).

The implementation of transitional justice in the communities

Different transitional justice measures were applied in the ten communities. Out of the communities analyzed, Lucanamarca, Chuschi, and Uchuyri have seen the highest attention from the TRC and reparation program. The three communities Quispillacta, Alanya, and Julo had medium attention and the communities of Santa Rosa, Querobamba, Kimbiri, and Nuevo Progreso only low attention.

In Lucanamarca, the TRC collected 70 testimonies, carried out exhumations, held a re-burial ceremony, and prepared a trial with the participation of community members. A communal memorial was installed by the human rights organization *COMISEDH*. A collective reparation project was implemented, but did not succeed, and only some individual reparations were paid. The high attention is partly due to the work of the NGO that acted as an intermediary between the applicants and state institutions.

In Chuschi, an exhumation and reburial were also carried out by the TRC, testimonies collected, a trial prepared, a collective reparation project was implemented and a few individual reparations paid. This work was also supported by the human rights organization *Paz y Esperanza*.

The exhumation carried out in Chuschi was on the boundary to Uchuyri, and some testimonies were collected here as well, a collective project was implemented after the local authorities had fought for it, and a few individual reparations were paid.

The community Quispillacta was part of the exhumation because the people exhumed on the border of Chuschi and Uchuyri were mainly from Quispillacta. Some of its *anexos* have experienced collective projects but not Quispillacta itself, at least no one knew about it. Only a few individual reparations have been paid until today.

The communities Alanya and Julo have received a collective reparation project but the TRC did not come there. However, some community members noticed it or were participating in its work in the capital of the district, Lucanamarca. They did not seem to have received individual reparations yet although some rumors exist of someone having receiving something. The collective projects came to the villages because of the high attention the district of Lucanamarca received and the support from the NGO.

Santa Rosa was visited by the TRC for a couple of days to collect testimonies, and some community members have also received individual reparations. The number of registered people had risen because the municipality installed an office for attention. The money transferred to the municipality of Santa Rosa for the implementation of the collective projects seems to have been misused for other purposes. Projects were implemented in neighboring villages.

Querobamba was visited by the TRC as well, some people are registered in the RUV but only very few have received individual reparations. There are hardly any collective projects in the area, and I could not observe attempts to change it on behalf of the local authorities. There were, however, plans to install an office to offer help with registration and information to affected people.

Kimbiri and Nuevo Progreso were not visited by the TRC. Some community members gave their testimony in other places. Only recently, they applied for some collective projects in the area but because the region receives the *Canon* interest in this type support is not so high. However, recently the interest in individual reparations is rising and the municipality of Kimbiri also tried to offer help to victims to register and receive information. Some community members received a payment already. In Nuevo Progreso, there were no such initiatives for reparations.

The community of San José de Huyma (only six interviews conducted, in the district of Lucanamarca) faces the problem that they were only recently recognized as a community and are therefore not listed in the register for affected communities that would allow them to demand collective reparations, although community members have been affected.

The implementation or non-implementation of transitional justice measures depends on national politics on the one hand and on local authorities and initiatives on the other. Furthermore, NGOs or victims' associations can influence the process. The attention from the TRC was influenced by the preparatory work done by NGOs in Chuschi and Lucanamarca (Exp36; Exp37). It did not have the resources nor the time to visit every affected community, investigate every case, and carry out more exhumations and had to choose cases. The reparation program was also supported by NGOs in Lucanamarca, Chuschi, Alanya, and Julo. In Uchuyri, local authorities were important with their insistence. In the other communities, there was no NGO presence, and the local authorities were not focused on reparations. The very diverse number of people registered individually in the districts is also due to the support or non-support by the municipality and/or NGOs and/or special attention of CMAN functionaries.

The awareness of transitional justice

Awareness of transitional justice is also very diverse in the different communities. However, it is not necessarily correlated with the level of attention a community received.

More than 60% of all community members have heard of the TRC, with the exception of Julo and Nuevo Progreso. Knowledge about the work, the commission carried out in the different communities, is low, though. People only in Lucanamarca, Chuschi, and Uchuyri are a bit better informed. This is not surprising as these are the communities where the commission did most of its work. Many interviewed people confuse the commission with the reparation program or think that the commission's first aim was to bring reparations. Of the nearly 100 people who knew of the commission, 50% said that it came only to give money to the victims.

The reparation program is known by more than 90% of the interviewed people in Lucanamarca, Chuschi, Santa Rosa, Kimbiri, and Alanya. Quispillacta, Uchuyri, Querobamba, and Nuevo Progreso have the lowest awareness with 60%–70%. Knowledge is only higher in Lucanamarca, Chuschi, Santa Rosa, Kimbiri, and Uchuyri. There is no strong correlation between the level of the attention from the program and the knowledge about it. The collective aspect of the reparation program is known more in Chuschi, Lucanamarca, and Uchuyri.

About 70% stated that some form of reparations had been paid in their community. Only in Querobamba and Nuevo Progreso had people not heard of reparations, which is not surprising given the low implementation in those locations. In all villages, the people's focus was on individual reparations, only 45 people mentioned collective reparations.

The information available in the communities is very limited. Sometimes not even the responsible person in the municipality is well informed. Or, if the person is informed he/she does not pass the information on to the affected people. This is not only the case for reparations but for social programs as well. It depends on the local authorities whether they themselves and community members are well informed about requirements and procedures for the inscription and payments. Only few people have direct access to the regional capital of Ayacucho, where all the offices are located. Some ask their children or an NGO to help with the administrative procedure – this is especially common in Lucanamarca. People without this special access can often not access reparations or do not even know about the program, as explained above. Even in the communities with high attention such as Julo or Alanya, the knowledge is very low. Again, Lucanamarca, Chuschi, and Uchuyri are communities that are the most informed.

The perception of transitional justice

The people who know the work of the TRC, mostly welcome the general idea to write a history and investigate what happened but criticize its implementation. According to them, it did not investigate enough, disappeared family members are still not found, testimony giving was difficult and did not bring anything. Many interviewees said that its work had not been concluded and that it should carry on. Moreover, it is interesting to note that the commission is only referred to as "Comisión de la Verdad" – the appendix "reconciliation" does not seem to be important to the people. The TRC is perceived as the entity to bring reparations in nearly all communities and is evaluated accordingly.

Regarding individual reparations, I find the same problems and patterns throughout all the communities: the lack of information, confusion with social programs, many rumors, high requirements and documentation, different treatment of different victims, different and insufficient amounts of reparations paid, late compliance to the degree that at the time some victims have already died and the problem of non-transference of reparations.

Regarding collective reparations, four projects (Lucanamarca, Julo, Alanya, Uchuyri) were not successful. Those who perceived it as reparations therefore judged it negatively. And it is not only the money of the reparation program that was lost but in the cases of Lucanamarca and Uchuyri municipality funds as well. In Julo and Alanya, only very few people, three of my interview partners, are satisfied with their cow. They still see that it did not work out for their fellow community members. And there are still many affected people who do not perceive the projects as reparations. This is also true for Chuschi, where a communal house was built. This was only mentioned by one of my interview partners, the awareness, and subjective exposure to the TJ measure is very low. Furthermore, there are some rumors about neighboring villages receiving some cows or other projects, which makes community members of Chuschi jealous and even more discontent.

In Chapter 5, the analysis of the perception of the reparation program was divided in reparation receivers, non-receivers, and observers. It is difficult to classify the entire communities. Certainly, Lucanamarca and Chuschi would be receivers and Uchuyri, Julo and Alanya as well because of the collective projects received although barely any individual reparations were paid. The other communities would be non-receivers because they all have been highly affected by the internal armed conflict and did not receive compensation – apart from a few individuals. Due to the chosen research design, there are no observer-communities.

Regarding the perception, it is interesting to see that there are identical impressions in all the communities. In all communities, the majority of the people are not satisfied with the form of implementation of the reparation program, and that includes both the collective and the individual part. Most of them approve of the general idea of reparations but not its implementation. More alarmingly, they state that the way implemented had rather a negative effect because expectations were not fulfilled and new conflicts and discontent created. In all villages, I heard complaints about some people receiving something and others not – for non-transparent reasons. This differentiation created a hierarchy of victims that goes against the criteria of reparation theory. The communities with higher attention have still not been attended in the form they expected, and projects were not successful.

Most important seems to be the perception of the individual reparations because people were waiting for those in particular. However, the overall satisfaction with the reparation program is low in 2/3 of the people that know the program and low in the rest. Higher satisfaction was only found in two observers in Santa Rosa that will be analyzed more in detail in Chapter 6.

It becomes clear that the reparation program was not implemented in the form the affected people were expecting it in any of the communities. All the villages investigated did not feel properly attended to by the TRC or the reparation program.

The impact on social cohesion

The analysis of the situation of social cohesion in the different communities revealed some similar problems and developments and some particularities for each community.

Overall, I analyzed weak social cohesion in all ten communities. On the horizontal level, the interpersonal trust within families is still high but toward neighbors it is rather low. Community members stated that their fellow community members were only interested in their own matters and did not look out for the common good anymore. Solidarity had decreased and only in extreme cases like accidents and deaths did people still help each other. In Lucanamarca, Chuschi, Kimbiri, and Julo, the majority of the community members complained that solidarity was down. They stated that in the old days life in the communities had been different with more trust and solidarity. The only different case is Santa Rosa, here, trust and solidarity seem even lower as in the other communities and only recently rising again. One reason for this might be that in Santa Rosa, the memories of the "good times" before the conflict were not as present as in Lucanamarca and Chuschi. In Santa Rosa, 90% of the people stated that the situation changed positively, Kimbiri and Nuevo Progreso also have high percentages. The communities in the VRAEM were settled during or even as a result of the conflict and did not exist in this form before. In Lucanamarca and Chuschi, the conflict is seen as having destroyed everything (Falconí, Jímenez, and Alfaro 2007). This is also the official political narrative. But, when taking a closer look, it becomes clear that it is not only the conflict that caused changes in the social cohesion of the villages. Before the internal armed conflict, there were conflicts present as well and traditions and solidarity were already in decline:

The most influential factors causing changes in the social structures are the introduction of money and paid work, migration and interchange with the cities, and to a lesser degree also climate change and decentralization (Gomez Tineo and Huancahuari Evanan 2015). These phenomena are not limited to conflict prone communities nor to Peru. However, I conclude in my analysis that the conflict certainly reinforced these developments especially due to higher migration, loss of social and political leaders and the distrust spread by the violence.

The narratives of the past conflict are very diverse. Within the communities, there are different memories (the "victim-village" and the "hero-village") and perceptions of who was the main perpetrator of violence differ as well. In Lucanamarca, with its *anexos* Julo and Alanya, the victim narrative prevails, the symbol of which is the memorial for victims on the central square. Active involvement of community members is neglected. But this is not a unifying narrative because there are different kinds of victims who suffered different kinds of violence. These differences were reinforced by the TRC and reparation program focusing on the victims of the massacre only and thus creating a new hierarchy of victims, which in turn had a negative impact on social cohesion. The wish to be a victim to be eligible to receive the "reparation gift" led to a new kind of victimization. Furthermore, the state perceives victims as passive receiving "objects" not as active agents (Ulfe 2013). Attention from the state was not used to create agency. Lucanamarca and Chuschi use the notion of the victims' village to demand support but do not build agency. Interesting was the different reactions of both villages when the state planed a high-voltage power line totaling about 900 km across the district of Chuschi and Lucanamarca. Chuschi and Quispillacta both negotiated with the company in charge about the price to be paid for using the territory. Lucanamarca accepted the first offer – maybe a sign for low agency.[6]

In the district of Chuschi with the villages Chuschi, Quispillacta and Uchuyri, the narrative of the passive villages that suffered from the violence is present with Fujimori being the pacificator. In Querobamba, community members do not wish to remember the past in which they stood against Shining Path after they had first supported them. No dominant narrative can be found there.

Now, a different narrative is present in the VRAEM region. Here, the "hero-discourse" is very strong and community members want to tell their children about the fights for pacification. In these times, everyone participated in reunions, communal work, and in the fighting. People in Kimbiri, Santa Rosa, and Nuevo Progreso said that the past should be remembered and have themselves created memorials or symbols of the pacification.

Identification with the community is high in all visited communities, the lowest was found in Alanya and the highest in Chuschi and Querobamba. However, overall the differences are marginal. On the objective level changed attitudes can be observed. Participation in social and communal activities is rather low today and the people only participate if there are penalties for not doing so. Community members pursue their own interests and only want to work for money. In all communities, there are conflicts present, mainly about territory or water. Levels of envy are very high in all the communities observed. Envy is directed toward community members who are advancing economically or personally and also to the ones receiving reparations as I already elaborated. Violence is still a problem and includes violence between community members and domestic violence as well. However, people state that thanks to leys, institutions and alcohol bans it was reducing. Conflicts are mainly resolved by the local authorities.

A special situation occurs in the communities with coca. Coca offers a special income possibility for community members and brings development in form of roads but at the same time drug trafficking brings a lot of violence and conflicts. This was reported especially in Santa Rosa, where incidents already occur in the secondary school. In Kimbiri, violence increased as well while the situation in Nuevo Progreso is fairly quiet. The problem with the coca and drug trafficking also changes the state presence. In these three communities, the military and police are much more present than in the other communities although Querobamba and Chuschi also have police stations.

The main problems they mentioned were unreliable water supply, malnutrition, education, violence, poverty, and unresolved conflicts over territory. Communal development is judged mainly positively in terms of infrastructure, basic service, and education but negatively in social terms. Community members see mainly the state, local authorities, and the municipality but also NGOs as the actors responsible for this change. The relationship toward the state, however, remains difficult. The state is expected to bring projects, and good governance is measured in the attention given. Confidence in political institutions is very low. The people do not feel the presence of the state in the villages. Visits are scarce but have taken place in Lucanamarca, Chuschi, and Querobamba recently. However, people were rather disappointed that president Humala did not listen to them or fulfill their demands. Therefore, the state's importance is rated as low or medium. The community members expect social programs and improvements in infrastructure, the only form in which the state is present. Interestingly, providing security is not one of their expectations toward the state as it is in state theory and in other countries. Kimbiri is an exception again, here the community members give the state higher importance because they receive the *Canon* budget and see its importance. Santa Rosa also gives the state a fairly high importance rating because of the presence of special units to combat drug trafficking.

Due to compulsory voting, voter turnout is relatively high but apart from elections, there is hardly any political participation.[7] Moreover, the people in the rural area have a high identification with Peru as a nation but do not see themselves as active members of the state with rights or as its agents.[8] The narrative that is predominant in Chuschi matches with this perception. They see Fujimori ("*the chino*") as the one bringing the peace (without active participation from the community members). This community member stated her expectations toward the state: "The 'chino' brought the peace. The actual mayor of Peru, the president, is not doing anything for Chuschi" (CH21: 23). In Kimbiri and Santa Rosa, a different narrative is told of "how our parents have fought in the self-defense committees" (K2: 49), which is proudly displayed in memorials as well but does not lead to a different state-society relation. Identification with Peru is high in all communities referring only to the nation and not to the state, and there exist only slightly differences.

In summary, social cohesion is weak in all the ten communities investigated. As discussed, the conflict was not the only reason but an important factor for this low cohesion. All the communities experience the influence of broader education and migration to and from the cities, the change from agriculture as the main source of income to other professions, the interconnection, and communication ways, the increase in paid work and income, leading to less interest in communal activities. The conflict reinforced some of those developments. With the exception of those in Quispillacta and Querobamba interviewees stated that the violence their communities suffered still held significant importance for the community today.

Some literature overestimates the possible effects of transitional justice in this regard. However, the truth commission (CVR 2003, Vol. IX, Ch. 2.2) also stated clearly that the reparation program was neither meant nor able to solve the structural problems of poverty, inequality, and exclusion. Still, TRC and reparations were meant to facilitate civic trust and social cohesion. Both, within the concept of transitional justice and in the conception of the Peruvian reparation program, reparations are implemented to compensate for harm suffered. They should lead to satisfaction in the affected people and help them to reconcile with the past. Collective projects should increase communal trust and solidarity and the interest in communal work. Reparation receivers should feel that their needs have been attended to by the state and increase their confidence in the state and its institutions (see Chapter 2).

In the ten communities reviewed, none of these aims could be reached due to the shortcomings in the implementation and their negative perception. This low objective exposure is reinforced by the problem of low subjective exposure. Reparations only had small influence on the social cohesion within the communities. It is a form of state attendance, but it was not successful and was therefore rather destructive for the state-communal cohesion. Expectations were not fulfilled. The social relations within the community were not enhanced.

It is worth looking at reparations in parallel to social programs. These are applied to improve the lives of poor people in the villages and focus on nutrition, health, or housing. The most well-known is the program *Juntos* in which mothers of young children receive a monthly payment of 33 US$ (100 PEN) when their children fulfill the requirements of regular school attendance and regular health checks. In all communities investigated the number of families receiving *Juntos* is very high. Now, opinions about the program are very diverse as I mentioned in the single villages already. Some people saw it as an important support for the families to buy necessary things such as clothes or school material for the children. Women who received *Juntos* complained that the money was not sufficient. Others, however, stated that it was too much and instead encouraged laziness because the women did not care about agricultural work and got used to receiving money for nothing. Some said that the women spent the money on their own clothes or on sweets instead of on healthy food. Other critics referred to the way in which it is implemented and how some families who were in need did not benefit from the program whereas others with comparatively higher incomes were. Interviewees demanded that the program should be accompanied by workshops teaching women handicrafts or agriculture to generate their own income instead of making them getting used to receiving money for nothing.

Similar to the reparation program, the requirements and procedures how to get a benefit from social programs were unclear. The money was also perceived as a gift and not as part of the state's duty of care. The perceived unequal distribution led to envy and conflicts. The same happened to the reparation program. It was perceived as assistentialism as well. Critics condemned the lack of information, its implementation and the perceived unequal distribution. In some interviews reparations were confused with social programs and in practice, the health insurance for victims is the same as the health insurance for poor people. One should keep that in mind when evaluating the reparation program. The state uses social or development programs as a form of reparation and fails "to recognise the essential notion of reparation as constituting part of a process toward peace, justice and reconciliation" (Von Boven 2013, 26).

Both are implemented on an assistance basis and without creating agency in the receiving population. Only one interviewee stated that women's groups now met regularly because of the reunions organized by the program *Juntos*. This could be important for them.

The analysis in this study made clear that a lot depends on the local authorities. Concerning individual reparations, real knowledge is low, there are more rumors and only limited information available. The level of information depends on local authorities. It also depends on them whether they offer advice and support for any individual's reparation application and process and whether they attempt to implement a collective reparation program. Diez Hurtado (2012) stresses that local authorities are generally the most decisive entity for the well-being of a community. This might not be so surprising. There is, however, no direct interaction between the state and the community but only with the municipality as intermediators. For reparations, I concluded that it depends highly on the local authority members' knowledge, initiative, and ability (sometimes supported by an NGO) whether they engage with the topic of reparations and transmit information and possibilities of benefits to the community members.

The collective projects investigated did not succeed and did not lead to communal work or cooperation. Individual reparations have led to new envy, conflicts, and distrust due to the manner in which they were applied. The results of the four communities in Chapter 4 have been confirmed in all ten communities.

Notes

1 The communities of San Antonio de Julo and Carmen de Alanya were analyzed more in detail in a Spanish article: Elisabeth Bunselmeyer (2017): *"¿Una vaca = una vida? Reparaciones y desigualdad en comunidades post-conflictos del Perú* "(in: Svenja Blanke and Sabine Kurtenbach (eds.): Violencia y desigualdad: Adlaf Congreso 2016, Buenos Aires, Adlaf; Friedrich-Ebert-Stiftung, Nueva Sociedad, pp. 52–63).

2 Important to note is that an association of women producing handicrafts was formed with the help of the NGO COMISEDH which, at least for a while, worked better than the other association.

3 Quispillacta is also known for the successful project *ABA (Asociación Bartolomé Aripaylla)* founded in 1991 by two women who returned after their studies in agro-engineering and aimed at reinforcing old Andean agricultural traditions and especially focused on the creations of ponds in which water is collected with the help of special plants. This allows community members to enhance their agricultural production. They did, however, not work in the village itself but in the upper part (*puna*). The project has been supported by the German NGO *terre des hommes* and won several prices: www.tdh.de/was-wir-tun/projekte/suedamerika/peru/das-entwicklungsgeheimnis-von-quispillacta-teil-1/; http://diariocorreo.pe/edicion/ayacucho/siembra-y-cosecha-de-agua-de-lluvia-recibe-galardon-549183/; www.elpopular.pe/series/mujeres-batalla/2014-11-22-magdalena-machaca-de-aba-hemos-restablecido-el-respeto.

4 Project Proposal: *Instalacion de pequeño sistema de riego por aspersión Uchuyri*, 2009.

5 http://infomidis.midis.gob.pe/formatos/documentos/05_20170914_F3_AYACUCHO.pdf.

6 www.proyectosapp.pe/modulos/JER/PlantillaProyecto.aspx?ARE=0&PFL=2&JER=5640.

7 An exemption is the mobilization of community members of Chuschi and the neighbor community of Quispillacta regarding the question of creating a new district, for example in the session of the regional government in Cangallo, March 25, 2015.

8 In the case of Chungui the communities used the attention from the TRC and the reparation program to enhance their political and social status (Koc-Menard 2014).

References

CVR (Comisión de la Verdad y Reconciliación). 2003. "Informe Final." Lima.

Diez Hurtado, Alejandro. 2012. "Inversiones Privadas y Derechos Comunales." *Tiempo de Opinion* 2 (4): 22–31.

Falconí, Carola, Edilberto Jímenez, and Giovanni Alfaro. 2007. *Lluqanamarka: Llaqtanchikpa Yuyariynin. Lucanamarca: Memorias de Nuestro Pueblo.* Lima: Asociación de Familiares Víctimas de la Violencia Política del Distrito de Santiago de Lucanamarca, Municipalidad Distrital de Santiago de Lucanamarca, Comisión de Derechos Humanos (COMISEDH).

Gomez Tineo, Gabriel, and Edgar Huancahuari Evanan. 2015. "Reflexiones Sobre El Allin Kausay Desde Lucanamarca." unpublished paper.

Koc-Menard, Nathalie. 2014. "Sufrimiento humano y representación de víctimas. El caso de Chungui en la posguerra peruana." *Bulletin de l'Institut français d'études andines* 43 (2): 209–26. doi:10.4000/bifea.5189.

Marcos, Sylvia. 2010. *Women and Indigenous Religions.* Santa Barbara, CA: ABC-CLIO.

Ulfe, Maria Eugenia. 2013. *¿Y después de la violencia que queda ? víctimas, cuidadanos y reparaciones en el contexto post-CVR en el Perú.* Buenos Aires: CLACSO.

Von Boven, Theo. 2013. "Victim-Oriented Perspectives: Rights and Realities." In *Victims of International Crimes: An Interdisciplinary Discourse*, edited by Thorsten Bonacker and Christoph Safferling, 17–27. The Hague: T. M. C. Asser Press.

Zamora Castellares, Gabriela. 2014. *La Constitución de Comunidades En El Contexto de Violencia Política En El Valle Del Rio Apurímac, Ene y Mantaro 1980–2000. Informe de Proyecto de Tesis Para Optar El Grado de Bachiller En Historia.* Thesis, Ayacucho: Universidad Nacional de San Cristóbal de Huamanga.

Chapter 6

Individuals, truth, reparations, and social cohesion

In the previous chapters, I analyzed the effects of transitional justice on social cohesion in different communities and discovered a very diverse situation. Within the communities, I found a few people who had received reparations, those who had not received anything, those who evaluated the TRC and reparation program positively, and those who criticized the measures. I met community members with high levels of trust and solidarity and those who were focused on their own circumstances. The purpose of this chapter is to investigate whether people with similar characteristics show similar opinions and attitudes, regardless of their village of origin. I am interested in their evaluations of the TRC and reparation program, their perceptions of the past conflict, their attitudes toward trust and solidarity, and, lastly, their behavior within the community and attitudes toward the state. Moreover, I want to discover what characterizes people with very positive attitudes toward social cohesion and those who think very positively of the TRC and reparations. I am interested to see whether these two groups are the same.

I offer new insights with my analysis as the perception and the impact of transitional justice on the individual level have barely been researched. Only very few surveys have been conducted to capture the opinion of affected people toward transitional justice processes (see Chapter 2).

Based on the theoretic assumptions laid out above, I will look at the individuals from six different angles.

First, I will analyze whether receivers [35] have different attitudes from non-receivers [67] or observers [58] of the reparation program.[1] A more positive attitude toward social cohesion would confirm that reparations achieved their aims.

Following, I will investigate whether victims [95] have different opinions than non-victims [65]. This classification is based on their self-classification as victims. One would assume that victims show lower attitude toward social cohesion than non-victims.

A topic that has not been touched upon in this study until now are differences between women [75] and men [85] in their opinions and attitudes. TJ research and practice claims to act gender-sensitive and extra units are created so that it is important to evaluate the perceptions from this angle.

Another interesting angle is to examine the people taking responsibility in the form of authority positions within the communities. Half of my interviewees are local authorities [88], half of those hold voluntary positions, the other half was in paid positions at time of the interview. However, before that this latter group also held voluntary positions before. Therefore, I expected to find higher attitude toward social cohesion in this group. I also expected in-depth knowledge of the TRC and the reparation program in authorities.

I then specifically look to understand who the people are that evaluate the TRC and reparation program as highly satisfying, the "contented", and see whether certain characteristics or attitudes influenced this perception. I will also discuss whether better knowledge of transitional justice measures leads to higher satisfaction.

Lastly, I examine those who are very sociable, trusting, and highly committed to the community, the "socially-minded", and then look what their characteristics are. I expected to see a higher number of young people, members of the local authorities, or the non-victims in this group. And finally, I discuss the findings on the different groups of individuals in comparison.

The analysis is based on the 160 interviews conducted in the 11 villages.[2] As dependent variables or factors of interest, I use the indicators for satisfaction with the TRC and the reparation program and the indicators for social cohesion developed. Here, it is not the communal level of social cohesion but individual attitudes toward social cohesion that I am interested in. I use descriptive statistics, typology tables, analysis of variance, and regression models. Data used for this study were collected according to the criteria for good research. However, it must be kept in mind that the selection of individuals is neither random nor representative. Nevertheless, results confirm patterns found on the community level in Chapters 4 and 5.

Receivers, non-receivers, and observers

As I am interested in the possible effect of reparations, I divide the individuals into subgroups according to the levels of attention received by the reparation program as it was already done in Chapters 4 and 5. I only focus on the attention from the reparation program, not from the TRC. As already explained before, the TRC is not very present in the perception of the people. Community members connected it directly to the reparation program, which is at the forefront of people's minds. I divide all interviewed people into groups of receivers of reparation benefits, non-receivers, and observers. Only 10 of the interviewed people were individual receivers, plus 25 receivers of collective reparations; there were 67 non-receivers, victims that have been affected but did not receive any form of reparation, just over a third of all people interviewed, of whom only 12 were registered in the RUV. There were 58 observers, which equals 36%. The highest percentage of interviewed observers came from the villages of Chuschi, Querobamba, and Kimbiri; the collective receivers from Alanya, Uchuyri,

Lucanamarca, and Julo; the non-receivers are mainly from Santa Rosa, Kimbiri, Querobamba, Quispillacta, and Nuevo Progreso. I look at the three groups in comparison with the analytical tools of cross tables and typology tables in MAXQDA.

There is an unequal distribution of the groups among the different communities. As mentioned earlier, the initial research design I was expecting to find five villages of receivers – at least of collective reparation projects. However, as these were mainly not perceived as reparations, only 27 interviewees considered themselves as collective reparation receivers. And against my expectations, I could only find and interview 10 individual receivers, two of whom were also collective receivers.

Regarding their general characteristics, in the group of receivers and non-receivers are more men than in the group of observers. Members of the authorities are more represented in receivers and observers. This is partly due to the fact that the collective projects are mostly known and perceived as such by this group, who are mainly men. The observer-authorities are often people who fled from the community, studied in a city, and have returned to serve the village. They do not consider themselves to be victims.

The receivers and their perception of transitional justice

Only ten of all the interviewed people have received individual reparations, two of them also received collective reparations and twenty-five further people only collective reparations. Those are the ones that are aware of the collective reparation projects, those with subjective exposure. The number of the interviewed inhabitants of the villages of Chuschi, Lucanamarca, Uchuyri, Alanya, and Julo, which were objectively exposed to TJ, is much higher but only very few knew about the projects. This lack of awareness was already described earlier. Within the ones receiving collective reparations are some that would also be entitled to individual reparations but have still not received them. Only five of them are registered in the RUV already. So they are collective-receivers but individual-non-receivers. There are 18 people in this group. It is also important to note the fact that some of the families who received cows have not been affected by the armed conflict nor do they see themselves as victims (seven of the 17 people who received collective reparations did not classify themselves as victims). This is due to the regulations of the collective reparation program – the whole community profited from the project. I heard some critics referring to this distribution of reparation to non-victim families as well. In this part, I will look at the whole group of receivers as one, and, in the next subchapter, I will investigate whether it makes a difference whether people classify themselves as victims or not.

Regarding their knowledge of and satisfaction levels with the reparation program, there are no differences between those receiving individual or collective reparations. However, it must be kept in mind that half of these people [11] received milk cows as collective project and so this project resembles individual reparations as the cows were given to each family. Among collective receivers, the percentage of authorities is very high, due to the fact that in some villages only the authorities knew about the collective projects.

Those receiving individual economic reparations see it as a support but criticize them as being too little, too late, or unfair. Many have heard of others receiving more and do not understand the reasons. This feeling was even stronger where (supposed) perpetrators of violence received reparations (SR2). Knowledge among individual receivers is also low [5] or medium [3]. Only one person, the former president of the victims' association of Lucanamarca, had higher knowledge. It is really surprising and alarming, when even the receivers are not well informed about the program. There have been some new developments in the implementation on the national level such as the transferability of the scholarship program to children or grandchildren of victims, but this information had not reached the affected people at the time of the interview.

In one case, only half of the 10,000 PEN (3,000 US$) was paid to two brothers (2,500 PEN each) because their mother died during the application process and her part could not be transferred. After all the testimony giving, registering, providing documents again and again, the amount of 750 US$ seems very little, even for Peruvian conditions (L13). When there are more siblings, the amount reduces even further and most of the families in the villages have many children (L7). In another case, a man received reparations but has to split the sum with his half-sister although it was not her father who died. As in this case, reparations can lead to family conflicts (L21).

Receivers still stated that the money was a support but the amount seemed too little in return for a human life. Whether this is even an appropriate equation is another question. But, as already explained, only very few interviewed victims reject the general idea of reparations. They express that all the money they received from the state could not replace the person lost. However, they see it as some support (K19). The affected people would prefer either a higher amount or long-term support in the form of health insurance or scholarships or help with the construction of a family home, which is part of the reparation program but barely implemented.

Regarding the collective reparations, projects that worked well such as the communal house in Chuschi were not perceived as reparations. The water system in Uchuyri and the fish farm in Lucanamarca did not succeed due to technical problems and the invested money was lost. The cows given in Alanya and Julo were not of the high quality that was promised and many have died already. None of those projects led to high levels of satisfaction.

All of the receivers stated that they did not feel repaired. This "feeling repaired" is definitely a difficult goal to reach and different for every single person. However, the people interviewed do not even feel properly attended to. The idea of reparations is that those people receiving them are more satisfied and consolidated. In the design of this study, I expected to find higher attitudes toward social cohesion in the receivers. However, as none of the individual or collective receivers are completely satisfied with the reparations, this was not the case. Five of the individual and eighteen of the collective receivers have low levels of satisfaction and four individual and seven collective receivers medium, none of them is highly satisfied. The satisfaction levels resulting from individual reparations are, however, still the highest compared to the other groups, together with observers' satisfaction levels. This is an important result because it suggests that reparations can work.

The non-receivers and their perception of transitional justice

Non-receivers make up 67 of the interviewed people. They all classified themselves as victims of the internal armed conflict. Many of them would be eligible for reparations according to the criteria of the reparation program. However, only seven of them are already registered in the RUV. Eight of the non-receivers had never heard of the reparation program, only one of them knew the truth and reconciliation commission. This lack of information should be alarming for those responsible for the program. Those who are the program's main target group, the victims, did not even know about it. I classify all of them as non-receivers, those aware of the program and those not aware. In the last part of this subchapter, I look at the differences within this subgroup.

Those among the non-receivers, who knew of the TRC and reparation program have only little information and real knowledge about it is scarce. Half of them think that the commission came to bring reparations. Some of them had also given testimonies to the commission. Regarding the reparations, those with the RUV certificate thought that they would finally receive something. But now they are even more disappointed. I did not find any improved satisfaction because of the certificate and the acknowledgement it contains for the harm suffered. People refer to the certificate as a little paper "*papelito*" (L16), which seems only a means to an end and useful only for receiving reparations but useless in their case.

Affected people who want to register, face many administrative problems and limitations regarding the eligible victim group. In an informal talk in Ayacucho, a young man explained to my research assistant how he and his family had been captured and held in a Shining Path camp, where his father died when he tried to escape. His family, however, did not receive reparations. Scared of being blamed as belonging to Shining Path, they registered very late and have not received any form of reparation yet.

Expectations are very high among this group. Concerning the work of the TRC non-receivers demand further investigations and support (L3; L6; L12). They demand that the disappeared should be searched for (CH8; CH21). Moreover, they demand that all the histories should be investigated, violence by Shining Path, military, and other actors (SR5). They also expect the commission (or a successor institution) to work in all the affected communities (NP2; NP10).

The expectation of reparations is also very high. Most of the people demand extensive equal reparations for all victims. Others do not believe in reparations at all: "*You cannot repair those things*" (CH21: 69). Money alone seems difficult to "repair", many suggest psychological support (K13: 75). Some demand hospitals or universities especially for victims or museums and exhibitions to learn about the past (K12). The demand for education is very high because many experienced the consequences of the conflict due to the educational opportunities they missed out on (K14).

But the majority approves of the idea of material reparations or even demands it. The discontent with the reparation program mainly results from its implementation. People do not understand why reparations came so late, only in part, and why some people received reparations when they did not. Those who know of the reparation program feel, once again, disappointed from the state, which made promises to them that it did not fulfill. However, it fulfilled the promise of reparation to others and so this seems even worse than not paying anything and creates new envy and conflicts.

To summarize, of the 67 non-receivers, 26 are not at all satisfied with the commission, 6 have medium satisfaction, and most of them linked the TRC with reparations. Regarding the reparations, 46 have low satisfaction and, 6 people have medium satisfaction, and no one is highly satisfied with the program. In comparison, the non-receivers have the lowest levels of satisfaction with the reparation program. I, therefore, expect to find lower levels of trust in the state from the non-receivers and less trust toward community members as well as higher levels of envy and conflicts. As mentioned earlier, when analyzing their attitudes and opinions regarding social cohesion, it seems important to note the differences between those that aware of the reparation program [52], those not aware of it [8], and those that have registered already [7].

The observers and their perception of transitional justice

Observers are those not directly affected by the internal armed conflict and, who therefore, did not receive nor expect to receive any benefits of the reparation program. All of them classified themselves as non-victims. There were 58 observers among the people interviewed. However, only 40 knew about the reparation program. Observers are mainly found in Chuschi, Querobamba, and Kimbiri. The observers in Chuschi are also receivers of the collective reparation project in objective terms. A communal house was built there as collective reparation but is not perceived as such. Therefore, I classify them as observers. But this shows once again that the program can also benefit people who were not directly affected by the violence because they form part of the community nowadays. In Julo and Alanya, there are observers, non-victims, who were receivers of the milk cows as explained above.

Of the observers, 40 stated that they knew the program, their knowledge, however, is low in 33 cases. Only five people, all of them members of the authorities, have medium or high knowledge. People knew even less about the TRC: only half of this group (26) had heard of the commission. Of those, 18 had low knowledge, 6 medium, and only 1 authority had high knowledge. It is interesting to see that the commission is even less known than the reparation program. Among this group, 14 people confuse the commission with the reparation program and do not know other aspects of its work. The opinion on the TRC is, therefore, connected to the evaluation of the reparation program. And, as in the other groups, people demand that the commission should conduct further and more extensive investigations. They complained that it did not work in all places and said important histories were missing (CH 5: 61; K5: 68; K16: 66). Only one person was medium satisfied with the commission, and 11 had low levels of satisfaction.

Levels of satisfaction with the reparation program vary. About ten of the observers were fairly satisfied and thought the program is a good idea because it provides support for the victims (K6; SR3; SR6). Others stated that information was missing and that there were still many people, who had not received their reparations (CH5, K20: 71, Q5: 78). They complained about the requirements for receiving the benefits that were difficult to fulfill (NP4: 63). And some see as well the problems arising out of the unequal distribution of the reparations: "Whose life is worth more?" (CH5: 67). In Lucanamarca, one woman stated that reparations should be for the whole community because all suffered from the violence and that personal benefits would only bring problems (L11: 52). Others questioned the general idea of material reparations (CH22: 50) or reported misuse of reparations and people not being the "right victims" (CH13, CH12, QB2: 51).

Discussion: receivers, non-receivers, and observers and their attitudes toward social cohesion

When comparing these three groups, we can see some interesting results regarding their perception of transitional justice and their attitudes toward social cohesion. According to the ideas of transitional justice, receivers were expected to show higher social cohesion. However, due to the problems in the implementation of the program and the discontent with the reparation program analyzed before, receivers cannot be expected to have positive attitudes. The non-receivers would be expected to show negative attitudes because their expectations toward reparations were not fulfilled.

In the comparison, I found that receivers had the highest awareness and knowledge of the TRC and reparation program, which is not surprising because they were able to get individual reparations and/or know about the collective project received. Non-receivers have about the same awareness of the TRC but know less about the reparation program; many confuse the TRC with reparations and are therefore disappointed because the commission did not bring what they expected. Observers show low knowledge of both measures. Satisfaction is higher in observers and receivers than in non-receivers as was to be expected but the difference is rather small. The few people who are non-receivers but registered in the RUV are the ones with the lowest satisfaction because their expectations were not fulfilled (see also the next part on registered and non-registered victims). When they received the certificate, they expected it to be followed by reparations immediately, and the disappointment was even higher because nothing came. They show the lowest attitude toward social cohesion as well. This is an alarming result that higher expectations create higher disillusion.

Regarding trust toward authorities, families, and solidarity, there were barely any differences between the groups. Within the group of non-receivers, there was slightly lower solidarity. Attitudes toward envy, conflict and violence were the same. Receivers were more willing to share their harvest with the neighbors in the corn question while the lowest amount was given by the observers. Interestingly, more non-receivers believed that there could be a renewed violent conflict. And while receivers wanted to remember, observers wanted to forget. This is a thought-provoking result. When non-receivers state that new conflict could arise because of their unmet needs this is alarming. For receivers and non-receivers, both victims of the conflict, the past is more important than to observers. National pride and being proud to be a member of the community as well as trust in the state was slightly higher in receivers. State importance is rated lower in receivers and non-receivers than observers. This goes against the idea of using reparations to generate renewed trust in the state. Regarding social programs, the non-receivers have a more negative opinion toward *Juntos*, observers are more positive. This is quite interesting and could be due to the fact that non-receivers do not agree with programs they do not profit from. I addressed parallels between reparations and social programs in the previous chapter.

Overall, the social cohesion indicator shows similar levels for the three different groups, I could not find any significant differences in attitude toward social cohesion in receivers, non-receivers, and observers that could be traced back clearly to the receipt or non-receipt of reparations. It seems that the perception of the reparation program is more important, as I will analyze below.

Victims and non-victims in the focus

In this chapter, I analyze whether victims show different opinions and attitudes than non-victims. This differentiation was already important when dividing non-receivers and observers earlier. However, the focus on the victim perspective here offers new insight as no difference is made in this chapter between victims who received or did not receive reparations. With this classification, I want to find out whether victimhood itself could be the deciding factor for opinions and attitudes.

The differentiation between self- and external definitions of victims is already a huge topic in itself. The classification here is based on the self-classification of the interviewees. I asked them whether they considered themselves as victims of the internal armed conflict. Interestingly, interviewees perceive themselves as victims for various reasons. The death of a family member or direct violence or torture suffered are the most common reasons. Others stated that they were victims because of the fear they lived through for years, the loss of belongings, land, education, or living conditions. On the community level, the loss of social cohesion is mentioned as a consequence that turned the whole community into victims.

Apart from this self-definition, it is more often the external definition that creates conflict. Within transitional justice measures a definition of victims is mostly inevitable. Especially when designing a reparation program, the state – or the entity in charge – must have a concrete definition of who is a victim and who is, therefore, eligible for receiving reparations. The reparation program is an important public manifestation of this definition and is controversial. The certificate of being a victim that was handed to those successfully applied for the RUV seems hard to reach for many of the affected people. The process of becoming the "right good victim" seems difficult and the payment of reparations only to some victims creates huge problems. As elaborated earlier, even when victims manage to get the certificate, this does not lead to satisfaction because they expect reparations to come with it.[3] In this chapter, I am interested in whether victims have different opinions and attitudes than non-victims. I look at the two groups in comparison with the analytical tools of cross tables and typology tables in MAXQDA.

Of the 160 interview partners, 95 declared themselves to be victims. I interviewed most victims in the community of Lucanamarca. Only in Chuschi and Querobamba, the majority of the interview partners were self-declared non-victims.

Regarding their characteristics, the victims were on average older than the non-victims. This is due to the fact that the younger people did not experience the conflict themselves. There is also a slight majority of women and members of the authorities in the group of non-victims. The latter can be explained by the fact that members of the authorities moved to the communities to work there. Some of them grew up in the cities without direct exposure to the conflict.

Regarding their perception of the past, the violence experienced has more importance for victims than for non-victims and more victims state that it is important to remember what happened. This is not surprising. However, the risk of new violence is judged similarly by both groups.

Regarding their awareness of transitional justice measures, the awareness is higher in victims than in non-victims – which was to be expected. Seventy-four percent of the victims know the commission, and only 45% of the non-victims know the TRC. The reparation program is known by 92% of the victims, nearly all of them have heard about reparations but also 72% of the non-victims, which is high as well. It must be alarming for the people responsible for the reparation program that some victims have never heard of it. Another huge problem is that the real knowledge is low.

Of those who knew of the TRC [70 victims and 29 non-victims] about half thought that its purpose was to bring reparations [53% of the victims and 52% of non-victims]. Knowledge is about the same, with slightly higher knowledge in the non-victims group, this is again due to the higher number of member of the authorities in this group. Satisfaction is rather low in both groups while it is slightly higher in victims.

Within the group of those who knew of the reparation program [70 victims and 29 non-victims], 79% of the victims and 72% of the non-victims stated that reparations had been paid in the community, although in all communities individual and/or collective reparations had in fact been paid. About the same percentage of both groups knew of collective reparations [33% and 34%]. The knowledge about the reparation program is higher in victims, satisfaction levels, however, were higher in non-victims [1.2 and 1.5]. Satisfaction does, therefore, not depend on knowledge and vice versa higher knowledge does not necessarily lead to higher satisfaction. Statistical analysis does not show a significant correlation either.

Regarding their view of the communities, victims showed slightly more positive attitudes regarding solidarity, trust in authorities and in their fellow community members. They see more participation in communal activities and participate more often as well. Victims would give a little more corn to their neighbors than non-victims, they were more willing to share. But non-victims would also help neighbors in case of severe problems. The more positive attitude seems to result from the experiences of violence, which lead to a better evaluation of the situation today. Proud to be a member of the community and Peru is nearly equal, non-victims do trust the state more though. This is an important result because the attention of the TRC and reparation program was to be a way to take responsibility for what happened and renew trust in the political institutions. The summarized level of social cohesion is nearly equal in victims and non-victims.

A quick comparison of the differences between victims registered in the RUV and those not yet registered and the comparison between victims that have received and those who did not receive reparations yields interesting results. As expected, registered victims are very dissatisfied with the reparation program. They know surprisingly little about the TRC. Their attitudes toward social cohesion are, however, very similar to those who are not registered.

Regarding those that have received individual reparations and those victims that have not, there are slightly differences. The knowledge of the reparation program and satisfaction levels are higher in the receivers. The knowledge of and satisfaction with the TRC is the same. Receivers find the past violence more important than non-receivers, and non-receivers see a higher risk of new violence, which is alarming. Attitudes toward social cohesion are somewhat more positive in the receivers than among non-receivers – which would confirm the theory. However, these differences are only marginal and not significant.

Overall, victims regard the past as more important than non-victims. The knowledge of the reparation program is higher in victims, satisfaction levels, however, are higher in non-victims. Victims are disappointed in the program. Nevertheless, the attitudes of individuals toward social cohesion are nearly the same. Victims, and especially victims who received reparations, have slightly more positive attitudes toward social cohesion. Differences are, however, only very small and do not hold for a strong causal argument.

Men and women in the focus

In this chapter, I analyze whether women have different opinions and attitudes from men. Research on transitional justice with a gender dimension is a recent development. To my knowledge, there are no studies on the perception of TJ that have a gender dimension. Many of the implemented TJ measures have special programs for women who are often affected by armed conflict differently. The Peruvian TRC also had a special gender unit but critics claim that it did not operate properly and that the reparation program did not have a special gender dimension. Therefore, it is interesting to see whether women and men have different opinions and attitudes toward the TJ measures and social cohesion. Less than half of my interview partners were women [75 to 85]. I could not reach an equal percentage due to the fact that many authority positions are still held by men, only 30% of the authority members were women. In the next chapter, I take a look at the members of the authorities and also combine the gender with the authority-dimension to see whether male and female members of the authorities think differently and if it is their gender or the position that made the difference. In this subchapter, however, I will look at gender first.

The average age of the women interviewed was six years younger than that of men, fewer women considered themselves to be victims and fewer women were registered in the RUV because of the lack of information and problems in the procedure. Some interesting differences appear here. Fewer women think that new violence could reoccur than men. And women tended to want to forget the past. With regard to the other attitudes concerning the past, both groups had similar opinions. Awareness of the TRC is significantly lower in women than in men [48% and 74%], real knowledge is also lower and women are less satisfied, however not significantly so. Awareness of the reparation program is also lower [91% in men to 76% in women], and knowledge of and satisfaction with the reparations is also lower in women than in men. While the difference is marked in terms of knowledge, it is only marginal with regard to levels of satisfaction. Again, there is no correlation between knowledge and satisfaction of the TRC and reparation program. The higher knowledge in men is certainly connected to their positions within the authorities. Interestingly, in comparison, levels of awareness and opinions of the social program *Juntos* are nearly the same in men and women.

Men are more trusting toward community members, family, and authorities than women. Women see more violence, this would also include domestic violence against them. Regarding the problems in the community women mention poverty and malnutrition more often than men. Both groups see the change in the communities in a similar light. As actors responsible for the change men mention local authorities more often, probably because they occupied those positions more often. The perception of the participation in local assemblies and communal work is the same in both groups. But more men [93% compared to 68%] state they would participate themselves. However, interestingly, women describe that this has changed a lot in recent years and nowadays there were be more women participating than before. In some communities, men only send their wives because they are not interested in taking part.

Trust toward the state is higher in men and the feeling of being proud to be member of the community is also stronger in men. They see themselves as playing a more active role in it. Levels of national pride are nearly the same. The level of individual attitudes and communal social cohesion is a bit lower in women than in men. In most of the villages visited, there are still traditional role models present and only recently women participate more and take over authority positions as well. Women are nearly always less well-informed than men, I found that this applied to knowledge of TRC as well as the reparation program. Again, TJ reinforces existing power structures. This did not influence their satisfaction with the reparation program. In the next chapter, I will see whether working for the authorities created these differences or if it is the gender aspect.

Authorities and non-authorities in the focus

In this chapter, I analyze whether members of the authorities hold different opinions and attitudes than ordinary community members. Many of the positions within communal authorities are voluntary and unpaid. Paid positions such as mayors and those of the council members, governors, and teachers often held voluntary positions first. As this requires high initiative and effort, I assume more positive attitudes toward social cohesion in members of the authorities.

Overall 88 interviewed people were local authorities, the rest were ordinary community members. Both groups have a very similar average age although the age groups the members of the authorities were mainly 30 to 50 and non-authorities 20 to 40. The majority of authorities are men, victims and non-victims are distributed equally.[4] Regarding their perception of the past, authorities regard the past violence as more important than non-authorities. And a higher percentage of them than non-authorities believe that new conflict could arise.

The awareness and knowledge of the TRC is higher than in non-authorities [72%–50%], satisfaction also slightly higher. As for reparations, awareness and knowledge is also higher, nearly all authorities know the reparation program [93%–72%] but the satisfaction of non-authorities is slightly higher. That is quite interesting, showing once again, that knowledge and satisfaction do not necessarily correlate. I assume that this is caused by the collective projects not working that are more known within the authorities and that this is a source of discontent among that group.

The perception of the community life is a bit more positive in authorities than non-authorities. The problems mentioned are similar, members of the authorities mention malnutrition, violence, and disorganization more frequently. Factors causing change are also seen in a very similar light, the non-authorities mention the mayor more often while authorities mention NGOs more frequently. I assume that they are more aware of their work than the ordinary community members. Regarding the participation in communal activities, both have the same opinion. Individual engagement is obviously higher in authorities than among non-authorities. But in their attitudes toward helping each other and giving corn, non-authorities are more positive. Authorities have higher levels of pride in their community. Obviously, as a member of the authorities high levels of identification with the community are essential. Non-authorities have slightly higher levels of national pride. The state is judged as being more important for the community by authorities and trust in the state is also higher in authorities. State programs such as *Juntos* are equally well-known by both groups and judged in a similar manner as well.

In the summarized indicator, the communal cohesion is seen as more positive by authorities, and individual attitudes toward social cohesion is slightly higher in non-authorities. In the joint indicator, authorities have a marginally higher index.

It is very interesting to combine the two categories, members of the authorities and gender. There it becomes obvious that knowledge of the TRC and reparation program is the highest in male authority members, 80% for the TRC and 100% for the reparations, and the lowest in non-authority women, 40% and 70%, respectively. Even female members of the authorities only knew very little about the TJ measures. Satisfaction is also the highest in male authorities and male non-authorities. These groups have a higher number of victims as well. Female non-authorities have the worst perception of the community regarding trust, solidarity, conflicts, and violence. The joint indicator is higher for male authorities and non-authorities than for women.

Overall, it becomes clear that differences occur in members of the authorities and gender categories and are highest when both categories are combined. There are two main knowledge gaps leading to lower satisfaction levels and a more negative evaluation of the TJ measures and community life. TJ reinforced and did not overcome existing information gaps.

Getting to know the "contented" villagers

In this chapter, I take a look from the other side to understand who the people are that are highly satisfied with the TRC and reparation program. I am especially interested in their characteristics and attitudes toward social cohesion.

There is no correlation between satisfaction with the TRC and satisfaction with the reparation program and some people know only one of the measures. Therefore, I look at the two groups of contented interviewees separately, in total there are 34 people who are either medium satisfied with the TRC or medium or highly satisfied with the PIR.

There were only three people who are satisfied with the TRC and with the PIR: L1, victim and collective receiver; L4, non-victim and collective receiver; SR2, victim and individual receiver. All three were male members of the authorities and very well informed about the work and measures. They are the ones with the highest levels of satisfaction of all interviewed people but they were still only medium satisfied. They stated that the TRC and reparation program are still missing full investigation or implementation. These three show high attitudes toward social cohesion, which would confirm the theory. However, the number of cases is too small to confirm the hypotheses.

Concerning satisfaction with the TRC, there were ten people with medium satisfaction, without the three already mentioned, seven. These were from Chuschi, Santa Rosa, Kimbiri, and Quispillacta. Five of them are male members of the authorities, 80% are victims. Regarding the past, they stated that it was important but that they would rather forget it. They did not think that new violence is likely to occur. They were mainly non-receivers, which is surprising because they did not seem to judge the TRC according to the advances in reparations. In this group, only very few confused the TRC with the reparation program, only 30% compared to 60% of those with low levels of satisfaction. This shows that the connected expectation of reparations plays an important role. Only when not only connected to reparations, the truth commission is judged positively.

Most of the people who were satisfied with the commission had low levels of satisfaction with the reparation program but judged the two measures to be separate from each other. Knowledge of the TRC is fairly high but not in all cases. They showed medium to high attitudes toward social cohesion.

In total, 25 evaluated the reparation program with medium satisfaction, minus the three above, 22 people. They can be found in all communities apart from Nuevo Progreso, where there was only little attention from the reparation program. Here, I find the highest percentage of receivers, half of them have received individual or collective reparations and the lowest proportion of non-receivers. Knowledge was very diverse and not different from the ones rating the reparation program with low satisfaction. But in this group, they had higher knowledge of the TRC, however still confusing it with the reparation program. Those inscribed in the RUV rate the reparation program rather negatively – they are even more disappointed. In this group of medium, satisfied people they do not see it as very likely that new violence could occur and want to remember the past, which is very important in their opinion. The state is rated as having medium to high importance, trust is also rather high, which would confirm the proposed aim of the state to foster confidence. Finally, social cohesion is very high on the individual and collective level, which means that there could be a connection with satisfaction with the reparation program leading to better social cohesion unless these people have more positive attitudes in general.

The two people who are highly satisfied with the reparation program are two observers who knew someone personally that had received reparations. They have low knowledge and don't know the TRC. These two, one male member of the authorities and one female community member, also showed very high levels of social cohesion.

Overall, it is clear that male members of the authorities are overrepresented among those with higher levels of satisfaction. However, there is no correlation between knowledge and satisfaction for the reparation program, but there is one for the truth commission. There is also no correlation between satisfaction with the TRC and reparation program on this level because people medium satisfied with the commission know that it did more than bring reparations und evaluate them separately from each other.

The most important finding is that all these people with higher satisfaction showed also higher attitudes toward social cohesion, which suggests a connection between the two factors which is, however, statistically not significant.

Getting to know the "socially-minded" villagers

In this chapter, I take a look at the people with high trust and solidarity and what characteristics they have. Maybe they have a combination of characteristics that I did not think of. For this analysis, I use only those interviews where all relevant questions were answered. Therefore, the total number of interviews used for this analysis comes to 96. There are eight people with very low attitudes toward social cohesion, 57 with middle, and 31 with high attitudes toward social cohesion. The two last groups were split again.

Regarding their general characteristics, it is interesting to note that they are distributed equally within the 11 communities. That means that there is no community that has more social members than others, which is an important result. Older people and women have the lowest satisfaction rates. In the highest social cohesion category, there is only one woman. Most members of the authorities are in the groups with second or third highest cohesion. In the lowest groups, there are mainly non-authority women. The victims are spread evenly across all groups, whether registered in the RUV or not does not seem to matter. Interestingly, in the highest social cohesion group, 83% acknowledged the state for bringing positive change and judged it to be important for the community. In general, the groups with higher attitudes toward social cohesion rated the change that happened as very positive. The groups with lower attitudes toward social cohesion thought that new conflict was more probable. While the groups with higher attitudes toward social cohesion stated that the past should be remembered, the others were in favor of forgetting. The importance of the violence is judged similarly.

Now, interestingly the awareness of the TRC and reparation program is highest in the higher socially minded groups but knowledge is the highest in the lowest social cohesion category. Satisfaction, with the TRC, however, is distributed equally, for reparations, the people with the lowest satisfaction are also in the lower social cohesion groups. This would actually confirm the theory of dissatisfaction with the reparation program leading to lower social cohesion, which was also confirmed in the previous subchapter. Individual receivers, however, tended to higher attitudes toward social cohesion while collective receivers showed mainly low attitudes toward social cohesion. That could be triggered by the dissatisfaction with the projects that did not work.

Overall, on the individual level, I found evidence of a connection between satisfaction with the reparation program and TRC and the level of social cohesion, which could not be seen on the communal level.

Discussion

In the analysis of the villages, I did not find a community who was an outright receiver of the TRC and the reparation program. Nor did I find a community in which all the people were satisfied with the TRC and reparations. I could also not find a community with an overall high level of social cohesion. The case selection did not work out due to misinformation before the interviews were conducted.

Therefore, the analysis of the individuals forms an important supplement to the analysis on the community level. I divided the 160 interviewees in different groups and analyzed their characteristics, opinions on TJ and on social cohesion. This is another form of the quasi-experimental research design because I compared people who received reparations (the treatment) and those who did not receive them (non-treatment group). The third group comprised the observers, who were not the target group of reparations because they have not been affected by the conflict violence.

The comparison, of receivers and non-receivers and the observers, was insightful. While the knowledge about the TRC and reparation program was the highest in receivers this did not lead to higher satisfaction with the measures. Satisfaction levels were fairly equal across the three groups. Attitudes toward social cohesion were also about the same. This is a clear sign that the assumption of this study was not fulfilled. The attention from the TRC and reparations did not lead to higher social cohesion because of its negative perception.

In a second step, people classifying themselves as victims were compared with those not directly affected by the violence of the internal armed conflict. As expected their perception of the past varies but against all expectations knowledge about the TJ measures was not higher in victims. Satisfaction with the TRC was slightly higher because some of the victims valued the exhumations it carried out. Satisfaction with the reparations was lower because so many of them had still not received anything. I found slightly higher attitudes toward social cohesion in victims, which I referred back to the perception that the situation is better now than during the conflict.

The analysis by gender was also revealing. While the perception of the past is similar (although women tended to want to forget), women are often less well informed than men. I found this to be true for knowledge of the TRC and of the reparation program. There are more male members of the authorities among my interviewed population, who are more involved in community life. Satisfaction with the TJ measures is also higher in men but only slightly so. The indicator for individual and communal social cohesion is a bit lower in women than in men, they were less active and also more pessimistic about the situation in the communities.

The focus on authorities in comparison with non-authorities showed that knowledge on the TJ measures was higher in authorities as expected. Satisfaction with the TRC is fairly high but not with the reparation program. Here, satisfaction is higher in non-authorities, which I attribute to the problems with the collective projects and the resulting discontent. Social cohesion is higher in members of the authorities concerning the community level as was expected but nearly equal on the individual level, which was surprising. Now, in the analysis of members of the authorities and by gender there were clear differences between male members of the authorities and female community members. There exists a knowledge gap, which leads to lower satisfaction rates and a more negative evaluation of TJ measures and community life of women. This gap was not overcome by the transitional justice process.

In the last two subchapters, I analyzed those who were content with the TJ measures and the ones with high levels of social cohesion. Both analyses showed ones again that there was no correlation between high knowledge and high satisfaction with the TJ measures. However, good knowledge of the TRC leads to higher satisfaction while this does not apply to reparations. For the TRC, it seems to be important to understand the purpose of its work and that it involved much more than preparing the reparation program. There is no correlation between satisfaction with the TRC and with the reparation program either. Comparing receivers to non-receivers again, I conclude that it does not matter whether people received reparations but how they evaluate it. Neither individual nor collective receivers are automatically highly satisfied. This explains why I did not find a correlation with social cohesion in 7.1. The most important finding is that all the people with higher satisfaction with the TJ measures also report higher levels of social cohesion, which suggests a connection between these two factors. That means that the assumption holds true only when people have a positive perception of the respective measure.

The communities are composed of a mixture of those individuals, which explains the mixed picture regarding their opinion on the transitional justice process and attitudes toward social cohesion.

Notes

1 I had planned the analysis of the testimony-givers as well to further analyze the effects of truth telling. However, there were less than ten people in my cases that participated in the TRC. Moreover, the perception is rather focused on the reparation program following out of the testimonies so that this analysis was not done in the end.

2 In this chapter I also include the additional interviews conducted in the ten villages of Chapters 4 and 5 as well as interviews from the village Huyma, which was not included in the main part of the study as only six interviews could be conducted there. This inclusion adds 20 cases to a total of 160 cases. However, not all questions were answered by all the interviewees. I note the number of missing answers in the analysis when relevant.

3 For a further discussion on the construction of victim roles in the transitional justice process in Peru see: Elisabeth Bunselmeyer: *Victim = Victim? The Construction of (Non-)Victim Roles by Transitional Justice Processes in Peru.* Unpublished paper presented at the Zentrumstage 2016, Centre for Conflict Studies, University of Marburg, October 2016.

4 That means there is no higher activism of victims as Blattman found in Uganda: Christopher Blattman. 2009. "From Violence to Voting: War and Political Participation in Uganda." *American Political Science Review* 103 (02): 231–47.

Chapter 7

Conclusion

> But I don't agree with these reparations; they seem like a joke to me. First, many victims have not been considered. And second, they give reparations of 5,000 or 10,000 Soles for one life. That seems a joke to me. For example, if I had had my dad, my life would maybe be different. And if they told me to choose between 10,000 and my dad, obviously I would choose my dad. And individual reparations, a cow or a tractor, with this they want to console us for the destruction and trauma that was left in the communities, here in Lucanamarca. I think it would have been better, I mean, to give nothing because this creates new conflicts between community members. If he receives something and I do not, envy is created. I don't agree, to me it seems a joke.
>
> (L6: 70)

This interviewee's dissatisfaction stands in sharp contrast to the statement by Peru's former President Ollanta Humala cited in the beginning of this book, who claimed the reparation program for victims of the internal armed conflict as a success for his government. The immediate question that arises from these opposing views is: Why did the reparation program not meet the expectations of the affected people? But at the same time, some broader issues are addressed, including the varying impact of truth commissions and reparation programs, possible limitations of transitional justice measures, and their contribution to social cohesion in post-conflict communities.

This study aimed to disentangle these issues and to understand the dynamics and effects of transitional justice measures on society's micro level. Its extensive focus on the needs and perceptions of those people who are the target group of TJ measures constitutes a new perspective and offers valuable insights for practitioners and TJ scholars alike. Moreover, by connecting the concepts of transitional justice and social cohesion, I have developed a new indicator and elaborated a framework, which allows for an ambiguous evaluation of TJ instruments and aims. This conceptual framework was applied within an innovative quasi-experimental research design. For that purpose, I gathered a broad range of microlevel data both on the community and on the individual level. The results of this fieldwork allow for an in-depth account of the Peruvian case.

The book provides three important main results to the discussion on transitional justice. First, my analysis within the developed framework made very clear that the perception of the respective measure by its target group is the most important factor for its impact. This perception depends on knowledge and even more so on awareness of the transitional justice measures in the first place. A surprising result is that communities and individuals that have been objectively exposed to various transitional justice measures were not aware of them and this revealed a huge gap between objective and subjective exposure. Another important finding is that the transitional justice process and its measures were not able to overcome existing power structures but reinforced them. The Peruvian state barely interacted with the affected people directly but mainly via intermediators such as municipalities or NGOs. Many victims were dependent on those organizations to claim their reparations. Within the program, no agency of affected people was created and it seems that empowerment of victims was not desired.

Lastly, it was not expected to find weak social cohesion in all communities studied. Only very few individuals exhibited high attitudes toward social cohesion. This result invites to extend the analysis to villages that have high levels of social cohesion to compare the dynamics. The internal armed conflict turned out to be only one of many factors that influenced social cohesion in the communities.

In this section, I present the main results of my study and discuss their wider implications.

Assessing the impact of transitional justice on social cohesion in Peru

To assess the impact of transitional justice, I developed the social cohesion indicator that captures the horizontal level of cohesion within the community and the vertical level toward the state. It comprises individual attitudes such as trust, solidarity, and confidence in the state as well as behavior such as social and political participation.

Based on the concepts of transitional justice and social cohesion as well as the mandates of the measures, I assumed that the TRC and the reparation program contributed to social cohesion in the communities. Testimony giving and receiving reparations in particular were meant to create acknowledgement and satisfaction, confidence and trust as I have summarized in the conceptual framework.

To structure the analysis, an analytical framework of transitional justice impact was developed with the following stages:

I Conception

II Implementation (national and local)

- a Awareness → has the person heard about the measure?
  Knowledge → does the person know about the exact work or content of the measure?

b Perception → how does the person evaluate the measure?

III Impact → what impact did the measure have on the level of social cohesion?

I chose the Peruvian case where social cohesion on the local level had been greatly weakened by the conflict, and a TRC and a reparation program were applied to confront this consequence. The slow implementation of the reparation program allowed me to find regions with higher and lower levels of attention in accordance with the research design. For the quasi-experimental analysis, I chose ten post-conflict communities with different levels of attention from the TRC and the reparation program and interviewed 160 people in these villages and 43 experts. All of these villages are situated in the rural area of Ayacucho, the department most affected by the internal armed conflict. The analysis was made according to the quasi-experimental structured, focused research design, and guided by the stages. In the first level of analysis, I carried out four in-depth case studies (Chapter 4), followed by a comparison with six more communities (Chapter 5) and supplemented this with an analysis of the 160 individuals according to different categories (Chapter 6).

I and II) Conception and implementation of transitional justice

The design of both, the TRC and the reparation program, was very comprehensive, but it is the implementation that poses the first challenge (Moffett 2017, 401). Criteria for what constituted complete, comprehensive, and easily accessible reparations were met by the design of the program but already proved to be unsustainable during the registration process for affected people. Victims were supposed to receive preferential access to education and healthcare, but in order to gain this access they had to publicly identify themselves as victims and get registered in the RUV, which posed not only bureaucratic obstacles but carried a high risk of re-victimization (Roht-Arriaza 2004, 136; Waardt 2016).

The TRC carried out exhumations in two of the districts investigated; the communities of Lucanamarca, Chuschi, Uchuyri, and Quispillacta were directly involved. In all the others, apart from Kimbiri and Nuevo Progreso, testimonies were collected. Some community members of Chuschi and Lucanamarca participated in trials against Shining Path and military leaders.

Collective reparation projects were implemented in five of the communities in my sample. One was successful (communal house in Chuschi), two were not successful at all (the fish farm in Lucanamarca and the irrigation system in Uchuyri), and two were only successful in part (cows in Julo and Alanya). In one case, the money transferred for the implementation of a project disappeared (Santa Rosa). Whether communities received collective reparation projects depended entirely on the initiative of local authorities or NGOs. Symbolic reparations were only carried out in connection with the re-burial ceremonies. The restitution of civil rights in the form of restoring documentation had been partly accomplished.

Regarding individual reparations, in all the districts, there were some people who have received economic reparations according to the CMAN and community members. However, it was very difficult for me to identify or find them. I was only able to interview receivers in Lucanamarca, Kimbiri, Santa Rosa, and Uchuyri. I did not find anyone who benefitted from reparations in health, education, or housing although many people were eligible for these programs as well. The low number of people registered in the RUV in the districts of Lucanamarca, Chuschi, and Querobamba was surprising as well especially given the high number of registered people in the VRAEM. The lack of information and the difficult registration process were lamented in all communities. Whether individuals received reparations depended on local authorities, NGOs or well informed family members, mostly the victims' children, who often lived in the cities and had access to the institutions. This meant that the clientelistic power structures were reinforced and not overcome within the reparation program. As these political, economic, and social rifts in the Peruvian society were one of the reasons for the outbreak of the violence, this result can only be seen as alarming.

IIa) Awareness and knowledge of transitional justice

The analysis of this stage brought some unexpected results as well. Awareness of the TRC was lower than of the reparation program; more than 80% of all interviewed people had heard of the program regardless of the level of attention, which was surprising. It was assumed that only those regions with higher attention would show higher awareness. Awareness of the reparation program was extremely high, but mainly focused on individual reparations. Collective projects were oftentimes confused with development programs. The results here confirm the few existing studies (Paredes and Correa 2011; Ulfe 2013). Former presidents also classified the reparation program as social development policy and by doing so "it conflates two separate obligations of government: to make reparation for wrongs and to provide essential services to the population" (Roht-Arriaza 2004, 130).

Moreover, the confusion of the TRC with the reparation program was very high. Levels of knowledge were low for both measures in the communities, which poses a problem for the people that want to benefit from the reparation program. Furthermore, I observed a huge difference between objective exposure to TJ measures (there was a project implemented in the community) and subjective exposure (the person is aware of the TJ project). Less than half of the population in the communities with collective projects knew that it was a reparation project. This awareness was high only in male members of the authorities. Again it becomes clear that gender-specific measures and information would be necessary as demanded by Guillerot (2006) and Theidon (2016). The TRC did not comply with its gender-sensitive focus neither (Mantilla Falcón 2005; Theidon 2007). The persistent inequalities in gender and between people in positions of authority and those ordinary community members were not overcome, and the question arises whether the state and authorities really aimed to overcome them.

IIb) Perception of transitional justice

This lack of awareness and knowledge has implications for the perception of the TJ measures. Projects that are not perceived as reparation do not have any compensatory effect. I could, however, show that the level of knowledge about the program did not necessarily influence the level of satisfaction. In Chapter 6, I demonstrated that the people who were better informed did not necessarily judge the reparation program to be better. This was only the case for the TRC. Only those who knew more about its work and especially the exhumations evaluated it as important measure. The confusion of the TRC with the reparation program was very clear in the analysis, also in most of the testimonies given to the TRC the main expectations of the affected people toward the commission were focused on two things: reparations and the search for disappeared for those families who are still searching for their relatives. Against the backdrop of the literature on truth-telling another surprising result was that testimony giving was not seen as positive but negative by the interviewees because of these unfulfilled expectations connected with the TRC. So when the TRC was only connected to the reparation program, it was judged negatively as well.

Also, higher attention does not automatically lead to higher satisfaction. This is something found in another study for state attendance in infrastructure and public services as well (De Juan, Gosztonyi, and Koehler 2016). It is the perception of the measure that is decisive.

Satisfaction with the reparation program was very low, only reaching medium in a few members of the authorities, non-victims, and individual receivers. Interviewees criticized reparations for arriving late, not being universal, being incomplete, too little, and not adequate. The perceived "unjust" implementation of the programs stands in contrast to the claim by Laplante (2015, 163) that reparations must be perceived as fair and equal to have a positive impact. My main assumption was that transitional justice would contribute to social cohesion. These negative evaluations of the TJ measures, however, did not lead me to expect any positive impact on social cohesion.

III) Impact on social cohesion

Social cohesion was weak in all communities observed, which came as a surprise because at least two of selected cases, Quispillacta and Alanya, were said to have high levels. My analysis could not confirm this assumption. Social cohesion had diminished due to various factors, such as the change from agriculture as the only occupation together with paid work and the new budget for the municipalities that created the expectation that the municipality would carry out work and not the people themselves voluntarily. Migration and an active interchange with the cities brought new ideas and influences. The conflict reinforced those developments and, moreover, weakened confidence in fellow community members and toward local authorities. The communities that formed a self-defense committee to stand against external violence did also not show high levels of social cohesion. Violence from different sides led to fear and mistrust in those community members as well. Villagers were split between the different conflict groups, many local leaders died or fled during this time. The communities' social and political structures were destroyed. The communities had not been able to recover from that. Moreover, the interchange with the cities and the shift from voluntary to paid positions in the municipality who manage project budgets changed the relationships. The villages are not bonded together anymore.

These are factors that occur or have occurred in many communities worldwide. But here there is a Peruvian characteristic to it: The socioeconomic rifts that have marked the country for decades. These cannot be addressed by reparations alone, and it increases the likelihood of them being confused with development projects. Scholars demand a development-sensitive approach to transitional justice and argue that there is potential for development and reparation programs to be complimentary in order to overcome these rifts. This idea of socio-economic justice as well as civic justice in the sense of improving the relation between government and the governed were included in the design of the program in Peru but not implemented accordingly (Laplante 2014, 70–79). In the Peruvian case, this chance was missed by the state.

In theory, reparations are meant to benefit the community, bring them together in communal work, and contribute to individual satisfaction as well as acknowledge the individual's suffering, which would also have a positive influence on social cohesion in the village. The individual attitudes toward social cohesion, however, were very low as well. Only a very small group of people showed high attitudes toward social cohesion, which is an important finding that was analyzed in Chapter 6.

The TRC's influence on the communities was only marginal. The exhumations were judged as important in Lucanamarca, but usually in the same sentence they were also described as not concluded and seen to be privileging the victims of the massacre, which led to envy again. In Chuschi and Uchuyri, where only a few people mentioned the exhumations, people saw them in a critical light as well because so many other cases have not been investigated. For these individuals, the TRC did not lead to higher satisfaction, the pure act of testimony telling was not mentioned positively. Instead, those who gave testimonies are disappointed because the TRC was not followed by more exhumations or by reparations as was promised. The late, incomplete, and inadequate implementation of the reparations caused discontent in receivers, non-receivers, and observers alike. The process of re-victimization but also the development of a concurrence of different victim groups, which led to envy and new conflicts were particularly alarming. A reparation program entitling some victims to receive a benefit and excluding others poses strong problems and in the Peruvian case the various complex victim identities were not included, a relevant factor in reparation programs (Moffett 2016).

Collective reparations, even those projects that did work, were not perceived as reparations but confounded with development programs because they mostly did not have a communal or symbolic character. They may have an economic impact but its compensating effect is rather low. The weak social cohesion in the villages examined could not be improved through the reparation program. Neither trust nor solidarity within the community could be enhanced nor were attitudes toward the state improved by the program but it rather caused new envy, conflict and disillusion. This is why the program failed to achieve its objectives.

The ambiguity of truth and reparations in Peru

The findings presented earlier provided a detailed analysis on how the TRC and reparation program worked on the microlevel and highlighted the problems that ensued in those different conflict-affected settings. Furthermore, I was able to trace and disentangle the chain from the implementation to awareness and knowledge of the programs to the perception of the measures and their influence on social cohesion. In conclusion, I observed slightly negative effects due to the negative perception of the TRC and the reparation program. But what do we learn from these results?

First, it is important to note that the general idea of reparations was welcomed by most interviewees although some questioned how those damages could be repaired. All interviewees agreed that reparations can be a support and acknowledgement for violence-affected people but not in the way that they were implemented.

Second, when assessing the effects of the TRC and the reparation program on the basis of social cohesion, it became equally apparent that the high expectations that people have toward the reparation program are a crucial factor. The state and the reparation program did not satisfy the needs of the affected people. It is questionable, however, whether they are at all able to do so. In one of the very few needs assessment carried out by Rettberg and Prieto (2010, 17) in Colombia, they find: "Regarding reparation needs and expectations, most victims prioritize material reparations, but finding out the truth about what happened to them and getting some assurance that they will not be re-victimized are also among their top concerns". Interestingly, in Peru, the term justice was something that I barely heard in my interviews; at least, it was not named as such. The reparation program in Peru aimed to achieve several of the "plural justice aims" (Laplante 2014). However, in my study, reparations were also not perceived as the fulfillment of a right that affected people had but rather as a present given to those "winners" who were able to complete the complex application procedure. I observed similar perceptions of the social programs.

Third, another important result is that existent power constellations were reinforced by the TJ measures on different levels. The state was not interacting directly with the population but with intermediaries and put victims in a position of "supplicants" (Ulfe and Málaga Sabogal 2015). Power structures are also visible in another step of the implementation of the program. The military checked all the cases of people registering for reparations and had a veto right for those how were suspected supporters of the subversive groups. The main causes for the internal armed conflict were poverty as well as social, economic, and political exclusion. These factors were combined with an important structural characteristic: the inequality that had marked the country for centuries. The conflict started and spread predominantly in the marginalized and rural parts of the country that were inhabited mainly by people with indigenous roots and Quechua speakers, occupied in agriculture and with low education levels. This group was the largest of all victim groups. So, being a victim coincided with belonging to a marginalized part of the population, which is an important factor in the transitional justice process and makes the re-victimization within the reparation process even more dangerous.

When looking at the overall aims of transitional justice to achieve peace and democracy, these results are also alarming. State-community cohesion was not enhanced by the transitional justice process. Quite the opposite, unfulfilled expectations resulted in disillusion with the Limenian state. New conflicts generated by the reparation program and unsolved conflict causes generate an underlying feeling of discontent, 30% of interviewees stated that new violence could occur. This is alarming. If these results hold true for other cases as well then transitional justice has to be applied even more carefully. In this regard, an important result of my study was also that the fulfillment of individual rights can stand against collective well-being in the creation of envy.

The construction and politicization of victimhood is one of the crucial aspects of transitional justice processes. Reparation programs constitute a materialization of victimhood. In the Peruvian case, the TRC and reparation program created a space only for passive, innocent victims. Perpetrators in the form of supporters of Shining Path (not leaders) or the self-defense committees did not have any public space. Mixed roles were not discussed and those people not entitled for reparations, which in turn created conflicts and envy as my analysis demonstrated. People and communities could choose to take the passive victim role or no role at all. Lucanamarca is one example. The community did not create agency from the attention received, and, as Ulfe (2013, 31–32) argues, COMISEDH prevented this and saw their role as intermediator demanding projects and attention for the poor victims. COMISEDH would protest and claim that they were building an association and a school of leaders to create agency. Its role and that of other NGOs should be investigated further.

It is true, however, that only very few victims' associations or communities profited from the attention in such a way that they changed their position toward the state or other entities as a result. The victims' organization ANFASEP in Ayacucho and the community of Chungui are two examples (Koc-Menard 2014; Waardt 2014). Several political leaders of today started out at the youth organization of the ANFASEP. Ayacucho, however, wants to rid itself of its image as a cradle of terrorism or a land of victims. In Peru victimhood is connected with passivity, and this perception was not changed by the reparation program or the by other measures implemented (Theidon 2013; Weissert 2016; Winter 2009). On the contrary, no empowerment was observed but rather a reinforcement of existing power structures. This is similar to social programs that are also given as assistance without hardly any empowerment in the form of workshops or trainings.

In social conflicts but also in the national strike of teachers in 2017, who demanded better payments and working conditions, opponents are often defamed as "terrorists" and their claims delegitimized. The situation of transitional justice in Peru can also be observed in the ongoing debate about a possible pardon for former president Fujimori, convicted for corruption and human rights crimes. His daughter came second in the presidential elections twice, and her party is currently the strongest in congress. Her father's conviction and his involvement in various crimes do not diminish either his or her popularity. But apart from this discussion about Fujimori, the topic of transitional justice has no importance. One of the interviewed experts put the Peruvian situation in a nutshell: "The TRC was always marginal". And this is true for the whole topic of the conflict, the violence-affected people, and the transitional justice process. It was never a topic at the center of Peruvian politics or society nor were the violence-affected people or communities. It has always been a marginal topic, raised only by the human rights movement. Some recent governments put emphasis on it, but it is still not a priority. The budget for the reparation program has to compete with social programs or programs for natural disasters such as the major rainfalls and landslides in 2017. Affected people are one of the groups rowing for state attention, and they are not the loudest group. Interestingly, the affected people themselves also did not expect the state to put reparations on the top of the agenda. Not a single interviewee referred to the reparation program but to infrastructure and basic services when asked about their demands toward the state. When even the affected people do not regard the realization of the reparation program as a primary task of the government, then how can the government be expected to put it high on the agenda? In the communities, the reparation program is also not the main focus of local politics. Some local authorities engaged more than others, but it was only one of the many issues on the local agenda and fulfilling people's basic needs and development are still the main concerns.

Nevertheless, the Peruvian government has already invested several million US$ in the reparation program and if this is not working, this is money wasted. The reparation program would have been an opportunity for the Peruvian state to establish itself as reliable, and in so-doing build the political trust that is crucial for long-term democracy. But the reparation program was not seen in this way and transitional justice is not high on the political agenda. Furthermore, the program was implemented within the existing power structures. The villages and its inhabitants were seen as poor passive receivers, which were waiting to be attended. The government did not implement the program in a way that could empower people and build agency. The claim of de Greiff (2006, supra n. 32, 476–477) and others were not met. There is also no direct interaction between the state and communities but the municipalities or NGOs acted as intermediaries. It seems that those are not entirely focused on empowering victims and villages either. Again, transitional justice does adjust to rather than transform traditional power structures and bring along transformative justice (Gready and Robins 2014; Lambright 2015; Lambourne 2009; Ulfe and Málaga Sabogal 2015).

After the research for this study was completed, some changes have been made regarding the reparation program such as the re-opening of the national registry for victims and the presence of the CMAN in rural communities. It is, however, too early to judge whether this commitment will continue long-term and change the perception of the people.

The challenge to assess social impact

I applied a new research design to transitional justice impact research. In a quasi-experimental focused, structured comparison I compared villages with a high level of attention from transitional justice measures and those with less attention. However, I could not implement the design entirely as planned. The communities chosen based on prior information turned out to also have received attention from TRC and from the reparation program. And the ones with high objective exposure turned out to be not quite as high receivers as anticipated because the subjective exposure was so low. Many people did not perceive reparations as such.

Regarding the dependent variable, social cohesion, results were also surprising. The two communities chosen for the suspected high level of social cohesion turned out to have a low level only. In the eleventh community, which was supposed to have high social cohesion as well, only six interviews could be conducted. These, however, show a similar level of social cohesion as in the other villages. This demonstrates the difficulties of case selection in regions that have barely been researched before. So I did not have a community with a high level of social cohesion, which would be interesting for a follow-up study. The research design still worked out as I was still able to analyze communities with very different levels of attention. The slightly different characteristics in the communities were not a problem either. In the in-depth analysis, I included all relevant factors, and this allowed me to recognize differences caused by factors such as coca farming or the *Canon* budget in the VRAEM region. Regardless of those characteristics, the same patterns for the transitional justice and social cohesion process were identified.

The quasi-experimental design with the subnational comparison proved very well-suited for analyzing the research question. The supplemental analysis of individuals in Chapter 6 also led to important insights. Here, I also used the idea of the quasi-experimental design when I compared receivers to non-receivers.

The experimental corn-question ("If you had ten sacks of corn, which you cannot consume alone, with whom would you share it?") was also very valuable and brought important results on the willingness to share. However, as some interviewees did not understand the question fully, I would resort to using symbolic miniature corn sacks and a card with the different actors on it to make them distribute it, when I asked for a second time. With this visual aid, the question would even work better and also allowed for follow-up questions. I already realized this during the interviews but did not want to change the format due to issues with comparability.

The data collected and used for this analysis are unique; 160 semi-structured interviews plus 43 expert interviews and additional informal talks provided a solid basis for analysis. Ethnographic field research and a long period in the communities allowed me to observe and understand the processes. The comparison of the ten communities with the help of descriptive statistics was an important second level to show that problems and patterns are common in different communities with different characteristic. Quantitative statistics were used to show correlations between certain characteristics and individual attitudes in Chapter 6. I do not claim to reflect the entire processes in the communities with the 10 or 20 interviews conducted there but I was able to trace part of it and I am confident that the picture drawn in this book reflects the local reality fairly closely. The combination of different levels of analysis and different methods of analysis proved very helpful and is unique in this research area. To my knowledge, there is no other up-to-date study that combines the comparison of a large number of villages with an analysis at the level of the individuals.

The (im)possible task to repair in post-conflict societies

This study is a contribution to the discussion on transitional justice impact research, social cohesion, and beyond. I added a new perspective to transitional justice research in Peru. Neither the local level nor the perceptions of measures by affected people have been analyzed in this way before. My comparative study gives insights on how the measures applied nationally worked and were perceived on the micro level. The study addresses the claims to localize transitional justice research (Baines 2010; Hinton 2010; McEvoy and McGregor 2008; Méndez

2016; Shaw, Waldorf, and Hazan 2010). The insights of the local level made clear, however, that a "victims turn" (García-Godos 2016) of transitional justice measures is not enough. It is not enough to install a reparation program but it is important to manage expectations and to implement it according to the local situation and needs and also to remain aware of dominant power structures. As Sott (2017) finds for the Colombian case, transitional justice is hardly able to overcome power structures or lead to social transformation.

I also addressed the fact that transitional justice lacks a comprehensive theory. What I attempted with this book was to derive assumptions based on the concepts of transitional justice and social cohesion and to conceptualize them in a framework. The analytical and empirical connection is a new contribution. It provides a new framework for researchers interested in the link between transitional justice and its overall aim. In the empirical application, I demonstrated that both are connected on the microlevel of society, however, with no positive connection for the cases studied. I was able to disentangle how the underlying mechanisms at the base of transitional justice measures and social cohesion work. The conceptual framework needs to be applied further now to further prove its usability.

Moreover, with my quasi-experimental research design and the frameworks developed, I contribute to transitional justice impact research. Ten years after the publication of Van der Merwe, Baxter, and Chapman (2009) demanding more advanced TJ impact research, I proposed a new approach to address the lack of research that is still persistent according to various researchers (Bonacker and Buckley-Zistel 2013; Duggan 2010; Skaar, Malca, and Eide 2015; Thoms, Ron, and Paris 2010). I constructed an analytical framework with its different stages of TJ impact, which introduces the new stages of awareness and perception. The development and application of these two frameworks contributes to theory development and the methodological debate. In this study, the framework was very useful. Moreover, the quasi-experimental comparison of regions with and without attention from TJ measures proved useful. Both, research design and frameworks are available for the application to other cases or regions to prove their usefulness. They could also be relevant for other policy areas such as the assessment of development programs.

This study of the transitional justice process on the microlevel based on a huge amount of first hand data adds to area research and particular to the research on post-conflict Peru. No comparative analyses in the combination of the community and individual level have been applied yet, and I hope to deliver new insights.

I provided an in-depth analysis of the situation of social cohesion in the post-conflict communities. The identification of influencing factors in this process is an important contribution. I could show how social cohesion and conflict are linked but that the experience of violence was only one of the influencing factors alongside modernization. Moreover, the further development and application of the social cohesion indicator contributes to theory development in this area as well. My analysis demonstrated that it is a long path to develop social cohesion in a community and toward the state but that it can be destroyed rapidly.

Transitional justice is a very relevant field for politics and practitioners. On the global level, the imperative of transitional justice in every post-conflict situation is now seen more skeptically in research. This study adds to this skeptical view and demands caution when applying TJ measures. Installing a reparation program at any cost, which is then badly implemented, is not necessarily better than having no reparation program at all. Decision makers but also NGOs pushing transitional justice should be aware of the effects such a program can cause on the micro level of society. My study delivered an analysis based on the Peruvian example. Insights however, may apply to other cases as well.

Regarding truth commissions, my analysis made clear that the information available at the local level influences the perception of the measure and that this is a deciding factor for its impact. Future commissions should keep that in mind. Another crucial factor are the expectations that are generated by the giving of testimony. In the Peruvian case, the expectations of the people toward reparations have been further reinforced by the commission and could only be disappointed. This led to unexpected and unintended effects. For TRCs it is, therefore, certainly important to think about how they plan to interact with the affected population and question the expectations that are raised by its work. Also the appendix "reconciliation" should be carefully used. The commission was expected to create truth, which was accomplished in a way that it delivered a comprehensive analysis of the internal armed conflict based on a huge collection of material. But this is not THE truth, but a part of the history.

Reparation programs are no panacea, and the mere installation of the reparation program or commission does not necessarily lead to positive effects. It depends entirely on the implementation of the program. Expectations should be adjusted accordingly. The importance of local actors and existing power structures should not be overlooked as well as the importance of the perception of the respective measure. It must be very clear for all parties involved that a certain measure, project, or payment forms part of a reparation program. Otherwise, the compensatory effect will be low.

Within Peru but also beyond my results are also of importance for decision makers and practitioners. In July 2017, I summarized the results of my investigation and developed several recommendations for the further development of the program. CMAN, the entity in charge for implementing the program in Peru, warmly welcomed this report and some of the recommendations such as better information for the affected communities and the better inclusion of local authorities have already been implemented. CMAN conducted various visits to communities that have not been in its focus so far, also in the VRAEM region and in Lucanamarca. The results of this study, are however, not only relevant for the Peruvian case but especially relevant to those countries, which are about to apply a new reparation program such as the Colombian case.

Research ethics also demand a reflection of the implications for the local population studied. In the case of the analysis of the implementation of a state program such as this, it is especially relevant. As mentioned, the results and recommendations developed based on this study might contribute to the improvement of the attention from the reparation program. This would be a positive effect for the researched population.

Within this project, I was able to do something that most research projects did not. I went back to the communities and presented my preliminary results there, on three occasions in the villages and in one discussion in Ayacucho at the end of 2015. Together with the participants, I discussed similarities and differences of the situation in the post-conflict village and post-war Germany. For the people, the discussion and my presentation were an important gesture. For me, it was both the completion of my ethical duties and a valuable feedback loop for my results.

Outlook

The analysis in this book demonstrated once more that transitional justice is always political. That is to say that the installation and implementation of TJ measures will always depend on political circumstances and support. The success that former president Humala claimed in the quote at the beginning of this book was not perceived as such by the affected people. After the research for this book has been completed, there have been important changes and improvements within the Peruvian reparation program under the governments of Kuczynski and Vizcarra. Whether those efforts will continue and change the perception of the people and influence social cohesion positively remains to be evaluated in the near future. Another evaluation next year as a follow-up study would be very interesting and would form part of a time line series. Also, the comparison of my results with other regions could be very rewarding. The only report (Paredes and Correa 2011) that studies the perception of collective reparations so far finds similar patterns. A survey to capture the opinions of a larger number of people would also be very informative, also in comparison with other countries. Firchow's studies (2014, 2017) in Colombia reveal very similar patterns. So maybe these are general and structural problems of reparations? The very few existing studies to-date confirm this impression.

Another topic worthy of further investigation is the role of local authorities and NGOs and their interactions. I only touched upon it for the case of Lucanamarca where COMISEDH had an important influence, which is seen critically as well. Without this NGO the community would perhaps not have received the exhumation. So its relationship with the TRC and the reparation program remains ambiguous.

Connected to NGOs as an actor is the question of how the state interacts or not interacts with its citizens in transitional justice processes. I found that power structures were reinforced instead of overcome and the question is whether this was wanted. Reparations are perceived as something coming as a present. Collective reparations equal development projects. The problems that this confusion brings were discussed by Roht-Arriaza (2004, 129). The state's presence in the communities is mainly perceived in infrastructure works or social programs. Good governance of the national government and local authorities is measured in projects (Huber et al. 2003). I did find little evidence of the perception of citizen's rights or security demands. Also in my question on the future of the community people ask for development. The presidents reinforced these perceptions in their visits to the communities to attend vulnerable populations. So what does this say about the state's perception by its citizens on the one hand and of the citizen's perception by the state on the other? This is definitely worth studying further.

Finally, a fundamental question is whether reparations are appropriate for harm suffered. Whether reparations – be it a cow or an economic payment, education or in symbolic form – can really "compensate" the harm suffered through the loss of a family member is a subjective matter. They cannot be expected to reverse consequences of violence but constitute a support for affected people. Feeling "repaired" is subjective. But even if they do not result in a feeling of "repairedness", reparations, if implemented rapidly and comprehensively, could be a very important tool in the rebuilding of lives after armed conflict as well as in the rebuilding of social relationships within communities and trust toward the state. However, in the Peruvian case as in other cases, this did not work out and transitional justice researchers, practitioners, and decision makers should question the normative assumptions behind a program and adjust their and the victims' expectations toward reparations. It is uncertain whether the recent advances in the Peruvian reparation program will bring at least some positive impact on individuals and their communities in the future.

References

Baines, Erin K. 2010. "Spirits and Social Reconstruction after Mass Violence: Rethinking Transitional Justice." *African Affairs* 109 (436): 409–30.

Bonacker, Thorsten, and Susanne Buckley-Zistel. 2013. "Introduction: Transitions from Violence. Analysing the Effects of Transitional Justice." *International Journal of Conflict and Violence* 7 (1): 4–9.

De Juan, Alexander, Kristof Gosztonyi, and Jan Koehler. 2016. "From Civil War to Social Contract? – Associations between Basic Service Delivery and Political Trust in Conflict-Affected States Final Report." unpublished project report.

Duggan, Colleen. 2010. "Editorial Note. Special Issue: Transitional Justice on Trial - Evaluating Its Impact." *International Journal of Transitional Justice* 4 (3): 315–28.

Firchow, Pamina. 2014. "The Implementation of the Institutional Programme of Collective Reparations in Colombia." *Journal of Human Rights Practice* 6 (2): 356–75.

———. 2017. "Do Reparations Repair Relationships? Setting the Stage for Reconciliation in Colombia." *International Journal of Transitional Justice* 11 (2): 315–38.

García-Godos, Jemima. 2016. "Victims in Focus." *International Journal of Transitional Justice* 10 (2): 350–58.

Gready, Paul, and Simon Robins. 2014. "From Transitional to Transformative Justice: A New Agenda for Practice." *International Journal of Transitional Justice* 8 (3): 339–61.

Greiff, Pablo de. 2006. "Justice and Reparations." In *The Handbook of Reparations*, edited by Pablo de Greiff, 451–77. Oxford: Oxford University Press.

Guillerot, Julie. 2006. "Linking Gender and Reparations in Peru: A Failed Opportunity." In *What Happened to the Women? Gender and Reparations for Human Rights Violations*, edited by Ruth Rubio-Marín, 136–91. New York: Social Science Research Council. www.ssrc.org/publications/view/D6D99C02-EA4A-DE11-AFAC-001CC477EC70/.

Hinton, Alexander Laban, ed. 2010. *Transitional Justice: Global Mechanisms and Local Realities after Genocide and Mass Violence*. Genocide, Political Violence, Human Rights Series. New Brunswick, NJ: Rutgers University Press.

Huber, Ludwig, Karin Apel, Iván Caro, Lenin Castillo, Enver Quinteros, and Hugo Rodríguez. 2003. "Centralismo y descentralización en Ayacucho." In *Centralismo y Descentralización en Ayacucho*, edited by Ludwig Huber, 15–104. Estudios de la Sociedad Rural, 22. Lima: IEP.

Koc-Menard, Nathalie. 2014. "Sufrimiento humano y representación de víctimas. El caso de Chungui en la posguerra peruana." *Bulletin de l'Institut français d'études andines* 43 (2): 209–26.

Lambourne, Wendy. 2009. "Transitional Justice and Peacebuilding after Mass Violence." *International Journal of Transitional Justice* 3 (1): 28–48.

Lambright, Anne. 2015. *Andean Truths: Transitional Justice, Ethnicity, and Cultural Production in Post-Shining Path Peru*. Liverpool: Liverpool University Press.

Laplante, Lisa J. 2014. "The Plural Justice Aims of Reparations." In *Transitional Justice Theories*, edited by Susanne Buckley-Zistel, Teresa Koloma Beck, Christian Braun, and Friederike Mieth, 66–84. London: Routledge.

———. 2015. "Just Repair." *Cornell International Law Journal* 48: 101–74.

Mantilla Falcón, Julissa. 2005. "The Peruvian Truth and Reconciliation Commission's Treatment of Sexual Violence against Women." *Human Rights Brief* 12 (2): 1.

McEvoy, Kieran, and Lorna McGregor, eds. 2008. *Transitional Justice from Below: Grassroots Activism and the Struggle for Change*. Oxford: Hart Publishing.

Méndez, Juan E. 2016. "Editorial Note. Special Issue: Victims as Protagonists in Transitional Justice." *International Journal of Transitional Justice* 10 (1): 1–5.

Moffett, Luke. 2016. "Reparations for 'Guilty Victims': Navigating Complex Identities of Victim–Perpetrators in Reparation Mechanisms." *International Journal of Transitional Justice* 10 (1): 146–67.

———. 2017. "Transitional Justice and Reparations: Remedying the Past?" In *Research Handbook on Transitional Justice*, edited by Cheryl Lawther, Luke Moffett, and Dov Jacobs, 377–401. Cheltenhem: Edward Elgar Publishing.

Paredes, Sonia, and Cristián Correa. 2011. "Perú: ¿Cuánto Se Ha Reparado En Nuestras Comunidades?" ICTJ. www.ictj.org/publication/per%C3%BA-%C2%BFcu%C3%A1nto-se-ha-reparado-en-nuestras-comunidades.

Rettberg, Angelika, and Juan Diego Prieto. 2010. "Reparations of Victims of Armed Conflict in Colombia." Conference Paper. ISA Annual Convention.

Roht-Arriaza, Naomi. 2004. "Reparations in the Aftermath of Repression an Mass Violence." In *My Neighbor, My Enemy: Justice and Community in the Aftermath of Mass Atrocity*, edited by Eric Stover and Harvey M. Weinstein, 121–40. Cambridge: Cambridge University Press.

Shaw, Rosalind, Lars Waldorf, and Pierre Hazan, eds. 2010. *Localizing Transitional Justice: Interventions and Priorities after Mass Violence*. Stanford Studies in Human Rights. Stanford, CA: Stanford University Press.

Skaar, Elin, Camila Gianella Malca, and Trine Eide. 2015. *After Violence*. London: Taylor & Francis Ltd.

Sott, Sarah Helen. 2017. *Desartikulation statt Transitional Justice? subalterne Perspektiven in der kolumbianischen Vergangenheitsbewältigung*. Postcolonial studies, Band 30. Bielefeld: transcript.

Theidon, Kimberly. 2007. "Gender in Transition: Common Sense, Women, and War." *Journal of Human Rights* 6 (4): 453–78.

———. 2013. *Intimate Enemies: Violence and Reconciliation in Peru*. Pennsylvania Studies in Human Rights. Philadelphia: University of Pennsylvania Press.

———. 2016. "A Greater Measure of Justice. Gender, Violence, and Reparations." In *Mapping Feminist Anthropology in the Twenty-First Century*, edited by Ellen Lewin and Leni M. Silverstein, 191–210. New Brunswick, NJ: Rutgers University Press.

Thoms, Oskar N. T., James Ron, and Roland Paris. 2010. "State-Level Effects of Transitional Justice: What Do We Know?" *International Journal of Transitional Justice* 4 (3): 329–54.

Ulfe, Maria Eugenia. 2013. *¿Y después de la violencia que queda ?: víctimas, cuidadanos y reparaciones en el contexto post-CVR en el Perú*. Buenos Aires: CLACSO.

Ulfe, Maria Eugenia, and Ximena Málaga Sabogal. 2015. "Los Nuevos Suplicantes Del Estado Peruano: Las Víctimas y El Programa Integral de Reparaciones (PIR)." In *Políticas En Justicia Transicional. Miradas Comparativas Sobre El Legado de La CVR*, edited by Ludwig Huber and Ponciano Del Pino, 169–89. Lima: IEP.

Van der Merwe, Hugo, Victoria Baxter, and Audrey R. Chapman. 2009. *Assessing the Impact of Transitional Justice: Challenges for Empirical Research*. Washington, D.C: United States Institute of Peace Press.

Waardt, Mijke de. 2014. "In the Name of the Victims? Victim-Survivor Associations Negotiating for Recognition in Post-Conflict Peru." Dissertation. Amsterdam: VU University.

———. 2016. "Naming and Shaming Victims: The Semantics of Victimhood." *International Journal of Transitional Justice* 10 (3): 432–50.

Weissert, Markus. 2016. "Memories of Violence Dreams of Development - Memorialisation Initiatives in the Peruvian Andes." Dissertation. Berlin: Free University.

Winter, Franka. 2009. "Giving Voice to the Voiceless? Second Thoughts on Testimony in Transitional Justice." *A Contracorriente: Revista de Historia Social y Literatura En América Latina* 6 (3): 90–107.

Annexes

Annex 1 List of Interviews

Interview code	*Community*	*Age*	*Sex*	*Authority/community member*	*Date*
A1	Alanya	60–69	male	Community member	Apr2015
A2	Alanya	20–29	male	Authority	Apr2015
A3	Alanya	20–29	female	Community member	Apr2015
A4	Alanya	40–49	male	Authority	Apr2015
A5	Alanya	30–39	male	Authority	Apr2015
A6	Alanya	60–69	male	Community member	Apr2015
A7	Alanya	40–49	female	Authority	Apr2015
A8	Alanya	40–49	female	Authority	Apr2015
A9	Alanya	30–39	female	Community member	Apr2015
A10	Alanya	20–29	female	Community member	Apr2015
CH1	Chuschi	30–39	male	Authority	May2015
CH2	Chuschi	30–39	male	Authority	May2015
CH3	Chuschi	20–29	male	Authority	May2015
CH4	Chuschi	30–39	male	Authority	Apr2015
CH5	Chuschi	30–39	male	Authority	May2015
(CH6)	Chuschi	50–59	male	Authority	May2015
CH7	Chuschi	30–39	male	Authority	May2015
CH8	Chuschi	30–39	female	Authority	May2015
CH9	Chuschi	40–49	male	Authority	May2015
(CH10)	Chuschi	20–29	male	Authority	May2015
CH11	Chuschi	30–39	male	Authority	Apr2015
CH12	Chuschi	40–49	female	Authority	Apr2015
CH13	Chuschi	50–59	male	Authority	Apr2015
CH14	Chuschi	70-	male	Community member	Mar2015
CH15	Chuschi	70-	male	Community member	May2015
CH16	Chuschi	30–39	female	Community member	Mar2015
CH17	Chuschi	30–39	female	Community member	Mar2015
CH18	Chuschi	30–39	female	Community member	May2015
CH19	Chuschi	20–29	female	Community member	Apr2015
(CH20)	Chuschi	70–	male	Community member	Mar2015
CH21	Chuschi	50–59	female	Community member	Jul2015
CH22	Chuschi	20–29	female	Community member	Jul2015
CH23	Chuschi	50–59	female	Community member	Jul2015
H1	Huyma	40–49	female	Community member	May2015
H2	Huyma	20–29	female	Community member	May2015

(Continued)

Interview code	*Community*	*Age*	*Sex*	*Authority/community member*	*Date*
H3	Huyma	40–49	male	Authority	May2015
H4	Huyma	20–29	male	Authority	May2015
H5	Huyma	50–59	male	Authority	May2015
H6	Huyma	30–39	female	Authority	May2015
J1	Julo	30–39	male	Authority	Apr2015
J2	Julo	30–39	male	Authority	Apr2015
J3	Julo	30–39	male	Authority	Apr2015
J4	Julo	30–39	male	Authority	Apr2015
(J5)	Julo	20–29	female	Authority	Apr2015
J6	Julo	20–29	female	Authority	Apr2015
J7	Julo	20–29	female	Community member	Apr2015
J8	Julo	20–29	female	Community member	Apr2015
J9	Julo	40–49	female	Community member	Apr2015
J10	Julo	70-	female	Community member	Apr2015
J11	Julo	40–49	female	Community member	Apr2015
K1	Kimbiri	40–49	male	Authority	Mar2015
K2	Kimbiri	40–49	female	Authority	Mar2015
K3	Kimbiri	70-	male	Authority	Mar2015
K4	Kimbiri	40–49	male	Authority	Mar2015
K5	Kimbiri	30–39	male	Authority	Mar2015
K6	Kimbiri	40–49	male	Authority	Mar2015
K7	Kimbiri	60–69	male	Community member	Mar2015
K8	Kimbiri	40–49	female	Community member	Mar2015
K9	Kimbiri	50–59	female	Community member	Mar2015
K10	Kimbiri	30–39	female	Community member	Mar2015
K11	Kimbiri	30–39	male	Community member	Apr2016
K12	Kimbiri	20–29	male	Community member	Apr2016
K13	Kimbiri	30–39	male	Authority	May2016
K14	Kimbiri	40–49	male	Authority	May2016
K15	Kimbiri	50–59	male	Authority	May2016
K16	Kimbiri	20–29	female	Authority	May2016
K17	Kimbiri	20–29	female	Community member	Jul2016
K18	Kimbiri	30–39	male	Community member	Jul2016
K19	Kimbiri	30–39	female	Community member	Jul2016
K20	Kimbiri	20–29	female	Community member	Sep2016
L1	Lucanamarca	40–49	male	Authority	Apr2015
L2	Lucanamarca	30–39	female	Authority	Apr2015
L3	Lucanamarca	20–29	male	Authority	Apr2015
L4	Lucanamarca	30–39	male	Authority	Apr2015
L5	Lucanamarca	40–49	male	Authority	May2015
L6	Lucanamarca	30–39	male	Authority	Apr2015
L7	Lucanamarca	40–49	male	Authority	May2015
(L8)	Lucanamarca	40–49	male	Authority	Feb2015
L9	Lucanamarca	30–39	female	Authority	Apr2015
L10	Lucanamarca	40–49	male	Authority	Apr2015
L11	Lucanamarca	30–39	female	Authority	Apr2015
L12	Lucanamarca	30–39	female	Authority	May2015
L13	Lucanamarca	30–39	female	Community member	Apr2015
L14	Lucanamarca	20–29	male	Community member	Apr2015
(L15)	Lucanamarca	20–29	male	Community member	May2015
L16	Lucanamarca	50–59	female	Community member	Feb2015
L17	Lucanamarca	30–39	female	Community member	Feb2015

Interview code	*Community*	*Age*	*Sex*	*Authority/community member*	*Date*
L18	Lucanamarca	20–29	female	Community member	Feb2015
L19	Lucanamarca	30–39	female	Community member	Feb2015
L20	Lucanamarca	50–59	female	Community member	Feb2015
L21	Lucanamarca	20–29	female	Community member	Feb2015
L22	Lucanamarca	30–39	female	Community member	Feb2015
NP1	Nuevo Progreso	40–49	male	Authority	Mar2015
NP2	Nuevo Progreso	60–69	male	Authority	Mar2015
NP3	Nuevo Progreso	40–49	male	Authority	Mar2015
NP4	Nuevo Progreso	50–59	male	Authority	Mar2015
NP5	Nuevo Progreso	50–59	male	Authority	Mar2015
NP6	Nuevo Progreso	40–49	female	Authority	Mar2015
NP7	Nuevo Progreso	20–29	female	Community member	Mar2015
NP8	Nuevo Progreso	60–69	female	Community member	Mar2015
NP9	Nuevo Progreso	30–39	female	Community member	Mar2015
NP10	Nuevo Progreso	30–39	male	Community member	Mar2015
Q1	Quispillacta	40–49	male	Authority	Apr2015
Q2	Quispillacta	20–29	female	Authority	Apr2015
Q3	Quispillacta	60–69	male	Authority	Apr2015
Q4	Quispillacta	60–69	male	Authority	Apr2015
(Q5)	Quispillacta	50–59	female	Authority	Apr2015
Q6	Quispillacta	40–49	female	Authority	Apr2015
Q7	Quispillacta	50–59	male	Authority	Apr2015
Q8	Quispillacta	30–39	male	Community member	Apr2015
Q9	Quispillacta	50–59	female	Community member	Apr2015
Q10	Quispillacta	50–59	female	Community member	Apr2015
Q11	Quispillacta	40–49	female	Community member	Apr2015
(Q12)	Quispillacta	50–59	female	Community member	May2015
(QB1)	Querobamba	60–69	male	Authority	Apr2015
QB2	Querobamba	50–59	female	Authority	Apr2015
QB3	Querobamba	50–59	female	Authority	Apr2015
QB4	Querobamba	70-	male	Community member	Apr2015
(QB5)	Querobamba	70-	male	Authority	Apr2015
QB6	Querobamba	60–69	male	Authority	Apr2015
QB7	Querobamba	70-	male	Authority	Apr2015
QB8	Querobamba	30–39	female	Authority	Apr2015
QB9	Querobamba	60–69	male	Community member	Apr2015
QB10	Querobamba	70-	male	Community member	Apr2015
QB11	Querobamba	50–59	male	Community member	Apr2015
QB12	Querobamba	50–59	male	Community member	Apr2015
(QB13)	Querobamba	50–59	female	Authority	Nov2015
SR1	Santa Rosa	40–49	male	Authority	Apr2015

(Continued)

Interview code	*Community*	*Age*	*Sex*	*Authority/community member*	*Date*
SR2	Santa Rosa	30–39	male	Authority	Apr2015
SR3	Santa Rosa	40–49	female	Authority	Apr2015
SR4	Santa Rosa	30–39	male	Authority	Apr2015
SR5	Santa Rosa	30–39	male	Authority	Apr2015
SR6	Santa Rosa	40–49	female	Community member	Apr2015
SR7	Santa Rosa	40–49	female	Community member	Apr2015
SR8	Santa Rosa	40–49	male	Community member	Apr2015
SR9	Santa Rosa	30–39	male	Community member	Apr2015
SR10	Santa Rosa	40–49	female	Community member	Apr2015
SR11	Santa Rosa	60–69	male	Authority	Mar2016
SR12	Santa Rosa	20–29	male	Authority	Mar2016
SR13	Santa Rosa	40–49	male	Authority	May2016
SR14	Santa Rosa	30–39	female	Community member	May2016
SR15	Santa Rosa	60–69	female	Community member	May2016
SR16	Santa Rosa	40–49	female	Authority	May2016
SR17	Santa Rosa	30–39	male	Authority	Jul2016
SR18	Santa Rosa	60–69	female	Community member	Jul2016
SR19	Santa Rosa	20–29	female	Community member	Aug2016
SR20	Santa Rosa	30–39	female	Community member	Sep2016
U1	Uchuyri	30–39	male	Authority	May2015
(U2)	Uchuyri	40–49	male	Authority	Apr2015
U3	Uchuyri	60–69	male	Authority	Apr2015
U4	Uchuyri	60–69	male	Authority	Mar2015
U5	Uchuyri	40–49	male	Authority	Apr2015
U6	Uchuyri	50–59	male	Authority	Apr2015
(U7)	Uchuyri	60–69	female	Authority	Apr2015
U8	Uchuyri	40–49	female	Community member	Apr2015
U9	Uchuyri	40–49	male	Community member	Apr2015
(U10)	Uchuyri	20–29	female	Community member	Apr2015
U11	Uchuyri	30–39	female	Community member	Apr2015
U12	Uchuyri	30–39	female	Community member	Apr2015
U13	Uchuyri	20–29	female	Community member	Apr2015

Note: Interviews in brackets are those not counted for the quantitative analysis.

Annex 2 List of Expert Interviews

Interview code	*Place*	*Sex*	*Institution*	*Date*
Exp1	Lima	female	NGO	Oct2014
Exp2	Lima	male	NGO	Oct2014
Exp3	Lima	female	NGO	Oct2014
Exp4	Ayacucho	female	NGO	Nov2014
Exp5	Ayacucho	male	NGO	Nov2014
Exp6	Ayacucho	male	University	Nov2014
Exp7	Lucanamarca	male	Local Authority	Nov2014
Exp8	Lucanamarca	male	NGO	Nov2014
Exp9	Lucanamarca	male	NGO	Nov2014
Exp10	Lucanamarca	male	Local Authority	Nov2014
Exp11	Ayacucho	male	University	Nov2014
Exp12	Ayacucho	male	University	Nov2014
Exp13	Ayacucho	male	NGO	Nov2014
Exp14	Ayacucho	male	University	Nov2014
Exp15	Ayacucho	male	CMAN	Nov2014
Exp16	Lima	male	Ministry	Dec2014
Exp17	Lima	male	University	Dec2014
Exp18	Lima	female	NGO	Dec2014
Exp19	Lima	female	University	Dec2014
Exp20	Lima	female	NGO	Dec2014
Exp21	Lima	male	University	Dec2014
Exp22	Lima	female	University	Dec2014
Exp23	Lucanamarca	male	Local Authority	Dec2014
Exp24	Ayacucho	male	NGO	Dec2014
Exp25	Ayacucho	female	CMAN	Feb2015
Exp26	Lima	female	CMAN	Feb2015
Exp27	Ayacucho	male	Ministry	Feb2015
Exp28	Lucanamarca	male	Ministry	Jul2015
Exp29	Chuschi	female	Church	Jul2015
Exp30	Chuschi	male	Local Authority	Jul2015
Exp31	Ayacucho	male	NGO	Jul2015
Exp32	Lima	male	Former TRC	Oct2015
Exp33	Lima	female	Former TRC	Nov2015
Exp34	Ayacucho	female	NGO	Nov2015
Exp35	Lima	male	NGO	Nov2015
Exp36	Ayacucho	male	Former TRC	Nov2015
Exp37	Lima	male	Former TRC	Nov2015
Exp38	Ayacucho	male	Local Authority	Mar2016
Exp39	Ayacucho	female	Local Authority	Mar2016
Exp40	Ayacucho	female	University	May2016
Exp41	Berlin	male	Former NGO	Aug2016
Exp42	Berlin	male	Former Consejo	Aug2016
Exp43	Berlin	female	Former Consejo	Aug2016

Annex 3 List of Testimonies

ID of testimony	*Place*
100005	Santa Rosa
100202	Santa Rosa
200357	Lucanamarca
200480	Santa Rosa
200492	Lucanamarca
200493	Chuschi
200801	Chuschi
201113	Lucanamarca
201149	Lucanamarca
201151	Lucanamarca
201153	Lucanamarca
201159	Lucanamarca
201165	Lucanamarca
201166	Lucanamarca
201167	Lucanamarca
201168	Lucanamarca
201170	Lucanamarca
201718	Kimbiri
201907	Kimbiri
201910	Kimbiri
202732	Santa Rosa
203161	Lucanamarca
203166	Lucanamarca
203167	Lucanamarca
203171	Lucanamarca
203172	Lucanamarca
203173	Lucanamarca
203179	Lucanamarca
203181	Lucanamarca
203183	Lucanamarca
203190	Lucanamarca
204065	Kimbiri
204368	Lucanamarca
204644	Kimbiri
204681	Santa Rosa
204708	Santa Rosa
204720	Santa Rosa
205105	Kimbiri
205146	Santa Rosa
205194	Lucanamarca
205244	Santa Rosa
732006	Kimbiri

Note: These testimonies were collected by the TRC in 2001/2002 and are available at the Defensoría del Pueblo in Lima.

Annex 4 Operationalization of Social Cohesion Indicator

	Subjective component (people's state of mind)	*Objective component (behavioral manifestations)*
Horizontal dimension (Cohesion within community)	**General trust with fellow citizens** (Trust Code + Trust Text + Trust Family Code + Envy Code + Envy Text) **Willingness to cooperate and help → solidarity** (Help Code + Corn Mem + Help Text + Sol Code) **Sense of belonging or identity** (proud Code + text) **Common narrative and perception of the past** (Actor Code + victim text + rem/forget code)	**Social participation** (asa part code + obs. + no part text+ associations + social events) **Voluntarism** (obs faenas + text part + Corn NGO) **Relationship towards local authorities** (auth trust code + auth caring code + corn auth) **Presence or absence of major inter-group alliances or cleavages** (conflict code + conflict solution code + violence code + newvio code + obs) **Crimes** (obs + violence text)
Vertical dimension (State-citizen cohesion)	**Confidence in political institutions** (trust code + trust text + rights awareness) **Importance/role of the state** (code importance + text importance + corn state) **Expectations towards the state** (code exp + text exp) **Sense of belonging or identity** (proud Code + text)	**Political participation** (voting + demonstration + parties) **State presence** (corruption) (visits, campaigns) (public goods, social programs)

Source: own elaboration

Annex 5 Operationalization of Analytical Framework

	II Implementation TJ		*IIa Awareness TJ*			
Indicator	TRC Attention	Ind.+ Coll. Rep. Att.	TRC Awareness	Ind. Rep. Awareness	Coll. Rep. Awareness	TRC Knowledge
Measures	High (exh + test)/Medium (exh or test)/Low (none)	High (coll+ind)/ Medium (coll or ind)/Low (none)	High (70–100% aware of TRC)/ Medium (30–70%)/ Low (0–30%)	High (70–100% aware of ind. Rep)/ Medium (30–70%)/Low (0–30%)	High (70–100% aware of coll. Rep)/ Medium (30–70%)/ Low (0–30%)	High (70–100% know what is TRC)/Medium (30–70%)/ Low (0–30%)
Sources	TRC/CMAN/ Interviews	TRC/CMAN/ Interviews	Interviews	Interviews	Interviews	Interviews

Source: Own elaboration

Annex 6 Results: Transitional Justice and Social Cohesion in Ten Post-Conflict Communities (Own Data)

	II Implementation TJ		*IIa Awareness TJ*			
	TRC Attention	*Ind.+ Coll. Rep. Att.*	*TRC Awareness*	*Ind. Rep. Awareness*	*Coll. Rep. Awareness*	*TRC Knowledge*
Lucanam.	high exh, test, trial	high coll + ind	high	high	med	med
Chuschi	high exh, test, trial	high coll + ind	high	high	med	med
Santa R.	med test	med ind	high	high	low	low
Kimbiri	low	med ind.	high	high	low	low
Julo	low	high coll + ind	low	high	high	low
Alanya	low	high coll + ind	med	high	high	low
Quisp	med test, exh	med ind	high	high	med	low
Uchuyri	med test, exh	high coll + ind	high	high	med	med
Nuevo P.	low	med ind.	med	high	low	low
Querob.	med test	med ind.	med	high	low	low

		IIb Perception TJ			*III Impact Social Cohesion*	
Ind. Rep. Knowledge	Coll Rep. Knowledge	Satisfaction TRC	Satisfaction ind. Rep.	Satisfaction coll. Rep.	Horizontal: Solidarity, Trust, Identity, Social Particip.	Vertical: Political Trust, State Importance Identity, Political Particip.
High (70–100% know what is ind Rep)/Medium (30–70%)/ Low (0–30%)	High (70–100% know what is coll Rep)/Medium (30–70%)/Low (0–30%)	High (70–100% pos)/ Medium (30–70% pos)/Low (0–30% pos)	High (70–100% pos)/Medium (30–70% pos)/Low (0–30% pos)	High (70–100% pos)/ Medium (30–70% pos)/Low (0–30% pos)	High/Medium/ Low	High/Medium/ Low
Interviews	Interviews	Interviews	Interviews	Interviews	Interviews and Observation	Interviews and Observation

		IIb Perception TJ			*III Impact Social Cohesion*	
Ind. Rep. Knowledge	*Coll Rep. Knowledge*	*Satisfaction TRC*	*Satisfaction ind. Rep.*	*Satisfaction coll. Rep.*	*Horizontal*	*Vertical*
med	med	low	low	low	low	low
med	low	low	low		low	low
med	low	med	med	low	low	low
med	low	low	low	low	low	low
med	high		low	med	low	low
med	high	low	low	med	low	low
low	med	low	low	low	low	low
med	med	low	low	low	low	low
med	low	low	low	low	low	low
low	low	low	low	low	low	low

Index

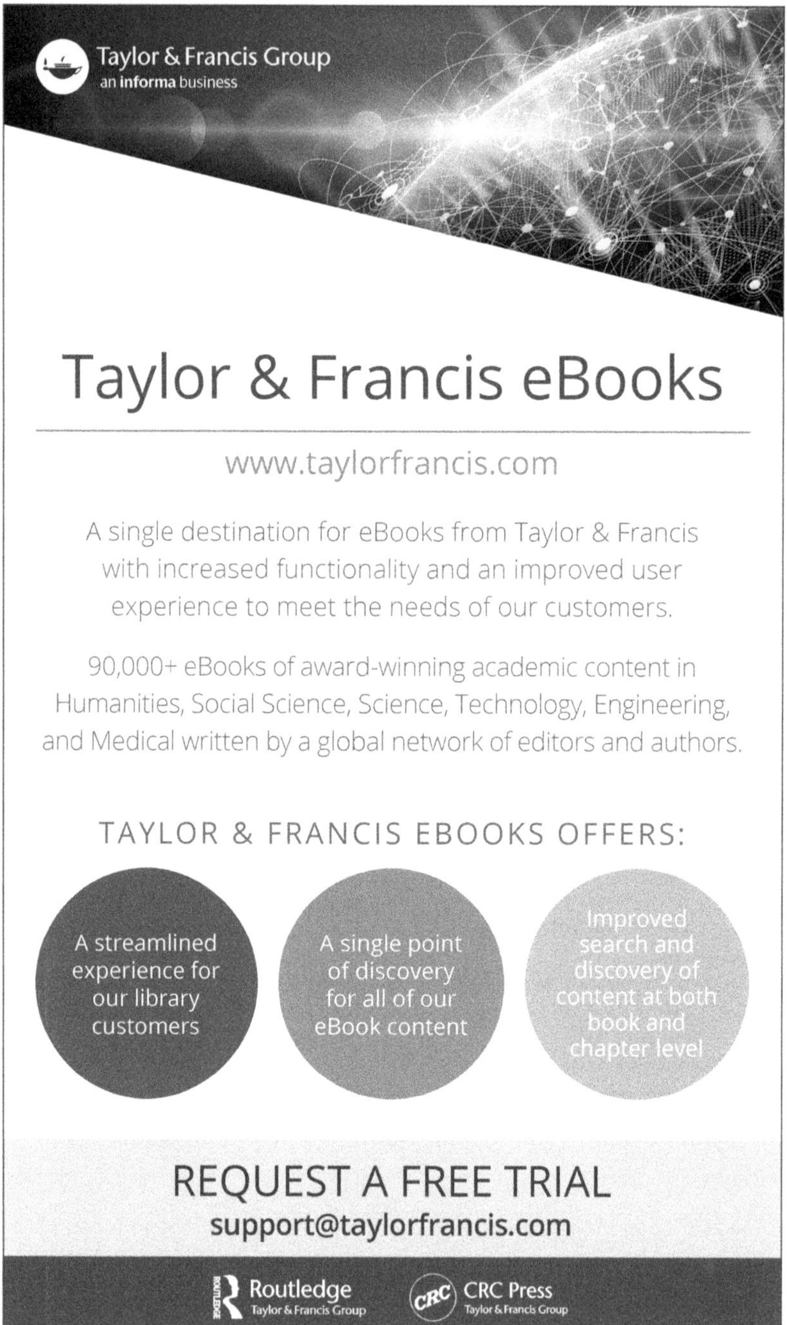

Taylor & Francis Group
an informa business
Taylor & Francis eBooks
www.taylorfrancis.com
A single destination for eBooks from Taylor & Francis with increased functionality and an improved user experience to meet the needs of our customers.
90,000+ eBooks of award-winning academic content in Humanities, Social Science, Science, Technology, Engineering, and Medical written by a global network of editors and authors.
TAYLOR & FRANCIS EBOOKS OFFERS:
A streamlined experience for our library customers
A single point of discovery for all of our eBook content
Improved search and discovery of content at both book and chapter level
REQUEST A FREE TRIAL
support@taylorfrancis.com
Routledge Taylor & Francis Group
CRC Press Taylor & Francis Group

For Product Safety Concerns and Information please contact our EU representative GPSR@taylorandfrancis.com
Taylor & Francis Verlag GmbH, Kaufingerstraße 24, 80331 München, Germany

www.ingramcontent.com/pod-product-compliance
Ingram Content Group UK Ltd.
Pitfield, Milton Keynes, MK11 3LW, UK
UKHW011005180926
475701UK00004B/563
9781032173894